■ *Life in America Series*

General Editor: **Richard C. Wade**

Editorial Adviser: **Howard R. Anderson**

HOUGHTON MIFFLIN COMPANY / *Boston*

CITIES IN AMERICAN LIFE

Selected Readings

RICHARD C. WADE

New York / Atlanta / Geneva, Ill. / Dallas / Palo Alto

■ *About the Editors*

RICHARD C. WADE

A graduate of the University of Rochester, Dr. Wade received his Ph.D. in history from Harvard University. Presently Professor of American History at the University of Chicago, he has also taught at the University of Rochester, Washington University in St. Louis, and the Salzburg Seminar of American Studies in Austria. He is the author of Slavery in the Cities, The Urban Frontier, and Chicago: Growth of a Metropolis, and is serving as general editor for the LIFE IN AMERICA series.

HOWARD R. ANDERSON

Past President of the National Council for the Social Studies, Dr. Anderson has taught at the University of Iowa and at Cornell University, and served as Provost of the University of Rochester. He began his teaching career in the public schools of Michigan and Iowa. Dr. Anderson, whose specialty is the teaching of history, is co-author of the widely used text, The History of Our World.

Copyright © 1971 by Houghton Mifflin Company

Printed in the U.S.A.

Library of Congress Catalog Card Number: 73–132975

Hardcover Edition ISBN: 0–395–11206–0
Softcover Edition ISBN: 0–395–11207–9

■ *Contents*

▪ *Life in America Series*

Almost a half century ago the philosopher George Santayana, writing about his fellow Americans in *Character and Opinion in the United States,* had this to say:

> . . . if there are immense differences between individual Americans . . . yet there is a great uniformity in their environment, customs, temper, and thoughts. They have all been uprooted from their several soils and ancestries and plunged together into one vortex, whirling irresistibly in a space otherwise quite empty. To be an American is of itself a moral condition, an education, and a career. . . .

One might express this idea another way by saying that there is indeed broad diversity in American life and yet enough similarity in the American experience to enable us profitably to explore that experience in its various facets — whether we are speaking of its rich cultural heritage or of the development of its political and social ·institutions. For "this soil is propitious to every seed," wrote Santayana. And it will be the purpose of the LIFE IN AMERICA series — of which the present volume is one — to trace the planting and the growth of those many seeds that go to make up American civilization as we know it today.

Coming originally from different — often disparate — national and social backgrounds, speaking a multiplicity of languages, our colonial forebears found on this broad continent the room and the freedom they sought. Here they shaped a new society while yet preserving much of their older heritage. From this interaction between the old and new, between the land and the people, a distinctively American civilization emerged.

For nearly two hundred years the mainstream of American life has remained sufficiently broad and open to contain a great variety of views and experience while continuing to add to — and thereby to enrich — our total cultural heritage.

This series examines what has come to be known as the American way of life by looking into the separate aspects of the American experience. It not only emphasizes the crises in the American past but traces the continuities as well. It discovers meaning in the life of ordinary people as well as in the achievements of their leaders. It illumines the great movements of history by viewing them first hand through the eyes of contemporaries. Most of all, it puts the student on the stage of history, making him a companion of the generations and the groups that have gone before.

Each volume in the LIFE IN AMERICA series deals with a particular facet of the American experience. In each, the story will begin by examining the way in which the people most involved with that aspect of national life have become part of the American story. Other selections will trace their development, chronicle their troubles and achievements and, finally, suggest present problems and prospects.

In this way the student will receive a balanced picture of the growth of his country. Instead of seeing American history as a series of crises and conflicts only, he will perceive also the continuing, if sometimes uneven, development of a free society. Instead of trying to find in Washington all the keys to understanding the American achievement, he will be encouraged to seek them as well in the many other sections of the country. And in searching for the significance of events, he will focus his attention not only on the prominent figures of history but on the experiences of ordinary citizens as well. He will be invited to participate vicariously, as he reads, in their struggles, hopes, aspirations, failures, and successes.

Today's America is a land of cities and city people, destined to become ever more urbanized. How did the first settlements — tender plants in forbidding soil — take root, flourish, and multiply? Why did new cities spring up where and how they did? What factors determined growth in population and commercial importance? Has three hundred years of city building resulted only in the transformation of the green wilderness into a more fearsome "asphalt jungle"? Selections in this volume record American's urban history in its full scope and variety, leaving the reader to seek his own answers, to interpret for himself causes and consequences.

Part One

New Cities in a New Land: 1630-1860

Part One: Introduction

Almost from the beginning of colonization, cities have played an important role in the American experience. Long before the rise of the modern metropolis of the nineteenth century, young commercial towns exercised a strong influence in the life of the colonies and the young nation. Soon after the first British settlements in the New World, towns appeared on the eastern seaboard and developed along with the back country. From Charleston in the South to Boston in the North, urban enclaves grew up and produced a style of life that contrasted sharply with the ways of farm, frontier, and plantation.

The Role of Colonial Cities

Cities very quickly became the centers of colonial life. Not only did they carry on extensive commerce with the outside world and engage in most of the manufacturing that took place in British North America, but they were also the setting and stimulus of cultural and intellectual activity. Here were found most of the newspapers, libraries, schools, social clubs, and museums. In the towns, too, churches flourished; music societies were formed; and debating and literary clubs appeared. And it is significant that the man most often referred to as the "first American," Benjamin Franklin, was a product of Boston and Philadelphia rather than of farm or plantation. (*See Section I, selections 4 and 5.*)

Of course, the first towns were small by modern standards, but sizable for the eighteenth century. Though Philadelphia had a population of only 40,000 at the time of the Revolution, it was larger than any other British city except London. And Boston, which would be the workshop of the Revolution, had only 16,000 residents in 1775. Yet their influence spread into the countryside and their strategic locations in the colonies magnified their importance. When trouble broke out with the mother country, the issues were shaped in the cities, which became the nerve centers of the colonies in the long struggle. (*See Section I, selections 11 and 12.*)

The Western Radiation

After the Revolution the young cities became commercial hubs of the new Republic. Philadelphia was the largest, but New York was chosen as the nation's first capital. While overseas trade continued to be the central concern of these ports, increasingly they turned their attention to the developing West. As the trans-Appalachian region filled up, eastern cities vied for their share of the market. In Philadelphia, Baltimore, Boston, and New York, businessmen and speculators drew up plans to tap the promising new lands. In Pennsylvania, a turnpike from Philadelphia to Lancaster set off a transportation revolution as eastern towns arranged to tie the western hinterland to their own marketplaces. The Erie Canal brought the Great Lakes to New York's doorstep. A little later Baltimore met the challenge with the Baltimore and Ohio Railroad, forging an iron link with the Ohio Valley. Within two generations, urban mercantile demand created an elaborate network of roads, canals, and railroads throughout the settled areas of the country. (*See Section II, selections 14, 15, and 16.*)

In the new regions, cities sprang up quickly. Indeed, they were established on the frontier line ahead of the line of settlement. When the British had drawn the Proclamation Line[1] across the Appalachians in order to stop the flow of settlers, a French merchant company was preparing to survey the streets of St. Louis, a thousand miles off in the wilderness. Whether as part of the activity of the French and Spanish from New Orleans or of the English and Americans operating from the Atlantic seaboard, the establishment of towns had actually preceded the breaking of soil in the West.

By 1830, the growth of Pittsburgh, Cincinnati, Louisville, and St. Louis had driven a broad wedge of urbanism into the new country. (*See Section II, selection 2.*) Rural regions supplied the cities with raw materials for their mills and packinghouses, and offered an expanding market for their shops and factories. In turn, urban centers serviced the surrounding areas by providing both the necessities and comforts of life as well as new opportunity for ambitious farm youths. Cities spread their economic power over the entire section, brought the fruits of civilization across the mountains, and insinuated their

[1] **Proclamation Line:** in 1763, when the British government declared the land west of the Alleghenies closed to white settlers and speculators, Daniel Boone was one of many who ignored the edict.

way into the countryside, thus speeding the transformation of the West from a gloomy wilderness into a richly diversified region.

The next generation saw the urbanization of the Great Lakes basin. Actually, places like Detroit, Cleveland, and Buffalo were founded much earlier, but their great growth followed the coming of the canals and the development of the lakes trade. Chicago and Milwaukee, late starters in the urban sweepstakes, flourished in the 1850's and 60's as the West filled up. (*See Section II, selection 5.*) Like the port cities on the Atlantic and the river towns of the Ohio Valley, these urban outposts owed their expansion to water commerce. They would all profit from the coming of the railroads, but their regional prominence was already established before the last phase of the transportation revolution.

Cities of the South and West

Southern cities shared this urban expansion. Resting on Dixie's irregular perimeter were New Orleans, Mobile, Savannah, Charleston, Richmond, Baltimore, Louisville, and St. Louis. These seaport and river towns shipped the area's produce to other regions, distributed necessary imports to the countryside, and provided enclaves of cosmopolitan life in a generally agricultural society. Scattered across the interior were smaller places, usually state capitals or trading towns with more than local importance. Then, too, there was Washington, the nation's capital but still very much a regional city. (*See Section II, selection 1.*) In fact, on the eve of the Civil War the census listed thirty places of over 8000 inhabitants throughout the South.

Even the West, which is generally thought of in terms of cowboys, Indians, and raw frontier conditions, produced important cities very early. In the Southwest, some Spanish towns grew after the coming of Americans. In Texas, Galveston, Houston, Austin, and San Antonio all had their important beginnings in the three decades before the war. San Francisco, Denver, Portland, and Seattle came into the urban census in the 1850's. Indeed, because the general population of these areas was so small and scattered, the cities made up a significant portion of the total number.

Social Dimensions of Urbanization

The surge of new population into cities aggravated the problems that had always confronted municipal governments. The lack of adequate housing meant overcrowding and unsanitary conditions.

Rapid building and congestion increased the chance of fire. The sources of water in use could no longer supply the amount needed for household and industrial purposes. More people, more wealth, and a high rate of transiency led to a rising crime rate and demands for better policing. The growing number of children forced local governments to set up more extensive school systems. Indeed, local governments themselves had to be reorganized to manage the broad range of problems occasioned by this first urban explosion. (*See Section II, selections 9–13.*)

But the spread of urbanization into all sections of the country was an important ingredient in the making of the nation. Though cities in different parts of the country had distinctive regional qualities, they shared characteristics which set them off from the surrounding countryside. That is, a resident of New York would be more at home in New Orleans than he would in a rural area of the Mohawk Valley in his own state. And a Chicagoan would find Boston more comfortable than the prairies of Illinois. Moreover, most of these cities were built on commerce, and leaders in each had business and personal contacts in other urban centers. Thus urbanization was a national movement that muted sectional differences and helped tie together a loosely knit federation. When the Civil War came, nearly all the cities in the South and the border states were reluctant to see these bonds snapped. ■

I. The Colonial City

When the British began the settlement of North America, the region was virtually without cities. Except for Spanish activity in Florida and the Southwest, the continent was only sparsely occupied by Indians, who, unlike those of Mexico and Peru, had no urban tradition. But by the beginning of the eighteenth century, New York (established by Dutch traders in 1625), Boston (1636), Newport, Rhode Island, (1639), Charleston (1670), and Philadelphia (1682) had been laid out and securely established. Some colonial towns developed spontaneously (Boston) while others followed strict plans devised by their founders (Philadelphia).

If colonial towns seem small by present standards, their problems were very contemporary. Almost all the issues we think are "new" or "modern" arose in the young cities. Housing was shoddy and crowded; disorder and crime were common, and police and fire protection inadequate; streets quickly became dirty and congested; schools were scarce and unsatisfactory; unsanitary conditions produced high death rates. Local governments complained that rural domination of colonial assemblies frustrated their attempts to improve conditions.

Despite their difficulties, the cities provided a focus for the intellectual and political life of the colonies. "Liberty, science, and commerce," wrote a visitor to North America in 1773, "always take up their chief residence in cities. . . . To them repair the patriots, the men of letters, and the merchants, who become the guardians of the people's rights, the protectors of learning, the supporters of their country's trade. Thus the cities . . . are the repositories, preservators, and nurseries of commerce, liberty, and knowledge."

The British were soon forcefully reminded of the importance of their colonial towns. When the leaders in London attempted to reorganize the empire after the wars with the French, it was American cities that were first to resist. The mother country tried to tighten up the loosely administered empire and put it on a self-sustaining basis. The program required the raising of revenue, the stationing of troops, and the reordering of customs collections in the colonies. These new

6

measures rubbed especially against the cities, where could be found powerful merchants whose usual profitable commerce was threatened.

The particular core of resistance to British policy was Boston, the central city of North America, which had fallen on difficult times after the imperial wars. Boston reacted quickly when the new program seemed to threaten its already precarious position. It took the lead in resistance and became the workshop of the Revolution. Other cities followed suit. Everywhere merchants were first to resist, with a radical movement rising behind them. The alliance between the two was always uneasy, and by 1770 the businessmen had withdrawn. But Britain again forced the issue with the Tea Act in 1773. The rebels replied with the Boston Tea Party, and the British countered with the Coercive Acts, which closed the port of Boston, moved the capital to Salem, and permitted the quartering of troops. The rest of the colonies supported Massachusetts, the back country joined the resistance, and events moved toward a final confrontation. In this perspective, the American Revolution can be said to have begun not on the rolling green at Lexington but on the cobblestones of Boston. ■

Population Growth of Colonial Cities, 1700–1790

	1700	1730	1775	1776	1790
New York	5000	8622*	25,000	5000	33,131*
Philadelphia	5000	11,500	40,000	21,767*	28,522*
Boston	6700	13,000	16,000	3500	18,320*
Charleston	2000	4500	12,000	12,000	16,359*

New York	16%
Philadelphia	18%
Boston	37%
Charleston	12%

1700 population as percentage of 1790 figure

* Denotes actual census figure; others are estimates from Carl Bridenbaugh, *Cities in Revolt: Urban Life in America, 1743–1776* (Capricorn Books, 1955).

Note the sharp decrease in the population of the three northern cities as a result of the Revolution. Many people went to live in the countryside, and some Tories fled to Canada or the West Indies.

1. Penn's Green Country Town[1]

✤ William Penn

America offered its immigrants a unique opportunity to control their environment through town planning. William Penn's design for Philadelphia is the best known of many such ventures. By proclamation of Charles II in 1681, Penn was made absolute proprietor of Pennsylvania, in which he promised to establish a "free colony for all mankind." In 1682 he laid out Philadelphia, and in 1683 concluded a treaty with the Indians which had the effect of protecting the colony from attack.

While Penn could not automatically create a new society, he was determined to provide a physical setting which would encourage the development of an excellent city. He benefited from a knowledge of various proposals advanced for the rebuilding of London after the great fire of 1666. The following excerpt from Penn's Instructions reveals his major aims: the city must be on a navigable river to insure its commercial prominence; it must be in a healthy area; and there must be a system of dividing the land equitably among the inhabitants. Also note the attempt to avoid the usual congestion by placing houses at the center of each plot, or "plat," as Penn called it, and providing for uniform streets. ■

. . . 2nd. That having taken what care you can for the people's good, in the respects abovesaid, let the rivers and creeks be sounded on my side of [the] Delaware River, especially upland, in order to settle a great town, and be sure to make your choice where it is most navigable, high, dry, and healthy; that is, where most ships may best ride, of deepest draught of water, if possible to load or unload at the bank or key[2] side, without boating and lightering[3] of it. It would do well if the river coming into that creek be navigable, at least for boats, up into the country, and that the situation be high, at least dry and sound, and not swampy, which is best known by digging up two or three [places] and seeing the bottom.

[1] Samuel Hazard, *Annals of Pennsylvania, from the Discovery of the Delaware,* 1609–1682 (Philadelphia: Hazard and Mitchell, 1850), pp. 528–531.
[2] **key**: place alongside water for loading and unloading vessels.
[3] **lightering**: transporting by means of barges.

3rd. Such a place being found out, for navigation, healthy situation, and good soil for provision, lay out ten thousand acres contiguous to it in the best manner you can, as the bounds and extent of the liberties of the said town.

4th. The proportion in the said town is to be thus: every share, or five thousand acres, shall have a hundred acres of land out of that ten thousand acres. If more than one be concerned in the share, as it may easily fall out, then they to agree of the dividing of the same, as they shall think fit, still keeping to proportion, as if one hundred pounds will have a hundred acres, five pounds will have five acres. . . .

12th. Be sure to settle the figure of the town so that the streets hereafter may be uniform down to the water from the country bounds; let the place for the storehouse be on the middle of the key, which will yet serve for market and statehouses too. This may be ordered when I come, only let the houses built be in a line, or upon a line, as much as may be.

13th. Pitch upon the very middle of the plat where the town or line of houses is to be laid or run, facing the harbor and great river, for the situation of my house, and let it be not the tenth part of the town, as the conditions say, viz., that out of every hundred thousand acres shall be reserved to me ten [thousand], but I shall be contented with less than a thirtieth part, to wit, three hundred acres, whereas several will have two by purchasing two shares, that is, ten thousand acres, and it may be fitting for me to exceed a little.

14th. The distance of each house from the creek or harbor should be, in my judgment, a measured quarter of a mile, at least two hundred paces, because of building hereafter streets downward to the harbor.

15th. Let every house be placed, if the person pleases, in the middle of the plat, as to the breadth of it, so that there may be ground on each side for gardens or orchards, or fields, that it may be a green country town, which will never be burned, and always be wholesome.

16th. I judge that you must be guided in your breadth of land by what you can get that is unplanted and will not be parted with, but so far as I can guess at this distance, methinks in a city, each share to have fifty poles[4] upon the front to the river, and the rest backward will be sufficient. But perhaps you may have more, and perhaps you will not have so much space to allow; herein follow your land and situation, being always just to proportion.

---

[4] **pole:** a rod, or 16½ linear feet.

17th. Lastly—Be sure to keep the conditions hereunto affixed, and see that no vice or evil conversation go uncomplained of or punished in any, that God be not provoked to wrath against the country.

In witness hereof, I do hereunto, the 30th of September, 1681, set to my hand and seal.

WILLIAM PENN

2. Oglethorpe's Healthful Place

James Oglethorpe had won distinction at a very early age as a soldier serving under Prince Eugene of Savoy in the war against the Turks. But he preferred to devote his talents to constructive and benevolent works of peace. In 1722 he became a member of the British Parliament, and in 1732 obtained a charter for a colony to be carved out of Carolina. Named Georgia in honor of the monarch, it was to be a refuge for the honorable poor and the persecuted. Oglethorpe intended to make Savannah its principal city.

The first excerpt given below contains a part of Oglethorpe's argument in favor of the establishment of such a colony. The second, taken from a letter he wrote to the Trustees in England, describes the site of Savannah. As Penn had done, Oglethorpe chose a place which afforded harbor facilities and seemed to be healthful. In the third selection, Francis Moore, a storekeeper in the colony, describes Savannah in 1736, three years after its founding. ■

A. THE INCORPORATION[1]

✤ James Oglethorpe

Let us . . . cast our eyes on the multitude of unfortunate people in the kingdom of reputable families, and of liberal or at least easy education; some undone by guardians, some by lawsuits, some by acci-

[1] James Oglethorpe, *A New and Accurate Account of the Provinces of South Carolina and Georgia,* in *Collections of the Georgia Historical Society,* Vol. I (Savannah, 1840), pp. 56–58.

dents in commerce, some by stocks and bubbles, . . . But all agree in this one circumstance, that they must either be burdensome to their relations, or betake themselves to little shifts for sustenance, which (it is ten to one) do not answer their purposes, and to which a well-educated mind descends with the utmost constraint. What various misfortunes may reduce the rich, the industrious, to the danger of a prison, to the moral certainty of starving! These are the people that may relieve themselves and strengthen Georgia, by resorting thither, and Great Britain by their departure. . . .

Having thus described (I fear, too truly) the pitiable condition of the better sort of the indigent, an objection rises against their removal upon what is stated of their imbecility for drudgery. It may be asked, if they can't get bread here for their labor, how will their condition be mended in Georgia? The answer is easy. . . . They have land there for nothing, and that land is so fertile that . . . they receive a hundredfold increase for taking very little pains. . . . If I make twenty pounds of the produce of a field and am to pay twenty pounds rent for it, it is plain I must perish if I have not another fund to support me. But if I pay no rent, the produce of that field will supply the mere necessities of life.

With a view to the relief of people in the condition I have described, his majesty has this present year incorporated a considerable number of persons of quality and distinction, and vested a large tract of South Carolina in them, by the name of Georgia, in trust to be distributed among the necessitous. These Trustees not only give land to the unhappy who go thither, but are also empowered to receive the voluntary contributions of charitable persons to enable them to furnish the poor adventurers with all the necessaries for the expense of the voyage, occupying the land, and supporting them till they find themselves comfortably settled. So that now the unfortunate will not be obliged to bind themselves to a long servitude to pay for their passage, for they may be carried gratis into a land of liberty and plenty; where they immediately find themselves in possession of a competent estate, in a happier climate than they knew before, and they are unfortunate indeed if here they cannot forget their sorrows.

B. THE PLAN[2]

✦ *James Oglethorpe*

GENTLEMEN:[3]

I gave you an account in my last [letter] of our arrival at Charles-town [Charleston]. The governor and assembly have given us all possible encouragement. Our people arrived at Beaufort on the 20th of January, where I lodged them in some new barracks built for the soldiers, while I went myself to view the Savannah River. I fixed upon a healthy situation about ten miles from the sea. The river here forms a half-moon, along the south side of which the banks are about forty feet high, and on the top flat, which they call a bluff. The plain high ground extends into the country five or six miles, and along the riverside about a mile. Ships that draw twelve feet [of] water can ride within ten yards of the bank. Upon the riverside in the center of this plain I have laid out the town. Opposite to it is an island of very rich pasturage, which I think should be kept for the Trustees' cattle. The river is pretty wide, the water fresh, and from the key of the town you see its whole course to the sea, with the island of Tybee, which forms the mouth of the river; and on the other way, you see the river for about six miles up into the country. The landscape is very agreeable, the stream being wide and bordered with high woods on both sides.

The whole people arrived here on the first of February. At night their tents were got up. Till the seventh we were taken up in unload-ing and making a crane, which I then could not get finished, so took off the hands, and set some to the fortifications, and began to fell the woods. I marked out the town and common; half of the former is already cleared, and the first house was begun yesterday afternoon. Not being able to get Negroes, I have taken ten of the independent company to work for us, for which I make them an allowance. I send you a copy of the resolutions of the assembly, and the governor and council's letter to me. Mr. Whitaker has given us one hundred head of cattle. Col. Bull, Mr. Barlow, Mr. St. Julian, and Mr. Wood-ward are come up to assist us with some of their own servants. I am

---

[2] James Oglethorpe, *Reasons for Establishing the Colony of Georgia,* in *Collec-tions of the Georgia Historical Society,* Vol. I (Savannah, 1840), pp. 233–234.

[3] **Gentlemen:** the Trustees.

so taken up in looking after a hundred necessary things, that I write now short, but shall give you a more particular account hereafter. A little Indian nation, the only one within fifty miles, is not only at amity, but desirous to be the subjects of His Majesty King George, to have lands given them among us, and to [educate] their children at our schools. Their chief, and his beloved man, who is the second man in the nation, desire to be instructed in the Christian religion.

I am, gentlemen, your most obedient, humble servant,

JAMES OGLETHORPE

C. A GROWING TOWN[4]

✦ Francis Moore

. . . I [Francis Moore] took a view of the town of Savannah. It is about a mile and a quarter in circumference; it stands upon the flat of a hill. The bank of the river . . . is steep and about forty-five feet perpendicular, so that all heavy goods are brought up by a crane, an inconvenience designed to be remedied by a bridged wharf with an easy ascent, which in laying out the town care was taken to allow room for, there being a very wide strand between the first row of houses and the river. . . .

The town of Savannah is built of wood; all the houses of the first forty freeholders[5] are of the same size with that Mr. Oglethorpe lives in, but there are great numbers built since, I believe 100 or 150. Many of these are much larger, some two or three stories high, the boards planed and painted. The houses stand on large lots, sixty feet in front by ninety feet in depth; each lot has a fore and back street to it. The lots are fenced in with split pales; some few people have palisades of turned wood before their doors, but the generality have been wise enough not to throw away their money, which, in this country, laid out in husbandry[6] is capable of great improvements. . . . There are some . . . [people] who have made but little or bad use of the benefits they received, idling away their time whilst they had

---

[4] Francis Moore, A *Voyage to Georgia, Begun in the Year 1735,* in *Collections of the Georgia Historical Society,* Vol. I, pp. 94–98.

[5] **freeholders:** a freehold is property held for life; therefore, property-owners.

[6] **husbandry:** proper management of resources.

provisions from the public store, or else working for hire, earning from two shillings, the price of a laborer, to four or five shillings, the price of a carpenter, per diem, and spending that money in rum and good living, thereby neglecting to improve their lands, so when their time of receiving provisions from the public ceased they were in no [position] to maintain themselves out of their own lands. . . .

. . . Their houses are built at a pretty large distance from one another for fear of fire; the streets are very wide, and there are great squares left at proper distances for markets and other conveniences. Near the riverside there is a guard house enclosed with palisades a foot thick where there are nineteen or twenty cannons mounted, and a continual guard kept by the freeholders. This town is governed by three bailiffs and has a recorder, register, and a town court, which is held every six weeks, where all matters civil and criminal are decided by grand and petty juries as in England. But there are no lawyers allowed to plead for hire, nor . . . attorneys to take money, but (as in old times in England) every man pleads his own cause. . . .

Restrictions on Inheritance

The freeholds are all entailed,[7] which has been very fortunate for the place. If people could have sold, the greatest part, before they knew the value of their lots, would have parted with them for a trifling condition, and there were not wanting rich men who employed agents to monopolize the whole town; and if they had got numbers of lots into their hands, the other freeholders would have had no benefit by letting their houses, and hardly of trade, since the rich, by means of a large capital, would underlet and undersell, and the town must have been almost without inhabitants. . . .

Free Whites Only

The mentioning the laws and customs leads me to take notice that Georgia is founded upon maxims different from those on which other colonies have been begun. The intention of that colony was an asylum to receive the distressed. This was the charitable design, and the governmental view besides that was, with numbers of free white people well settled, to strengthen the southern part of the English settlements on the continent of America of which this is the frontier. It is necessary, therefore, not to permit slaves in such a country, for slaves starve the poor laborer. . . .

[7] **entailed:** they could be passed on only to certain descendants.

Why Land Holdings Are Limited

In order to maintain many people, it was proper that the land should be divided into small portions, and to prevent the uniting [of] them by marriage or purchase. For every time the two lots are united, the town loses a family, and the inconveniency of this shows itself at Savannah, notwithstanding the care of the Trustees to prevent it. They suffered [a number] of lots to descend to the widows during their lives: those who remarried to men who had lots of their own, by uniting two lots made one be neglected, for the strength of hands who could take care of one was not sufficient to look to and improve two.

These uncleared lots are a nuisance to their neighbors. The trees which grown upon them shade the lots, the beasts take shelter in them, and, for want of clearing the brooks which pass through, the lands above are often prejudiced by floods. To prevent all these inconveniences, the first regulation of the Trustees was a strict agrarian law, by which all the lands near towns should be divided, fifty acres to a freeholder. The quantity of land by experience seems rather too much, since it is impossible that one poor family can tend so much land. If this allotment is too much, how much more inconvenient would the uniting of two be? To prevent it, the Trustees grant the lands in tail[8] male, that on the expiring of a male line they may regrant it to such man, having no other lot, as shall be married to the next female heir of the deceased, as is of good character. This manner of dividing prevents also the sale of lands and the rich thereby monopolizing the country.

Wards and Villages

. . . Every ten houses make a tithing,[9] and to every tithing there is a mile square, which is divided into twelve lots, besides roads: each freeholder of the tithing has a lot or farm of forty-five acres there, and two lots are reserved by the Trustees in order to defray the charge of the public. . . . Every forty houses in town makes a ward, to which four square miles in the country belong; each ward has a constable, and under him four tithing men. Where the town lands end, the villages begin; four villages make a ward without, which depends upon

---

[8] **tail:** limitation of an estate to a particular class of heirs.
[9] **tithing:** administrative division, often for the election of town officials or peace officers.

one of the wards within the town. The use of this is, in case a war should happen, the villages may have places in the town to bring their cattle and families into for refuge, and to that purpose there is a square left in every ward, big enough for the outwards to encamp in.

3. Growth along the Delaware[1]

✤ Benjamin Bullivant

Once settled, the new cities prospered as immigrants seeking a better existence poured in. The full panoply of urban life emerged in all its bustling vitality. Buildings rose rapidly to meet the needs of the growing population, ships crowded into port, and a daily routine quickly established itself. But within this general framework each city developed a distinct character which visitors were quick to detect. In the following account of Philadelphia, Benjamin Bullivant, a well-known Boston physician, describes with some amazement the Quaker City as he found it in 1697, only fifteen years after Penn's experiment began. ■

Philadelphia in Pennsylvania is [situated] on the Delaware River 150 miles from the sea. It is now but fifteen years since they began to build, and yet [they] do already show a very magnificent city. The streets are regularly laid out along the Delaware, and [extend] into the land, broad and even, leading forth into smooth roads that carry you into the country. At about two miles' distance from the River Delaware, direct from the city, is another large river, called Schuylkill [*skool'*kill], beyond which some are building. This is the extent of the city bounds to the land from the Delaware, and it is probable enough the vacancy between the two rivers may in time be made into fair streets and joined into one city as is designed and laid out by the Proprietor, and surveyed by Mr. Penn in his printed draft of the city of Philadelphia, which when it is finished will be almost a square in form.

[1] Adapted from "The Travel Diary of Dr. Benjamin Bullivant," as edited by Wayne Andrews, in *New-York Historical Society Quarterly*, Vol. XL, No. 1 (January 1956), pp. 69–71. Reprinted by permission.

The Delaware is fresh and good water; [there are] pumps and wells. Here is also sundry sort of fish, sturgeon and flesh of all sorts [being plentiful] enough. There are some few large and stately dwellings of some eminent merchants, but ordinarily their houses [do not exceed] our second-rate buildings in London, and many [are] lower. But [they are] generally very pretty, with posts in the streets as in London and shops after the English mode. They have a market twice a week, with butcher stalls and blocks and a market bell, rung also at certain hours of the day by a woman to give the time. . . . Here is a very large, tall, brick meeting house for the Quakers near the marketplace, and not far distant a neat little church for the Church of England, English fashion, handsomely [fenced] in, [with] a sufficient decent burial place annexed to it.

Philadelphia has somewhat upward of 500 families dwelling now in it, and very many buildings going forward. It seems already to exceed most shire towns[2] in England. . . . Philadelphia has the purest bread and the strongest beer in America; the beef, veal, and pork [are] tolerable, but short of England, mutton and lamb indifferent, but scarce at some times of the year. Butter and cheese are very good. . . .

It is at this instant very hot weather, which obliges people to go very thinly [clad]. Of the Negroes and Indians I saw many quite naked, except what covered the secrets of nature. Vessels of 500 tons lay their sides to the wharves and unload by their own tackle. The Quakers are very generous in their entertainments and furnish their houses very neatly. They [are willing] to marry their daughters to men of the world [non-Quakers], and indeed there are many of them very pretty women. Here are apples, pears, peaches, apricots, mulberries, and cherries in abundance. They pay little or no taxes of any sort whatsoever, nor any customs, or excises; they have no militia, only a night watch in Philadelphia, justices and constables, county courts, provincial courts, and assemblies.

The [next best] town in this province on the Delaware is Newcastle, forty miles below Philadelphia toward the sea. It is a pretty town, it builds ships and has merchants residing in it. Here live many Swedes formerly banished from their own country for misdemeanors. Here they live well, have good farms, and are under English government. . . .

---

[2] **shire towns:** county seats.

Thursday, July 8th. I went down the Delaware in the ordinary passage boat for Newcastle. . . . About halfway is Chester, an old settlement that has a good creek for [securing] sloops, a town house, a Quaker meeting house, a prison under the town house; [it] contains about fifty families. Thence to Newcastle is twenty miles. This is also an ancient settlement; here is the custom house, a small [ruined] church, a pretty town house on which they hoist the king's flag at approach of any three-masted vessel which may be espied coming in (at a good distance) out of Delaware Bay. They have six iron guns mounted on the bank but hardly large enough to command the river. Vessels also stop here going down to the sea. About eight miles below Newcastle is a creek, by which you may come to a neck of land across which are drawn goods to and from Maryland. Sloops also of thirty tons are carried overland in this place on certain sleds drawn by oxen, and launched again into the water on the other side.

4. New World Metropolis[1]

✦ *Joseph Bennett*

Trade was the lifeblood of the infant cities. One of the vital functions of such places as Boston and Philadelphia was to serve as centers for the exchange of goods between the growing hinterlands and world markets. Besides providing the reason for their existence, commerce brought more people and money to the cities, laid the foundation of a merchant middle class, and contributed to the cosmopolitan character of the ports.

An English observer, Joseph Bennett, describes the flourishing city of Boston, the capital of the New England colony, as it appeared a century after its founding. ■

This town [Boston] stands on a peninsula, or almost island, about four miles in circumference, at the bottom of a fine bay of the sea. . . .

[1] Joseph Bennett, "History of New England," *Proceedings of the Massachusetts Society* (Boston: Printed for the Society, 1862), Vol. V, pp. 108–112, 115–117, 124–126.

This town has a good natural security, in my opinion, for there is great plenty of rocks and shoals, which are not easy to be avoided by strangers to the coasts; and there is but one safe channel to approach the harbor, and that so narrow that three ships can hardly sail abreast, but within the harbor there is room enough for 500 sail to lie at anchor. . . .

At the bottom of the bay there is a fine wharf, about half a mile in length, on the north side of which are built many warehouses for the storing of merchants' goods; this they call the Long Wharf, to distinguish it from others of lesser note. And to this wharf ships of the greatest burden come up so close as to unload their cargo without the assistance of boats.

From the end of the Long Wharf, which lies east from the town, the buildings rise gradually with an easy ascent westward about a mile. There are a great many good houses and several fine streets, little inferior to some of our best in London, the principal of which is King's Street. . . . at the upper end of it stands the Town House, or Guild Hall, where the Governor meets the Council and House of Representatives, and the several courts of justice are held there also. And there are likewise walks for the merchants, where they meet everyday at one o'clock . . . round which there are several booksellers' shops. And there are four or five printing-houses which have full employment in printing books . . . that are brought from England and other parts of Europe.

This town was not built after any regular plan, but has been enlarged from time to time as the inhabitants increased, and is now, from north to south, something more than two miles in length, and in the widest part about one mile and a half in breadth. According to the best account I have been able to come at, which is from their muster-roll,[2] there is near three thousand houses and about thirty thousand souls. There are three Episcopal churches, one of which is called the King's Chapel and has a handsome organ and a magnificent seat for the Governor. . . . There are nine independent meeting-houses, one Anabaptist meeting, one Quakers' meeting, and one French church. There are sixty streets, forty-one lanes, and eighteen alleys, besides squares, courts, etc. The streets are well paved and lying upon a descent. The town is, for the generality, as dry and clean as any I ever remember to have seen. When we were upon the

---

[2] **muster-roll:** usually, a register of officers and men in military companies.

sea, that part of the town which lies about the harbor appeared to us in the form of a crescent . . . and the country, rising gradually from it, afforded us a pleasant prospect of the neighboring fields and woods.

A Center for Commodity Exchange

Boston is said to be not only the principal town of trade in New England, but also of any in all the British-American colonies. They employ annually between three and four hundred ships, great and small; and they also build abundance of shipping for the English and other European nations. They have likewise a whale and several cod fisheries, which are very considerable, which with their shipbuilding is the chief support of the country. They trade to the Carolinas and also to Jamaica and Barbados, and all the other West Indian islands and plantations in general, with whom they exchange their beef, port, fish, and other provisions, and also what they call lumber (such as deal-boards,[3] [cask] and hogshead staves, shingles, and such like commodities), for rice, pitch, tar, rum and sugar, and spices and logwood; great part of the last-named commodities they send to England in return for almost all sorts of English goods, but more especially clothing for men, women, and children. They have paper manufactured here, and some coarse woolen cloth, but workmen's wages are so high in this part of the world that they find it cheaper to import them from London. . . .

Boston being the capital of New England . . . the country people find their account in bringing . . . their choicest provisions to this town . . . this place is well served with all sorts of eatables. . . . Their beef, mutton, and lamb are as good as ever I desire to eat; and as to their veal, it is not so white and fine, in common, as at London. . . . As to their pork they challenge all the world. . . . They make but little bacon, and that, in my opinion, is not half so good as ours, but they pickle their pork so well that it answers the same end as fine bacon. Their poultry, too, of all sorts are as fine as can be desired, and they have plenty of fine fish of various kinds, all of which are very cheap.

Religious Observances and Charity

Their observation of the sabbath (which they rather choose to call by the name of the Lord's Day, . . .) is the strictest that ever I yet

---

[3] **deal-boards:** planks of specific measure, here probably six feet long.

saw anywhere. On that day, no man, woman, or child is permitted to go out of town on any pretense whatsoever; nor can any that are out of town come in on the Lord's Day. The town being situated on a peninsula, there is but one way out of it by land. [This] is over a narrow neck of land at the south end of the town, which is enclosed by a fortification and the gates shut by way of prevention there also. . .

But that which is the most extraordinary is that they commence the sabbath from the setting of the sun on the Saturday evening, and, in conformity to that, all trade and business ceases, and every shop in the town is shut up. Even a barber is [subject to fine] for shaving after that time. Nor are any of the taverns permitted to entertain company, for, in that case, not only the house but every person found therein is [subject to fine]. . . .

They also provide very well for their poor and are very tender of exposing those that have lived in a handsome manner. [They] therefore give them good relief in so private a manner that it is seldom known to any of their neighbors. And for the meaner sort they have a place built on purpose, which is called the Town Alms-house, where they are kept in a decent manner, and are, as I think, taken care of in every respect suitable to their circumstances in life. For the generality, there are above a hundred poor persons in this house, and there is no such thing to be seen in town nor country as a strolling beggar. And it is a rare thing to meet with any drunken people or to hear an oath sworn in their streets.

Sober Amusements

For their domestic amusements, every afternoon, after drinking tea, the gentlemen and ladies walk the Mall, and from thence adjourn to one another's houses to spend the evening—those that are not disposed to attend the evening lecture, which they may do, six nights in seven the year round. . . .

What they call the Mall is a walk on a fine green Common adjoining to the southwest side of the town. It is near half a mile over, with two rows of young trees planted opposite to each other, with a fine footway between, in imitation of St. James's Park [in London]. Part of the bay of the sea which encircles the town, taking its course along the northwest side of the Common, . . . forms a beautiful canal, in view of the walk. . . .

The government being in the hands of dissenters,[4] they don't admit of plays or music-houses; but, of late, they have set up an assembly, to which some of the ladies resort. But they are looked upon to be none of the nicest in regard to their reputation, and it is thought it will soon be suppressed, for it is much taken notice of and exploded by the religious and sober part of the people. But, notwithstanding plays and such like diversions do not obtain here, they don't seem to be dispirited nor moped for want of them, for both the ladies and the gentlemen dress and appear as gay . . . as courtiers in England on a coronation or birthday. And the ladies here visit, drink tea, and indulge every little piece of gentility to the height of the mode, and neglect the affairs of their families with as good a grace as the finest ladies in London.

[4] **dissenters:** Massachusetts Bay Colony was founded by Puritans, known as dissenters because they did not accept the dogma and ritual of the Church of England.

5. A Mutual Improvement Society[1]

✦ Benjamin Franklin

By the early 1700's a healthy urban economy had produced a small but important class of citizens with time and money for the "finer things of life." Those who had done well could indulge their taste for luxuries and at the same time advertise their newly found status. They commissioned artists to paint their portraits, patronized booksellers, and bought expensive jewelry and furnishings. Painters, silversmiths, cabinetmakers, wine merchants, and others who depended on this kind of clientele began to set up businesses in Boston and Philadelphia and New York. Thus colonial cities contributed to the emergence of a distinctly American culture.

One result of the growth of leisure time was the establishment of literary societies, such as Benjamin Franklin's famed Junto. (the word means "self-appointed committee"). In the following excerpt, Franklin describes members of the club and in so doing reveals something of the origins of the American leisure class. ∎

[1] *Autobiography of Benjamin Franklin,* edited by John Bigelow (Philadelphia: J. B. Lippincott & Co., 1868), pp. 168–170.

In the autumn of the preceding year, I had formed most of my ingenious acquaintances into a club of mutual improvement, which we called the Junto; we met on Friday evenings. The rules that I drew up required that every member, in his turn, should produce one or more queries on any point of morals, politics, or natural philosophy, to be discussed by the company, and once in three months produce and read an essay of his own writing on any subject he pleased. Our debates were to be under the direction of a president and to be conducted in the sincere spirit of inquiry after truth, without fondness for dispute or desire of victory. . . . [T]o prevent warmth, all expressions of positiveness in opinions or direct contradictions were after some time . . . prohibited under small [monetary] penalties.

The first members were Joseph Breintal, a copier of deed for the scriveners,[2] a good-natured, friendly, middle-aged man, a great lover of poetry, reading all he could meet with and writing some that was tolerable, very ingenious in many little knicknackeries, and of sensible conversation.

Thomas Godfrey, a self-taught mathematician, great in his way, and afterward inventor of what is now called Hadley's Quadrant.[3] But he knew little out of his way and was not a pleasing companion, as, like most mathematicians I have met with, he expected universal precision in everything said or was forever denying or distinguishing upon trifles, to the disturbance of all conversation. He soon left us.

Nicholas Scull, a surveyor, afterward surveyor-general, who loved books and sometimes made a few verses.

William Maugridge, a joiner, a most exquisite mechanic, and a solid, sensible man.

Hugh Meredith, Stephen Potts, and George Webb I have characterized before.

Robert Grace, a young gentleman of some fortune, generous, lively, and witty, a lover of punning and of his friends.

And William Coleman, then a merchant's clerk, about my age, who had the coolest, clearest head, the best heart, and the exactest morals of almost any man I ever met with. He became afterwards a merchant of great note and one of our provincial judges. Our friendship continued without interruption to his death, upward of forty years, and

[2] **scriveners:** they offered a public writing service.
[3] **Hadley's Quadrant:** an instrument for measuring altitude, used in navigation and astronomy.

the club continued almost as long and was the best school of philosophy, morality, and politics that then existed in the province. . . . [O]ur queries, which were read the week preceding their discussion, put us upon reading with attention upon the several subjects that we might speak more to the purpose, and here, too, we acquired better habits of conversation, everything being studied in our rules which might prevent our disgusting each other. From hence the long continuance of the club.

6. Cleaner Streets[1]

✢ Benjamin Franklin

As soon as there were cities, the constant dangers to public health and safety they posed were a matter of concern to responsible citizens. Town governments did not at first provide adequate thoroughfares; most streets were mere dirt paths, impassable after rain and filled with choking dust in dry weather. Residents habitually dumped garbage, human waste, and other refuse outside their doors, annoying passers-by and creating a health hazard. City officials hired scavengers to clear away the rubbish and contracted to pave some streets, but their early efforts were not impressive. In the following selection, Benjamin Franklin tells how he started a one-man movement to correct the condition of his street in Philadelphia. ∎

Our city, though laid out with a beautiful regularity, the streets large, straight, and crossing each other at right angles, had the disgrace of suffering those streets to remain long unpaved, and in wet weather the wheels of heavy carriages plowed them into a quagmire . . . and in dry weather the dust was offensive. I had lived near what was called the Jersey Market and saw with pain the inhabitants wading in mud while purchasing their provisions. A strip of ground down the middle of that market was at length paved with brick, so that being once in

[1] *Ibid.*, pp. 285–287.

the market they had firm footing, but were often over shoes in dirt to get there. By talking and writing on the subject, I was at length instrumental in getting the street paved with stone between the market and the bricked foot-pavement that was on each side next the houses. This for some time gave an easy access to the market dry-shod, but the rest of the street not being paved, whenever a carriage came out of the mud upon this pavement, it shook off and left its dirt upon it. . . . [Thus the street] was soon covered with mire, which was not removed, the city as yet having no scavengers.

After some inquiry, I found a poor, industrious man who was willing to undertake keeping the pavement clean by sweeping it twice a week, carrying off the dirt from before all the neighbors' doors for the sum of sixpence per month, to be paid by each house. I then wrote and printed a paper setting forth the advantages to the neighborhood that might be obtained by this small expense: the greater ease in keeping our houses clean, so much dirt not being brought in by people's feet; the benefit to the shops by more [business] . . . as buyers could more easily get at them, and by not having . . . the dust blown in upon their goods, . . . I sent one of these papers to each house, and in a day or two went round to see who would subscribe an agreement to pay these sixpences. [I]t was unanimously signed and for a time well executed. All the inhabitants of the city were delighted with the cleanliness of the pavement that surrounded the market, . . . and this raised a general desire to have all the streets paved and made the people more willing to submit to a tax for that purpose.

After some time I drew a bill for paving the city and brought it into the Assembly. It was just before I went to England, in 1757, and did not pass till I was gone, and then with an alteration in the mode of assessment, which I thought not for the better, but with an additional provision for lighting as well as paving the streets, which was a great improvement. It was by a private person, the late Mr. John Clifton, . . . giving a sample of the utility of lamps by placing one at his door, that the people were first impressed with the idea of lighting all the city. The honor of this public benefit has also been ascribed to me, but it belongs truly to that gentleman. I did not but follow his example and have only some merit to claim respecting the form of our lamps, as differing from the globe lamps we were at first supplied with from London.

7. Fire in the City[1]

✤ Cotton Mather

Another serious urban problem was the ever-present threat of fire. Because houses were so close together and often built of highly combustible material, a blaze could spread rapidly. Open fires for cooking and heating were the rule. The water supply was often scanty, and the bucket brigade and primitive pumper inadequate to deal with a serious fire. Sometimes authorities blew up buildings with gunpowder in order to halt the flames. Many lives and homes were lost in major conflagrations in Boston in 1676 and 1679, and in Charleston, South Carolina, in 1731 and 1740. Most fires were not as destructive as these, but they exacted a steady toll in lives and property throughout the colonial period. Here Cotton Mather, the famous Puritan preacher and writer, describes one of Boston's most serious fires. ◼

Beginning about seven o'clock in the evening, and finishing before two in the morning, the night between the second and third of October, 1711, a terrible fire laid the heart of Boston, the metropolis of New-English America, in ashes. The occasion of the fire is said to have been the carelessness of a sottish woman, who suffered a flame which took the oakum,[2] the picking whereof was her business, to gain too far before it could be mastered. It was not long before it reduced Cornhill into miserable ruins, and it made its impressions into King Street and Queen Street, and a great part of Pudding-lane was also lost, before the violence of it could be conquered.

Among these ruins there were two spacious edifices, which, until now, made a most considerable figure, because of the public relation to our greatest solemnities in which they had stood from the days of our fathers. The one was the town house; the other [was] the old meeting house. The number of houses, and some of them very ca-

---

[1] American Antiquarian Society, *Transactions*, VI (Albany, New York: Joel Munsell, 1874), pp. 247–248.

[2] oakum: loose fiber obtained by picking apart old rope; used for calking the seams of ships.

pacious buildings, which went into the fire with these is computed near about a hundred; and the families, which inhabited these houses, cannot but be very many more. It being also a place of much trade, and filled with well-furnished shops of goods, not a little of the wealth of the town was now consumed.

But that which very much added to the horror of the dismal night, was the tragical death of many poor men who were killed by the blowing up of houses, or by venturing too far into the fire, for the rescue of what its fierce jaws were ready to prey upon. Of these the bones of seven or eight were thought to be found; and it is feared there may be some strangers belonging to vessels, besides these, thus buried, of whose unhappy circumstances we are not yet apprised; and others have since died of their wounds. Thus the town of Boston, just going to get beyond fourscore years of age, and conflicting with much labor and sorrow, is, a very vital and valuable part of it, soon cut off and flown away.

8. Disease and Panic

Another dreaded enemy was disease. Epidemics of smallpox, cholera, yellow fever, and even measles swept away large numbers of city-dwellers until the late nineteenth century. In addition, many people, young and old, simply sickened and died of un-diagnosed ailments. As with fires, the defenses against the attacks of disease were rudimentary. No one knew why it occurred or how it spread. Filth in the streets, impure water supplies, and ships arriving with infected passengers insured the diffusion of harmful bacteria. Some cities were healthier than others, but all suffered at one time or another. Between 1670 and 1720, Boston, Newport, New York, Philadelphia, and Charleston experienced some twenty epidemics of serious diseases.

In the first selection below, the Reverend Hugh Adams of Charleston tells of the mortality among the people of that city when yellow fever struck. The number of deaths may seem small by present standards, but the total represented almost 9 per cent of the city's population. If this same outbreak had occurred in Chicago in 1970, and no more was known about the disease than in 1700, more than 300,000 persons would have died. The

second document *appeared as an advertisement in the* Boston
News Letter *in 1713 and reveals the fear which the mere rumor
of smallpox produced. The* News Letter *was the first regular
newspaper published in the colonies. It was started by John
Campbell, the postmaster, in 1704.* ■

A. THE REVENGING SWORD OF PESTILENCE[1]

✤ Hugh Adams

It is hard to describe the dreadful and astonishing aspect of our
late terrible tempest of mortality in our Charleston, which began
towards the latter end of August and continued till the middle of
November. In which space of time there died in Charleston 125
English of all sorts, high and low, young and old; 37 French; 16 Indians; and 1 Negro. Three ministers, viz., Mr. John Cotton, dissenter,
Mr. Samuel Marshal, conformist, Mr. Preolo, French minister, Mr.
Gilbert Ashly, an Anabaptist preacher, [and] Mr. Curtice, a Presbyterian preacher, died all in the beginning of the mortality for their
people's contempt of their gospel labors. After [their] decease, the
distemper raged and the destroying angel slaughtered so furiously
with his revenging sword of pestilence that there died (as I have read
in the catalogue of the dead) 14 in one day, September 28, and raged
as bad all October so that the dead were carried in carts, being heaped
up one upon another. Worse by far than the great plague of London,
considering the smallness of the town. Shops shut up for six weeks;
nothing but carrying medicines, digging graves, carting the dead, to
the great astonishment of all beholders.

B. AN ADVERTISEMENT[2]

Whereas in the week past one Braeman of Boston was taken ill
and had some pimples appearing in his face, some persons fearing
they might be the signatures of the smallpox, and accordingly re-

[1] Extract of a letter from Hugh Adams to Samuel Sewall, February 23, 1700,
in *The Diary of Samuel Sewall, 1674–1729*, Vol. II, *1699/1700–1714*, reprinted
in *Collections of the Massachusetts Historical Society*, VI, *5th Series* (Boston:
Massachusetts Historical Society, 1879), pp. 11–12.
[2] *Boston News Letter*, May 18–May 25, 1713.

ported the same, the rumor whereof may possibly have spread into the country, to the discouragement of the intercourse betwixt the town and country.

The Selectmen of Boston do hereby certify and assure all persons that the said Braeman was not visited with the smallpox or any malignant distemper, kept house only one day, is now in good sound health, and that there is no person in the said town sick of the smallpox, or has been for several years past.

9. "Outside Agitators" [1]

✦ Patrick Gordon

Along with every other urban problem, the law-and-order issue appeared early and persistently plagued city officials. As major seaports, colonial cities played host to irresponsible transients, rowdy sailors, and other undesirables. Taverns, the often denounced "dram-shops" and "groggeries," became centers for excessive drinking, gambling, and prostitution. The wharf area presented countless opportunities for petty theft, and the growing wealth of the cities attracted professional criminals such as burglars and counterfeiters. Riots and civil disorders were commonplace, especially during elections.

As towns grew, the means of dealing with threats to good order were inadequate. A few watchmen, constables, and an occasional sheriff were ill equipped to handle the situation. In 1729 Patrick Gordon, Pennsylvania's lieutenant governor, issued the following proclamation admonishing authorities to suppress the lawless tendencies of the populace. Interestingly enough, Gordon placed the blame on outsiders who traveled to Philadelphia to cause trouble—a charge often made today by local authorities when disorders occur in their communities. ■

By THE HONORABLE PATRICK GORDON ESQR., Lieut. Governor of the Province of Pennsylvania and counties of Newcastle, Kent, and Sussex, upon Delaware.

[1] _Minutes of the Provincial Council of Pennsylvania_ (Philadelphia: Jo. Severns & Co., 1852), Vol. III, pp. 251–352.

A Proclamation

WHEREAS, several dissolute and disorderly persons, pressed by their necessitous circumstances, do daily crowd into this Province as well from parts beyond the sea, as from our neighboring colonies, and bringing with them dispositions incompatible with that good order, peace, and unanimity which are acknowledged by all rational men to be the foundation as well as glory of all civil societies, and fomented by some restless persons amongst ourselves, disaffected to the peace and prosperity of this government, endeavor to raise heats and animosities amongst the inhabitants, instead of that mutual love and benevolence which has hitherto, under the Divine Providence, been their protection, and for which this Province has till of late years been remarkably conspicuous since its first settlement. . . . These persons, actuated by such principles and encouraged by such incendiaries, setting at naught the just powers of government and the obedience due thereto, have had the assurance even to menace some members of the Representative Body, now met in assembly at Philadelphia, as well as private persons, to the disturbance of the peace and delay of the public service, as has been fully represented to me by an address from that house, declaring their abhorrence of such practice and praying that the laws now in force in England against riots may, pursuant to a law of this province, be vigorously put in execution; THERE-FORE, being firmly resolved to proceed with all due severity against such offenders, their aiders and abetters . . . I do hereby strictly charge and command all persons whatsoever within this Province and particularly within the City of Philadelphia, that they carefully keep His Majesty's peace within the same. And for that end I strictly charge and require the Mayor, Recorder, magistrates, and other officers of the City of Philadelphia, all justices, sheriffs, constables, and other officers within the Province of Pennsylvania, to whom the conservation of the public peace doth more immediately belong, to be vigilant and careful in the discharge of their respective duties, and in case of any riots, tumult, or other disorder, they immediately put in execution against all such rioters, their aiders, and abetters, the statute made in the first year of the reign of our late sovereign Lord KING GEORGE . . . entitled "An Act for Preventing Tumults and Riotous Assemblies"; and for the more speedy and effectual punishing of rioters, hereby enjoining the Justice of His Majesty's Peace to cause the said Act to be published at the respective Courts of Quarter Sessions for each County of this Province and the Mayor and Recorder of Philadelphia to do the same at the Court of Quarter Sessions for the said city. And I do moreover strictly charge and command the respective sheriffs in this province to hold themselves and their officers in a readiness, upon occasion given, to raise the Posse Comitatus,[2] as the laws of Britain in such cases direct, to quell and reduce by force all tumults, riots, and disorders which may happen within their respective bailiwicks, and the offenders to seize and apprehend, in order to be committed to prison and proceeded against according to the direction of the said statute....

[2] **Posse Comitatus:** a body of men whom a peace officer may call to assist him in preserving order, making arrests, and serving writs; often shortened to "posse."

10. The Control of Urban Markets[1]

✦ *Provincial Council of Pennsylvania*

Fires, epidemics, and disorder were the dramatic problems of colonial cities, but urban governments also performed ordinary functions which were equally vital and often just as troublesome. The town market, the means by which the community fed itself day in and day out, provides one illustration. Because there was no way to preserve meat, except by salting, animals had to be slaughtered just before sale. If this activity were not centralized, people would kill pigs, poultry, and cattle whenever and wherever they wished. (As it was, unsalable remains of animals were often dumped in the streets where flies, dogs, and hogs were entrusted with their removal.) Sharp businessmen who bought up the available supply of a commodity before a market opened could extort high prices for their wares unless they were prevented by law. The following ordinance, issued in Philadelphia in 1693, attempted to regulate the activities of this important urban institution. ■

[1] Adapted from *Minutes of the Provincial Council of Pennsylvania* (Philadelphia: Jo. Severns & Co., 1852), Vol. I, p. 392.

1. That the place for the market be in the High-street where the second street crosses it, and in no other place.

2. That the market be kept two days in the week weekly, viz., Wednesday and Saturday.

3. That all sorts of provisions brought to this town for sale, viz., flesh, fish, tame fowl, butter, eggs, cheese, herbs, fruits, and roots, etc., be sold in the aforesaid marketplace; and in case any of the aforesaid provisions should come to the Town of Philadelphia on other days that are not market days, yet that they be sold in the market under the same circumstances, regulations, and forfeitures as upon the days on which the market is appointed; and in case any of the said provisions be exposed to sale in any other place in this town than the said market, they shall be forfeited, the one half to the poor of Philadelphia, the other half to the clerk of the market.

4. That the market begin and be opened at the ringing of the bell, which shall be rung from the first day of the second Monday of April to the first day of September, between the hours of six and seven, and from the first day of September to the first day of April, between the hours of eight and nine, and in case any of the aforesaid provisions, or any sort of marketing be sold (flesh excepted) before the ringing of the bell, unless it be for His Excellency the Governor Chief, or Lieutenant Governor, the same shall be forfeited, one half to the poor, the other half to the clerk of the market.

5. That no person cheapen or buy any of the aforementioned provisions by the way as it comes to the market, upon forfeiture of the same, besides the forfeiture of six shillings, both to the buyer and seller, one half to the poor, the other half to the clerk of the market.

6. That no hucksters (or persons that sell again) shall buy or cheapen any of the aforementioned provisions until it hath been two hours in the market after the ringing of the bell, upon forfeiture of the same and six shillings, one half to the poor, and the other half to the clerk of the market.

7. That the clerk of the market shall and may receive for all cattle killed for the market sixpence per head; for every sheep, calf, or lamb, twopence per head; for every hog or shoat brought to the market, or cut out for sale there, threepence; and that nothing shall be paid for what the country people bring to town ready killed.

8. That the clerk of the market shall and may receive for sealing of weights and measures one penny for each, great and small.

Lastly. That all persons concerned shall duly pay to the clerk of the market the several rates, fees, and forfeitures aforesaid, and that he shall from time to time deliver to the overseers of the poor their parts thereof; and that all justices of the peace, sheriffs, constables, and other officers be aiding and assisting him in the execution of his office. Given at Philadelphia, the first day of October, 1693.

11. A Merchants' Rebellion[1]

✦ John Rowe

Despite the fact that a depression swept the colonies at the end of the French and Indian War (1756–1763), the British ministry clamped down on colonial trade and western expansion. The cities, already suffering the brunt of the economic decline, were further grieved by these developments. Taxes fell most heavily on merchants, printers, lawyers, and others whose livelihood derived from urban commerce.

Boston had been in a bad slump even before 1763, and additional setbacks in the postwar years hit hard. Injured most by imperial policy, merchants naturally led the opposition to it. John Rowe, one of Boston's leading importers, served on various committees which protested against restrictions and harassment. Though he was opposed to any moves toward independence, Rowe believed that the British measures were wrong. In his diary he recorded the growth of American opposition to the British in the years 1768–1773. The excerpts below afford insight into the plight of Boston's merchants and their reasons for staging the famed Tea Party. ■

March 4. . . . The Committee of Merchants appointed at their meeting March 1, 1768, having duly considered what they had in charge, do report the following resolutions, viz.:

In consideration of the great scarcity of money which for several years has been so sensibly felt among us and now must be rendered much greater not only by the immense sums absorbed in the collec-

[1] Anne Rowe Cunningham, ed., *Letters and Diary of John Rowe, Boston Merchant* (Boston: W. B. Clarke Company, 1903), pp. 153–155, 254–256, 273–275.

tion of the duties lately imposed but by the great checks given thereby to branches of trades which yielded us the most of our money and means of remittance. — In consideration also of the great debt now standing against us, which if we go on increasing by the excessive import we have been accustomed to while our sources of remittance are daily drying up must terminate not only in our own and our country's ruin but that of many of our creditors on the other side of the water.

In consideration farther of the danger from some late measures of our losing many inestimable blessings and advantages of the British Constitution which Constitution we have ever revered as the basis and security of all we enjoy in this life, therefore voted

1st. That we will not for one year send for any European commodities excepting salt, coals, fishing lines, fish hooks, hemp, duck,[2] bar lead, shot, wool cards, and card wire,[3] etc., and that the trading towns in the province and other provinces in New England together with those in New York, New Jersey, and Pennsylvania be invited to accede hereto—

2nd. That we will encourage the produce and manufactures of these colonies by the use of them in preference to all other manufacturers—

3rd. That in the purchase of such articles as we shall stand in need of, we will give a constant preference to such persons as shall subscribe to these resolutions—

4th. That we will in our separate capacities inform our several correspondents of the reasons and point out to them the necessity of witholding our usual orders for their manufactures — the said impediment may be removed and trade and commerce may again flourish—

5th. That these votes or resolutions be obligatory or binding on us from and after the time that these or other singular or tending to the same salutary purpose be adopted by most of the trading towns in this and the neighboring colonies—

6th. That a committee be appointed to correspond with merchants in the before-mentioned towns and provinces and forward to them the foregoing votes and that said committee be empowered to call a meeting of the merchants when they think necessary. . . .

---

[2] **duck**: heavy cotton fabric, probably most used by the colonists in making sails.

[3] **wool cards and card wire**: implements used in combing fibers.

Nov. 29 [1773]. This morning there were papers stuck up to the following purpose: "Friends, Brethren, Countrymen: That worst of plagues, the detestable tea, shipped for this port by the East India Company is now arrived in this harbor; the hour of destruction or manly opposition to the machinations of tyranny stares you in the face; every friend to his country, to himself, and to posterity is now called upon to meet at Faneuil Hall at nine o'clock this day (at which time the bells will begin to ring) to make a united and successful resistance to this last, worst, and most destructive measure of administration. Boston, Nov. 29, 1773"

In consequence of the above notification about one thousand people met at Faneuil Hall where they passed a vote that they would at all events return this tea. From Faneuil Hall they adjourned to the Old South Meeting House. Afternoon they met again and adjourned until the morning—there were in the meeting this afternoon about 2500 people as near as I could guess.

Nov. 30. The body met again this morning. The governor sent them a message advising them to depart on their peril — they took but little notice of the message — they met again this afternoon. I told them I had purchased a cargo for Captain Bruce's ship, that it was on the wharf, and that Captain Bruce when he arrived would apply to the body and that I would endeavor to prevail on him to act with reason in this affair and that I was sorry that he had any tea on board — which is very true, for it had given me great uneasiness. I stayed some time at the meeting and was chosen a Committeeman much against my will but I dare not say a word....

Dec. 16. I being a little unwell stayed at home at day and all the evening. The body meeting in the forenoon adjourned until afternoon. Broke up at dark.... A number of people appearing in Indian dresses went on board the three ships, Hall, Bruce, and Coffin.[4] They opened the hatches, hoisted out the tea, and flung it overboard — this might, I believe, have been prevented. I am sincerely sorry for this event. 'Tis said near two thousand people were present at this affair....

June 2. I met the gentlemen merchants at the west side of the court house in Boston. While we were in the meeting Captain Williamson arrived at Marblehead from Bristol [England] and brought with him another Act of Parliament for the better regulating of the province

[4] **Hall, Bruce, and Coffin:** ships were often called by the names of their captains.

of Massachusetts Bay, which Act strikes the very charter granted to this province by King William and Queen Mary — and is, or will be, productive with many evils to the advancement of this, his Majesty's province, and sour the minds of most of the inhabitants thereof. I am afraid of the consequences that this act will produce. I wish for harmony and peace between Great Britain, our mother country, and the colonies — but the time is far off. The people have done amiss and no sober man can vindicate their conduct, but the revenge of the ministry is too severe.

12. Ordeal of Boston's Middle Class[1]

✤ John Andrews

Following the Tea Party in December, 1773, the British Parliament issued the so-called "Intolerable Acts" which closed Boston Harbor, quartered troops among the people, and reduced the powers of the colonial government. While the other colonies watched in amazement and fear, Boston's radicals rallied the townspeople and prevented capitulation to the British. The Committees of Correspondence, an intercolonial network begun by Sam Adams in 1772, spread the word of the plight of Massachusetts Patriots. Food and clothing to relieve them came from as far as Philadelphia. But Bostonians paid heavily for their resistance. Businessman John Andrews wrote long letters to his brother-in-law in Philadelphia, describing the suffering of those living in the blockaded port. ■

August 1, [1774] . . . Among the *innumerable* hardships we suffer, that of not being [allowed to] convey any sort of merchandise across the ferry is not the least; whereby we are necessitated to receive every kind of goods from Marblehead or Salem via Cambridge, which adds one third to the length of the way [and] is attended with the expense

---

[1] Winthrop Sargent, ed. and comp., "Letters of John Andrews, Esq., of Boston, 1772–1776," *Proceedings of the Massachusetts Historical Society* (Boston: Wiggin & Hunt, 1866), Vol. VIII, pp. 335–337, 343–344.

of eight dollars a load at the lowest rate it is done for. It is no uncommon thing to hear the carriers and wagoners when they pass a difficult place in the road to whip their horses and damn Lord North[2] alternately. Nor are the coasters who bring wood and grain allowed to carry away any more provisions and stores than will suffice to last 'em to Salem, much less permitted to carry any sort of merchandise or utensils for farming, whereby I am deprived of the sale of at least two thirds of the goods I usually used to vend, and of the other third I am in a manner totally deprived of, by the operation of the ill-judged policy of our committee in promoting that *bane to harmony*, the Solemn League and Covenant.[3] . . . Really, Bill, I think myself well off to take cash enough to supply the necessary demands of my family, and you may as well ask a man for the teeth out of his head as to request the payment of money that he owes you (either in town or country, as we are all alike affected) for you'll be as likely to get the one as the other. Notwithstanding which, there seems to be ease, contentment, and perfect composure in the countenance of almost every person you meet in the streets, which conduct very much perplexes the Governor and others, our lords and masters, that they are greatly puzzled, and know not what to do or how to act, as they expected very different behavior from us. I hope we shall have the resolution and virtue enough to observe a steady course, and not give them *the least advantage* by any misconduct of our own, much more to quiet any dissensions among ourselves that may tend to disturb that harmony so necessary to the welfare of us all.

—2nd Instant . . . The poor of the town are in general employed at present in mending the streets and cleaning the docks, for which they are paid three shillings fourpence a day, but some few of them grumble that they are obliged to work hard for that which they esteemed as their right without work. . . .

August 20th. When I seriously reflect on the unhappy situation we are in, I can't but be uneasy lest the trade of the town should never be reinstated again; but on the other hand, when I consider that our *future* welfare depends altogether upon a steady and firm adherence to the *common* cause, I console myself with the thoughts that if,

---

[2] **Lord North:** leader of George III's government from 1770 to 1782, he resigned when he lost a vote of confidence in Parliament concerning his colonial policy.

[3] **Solemn League and Covenant:** the Committee of Correspondence circulated this document. Those who signed it pledged themselves not to buy anything of English manufacture.

after using every effort in our power we are finally obliged to submit, we shall leave this testimony behind us, that, not being able to stem the stream, we were *of necessity* borne down by the torrent. You can have no conception how sensibly I am affected in my business. If you'll believe me (though I have got near two thousand [pounds] sterling out in debts and about as much more in stock) I have not received above eighty or ninety pounds lawful money from both resources for above two months past; though previous to the ports being shut, I thought it an ordinary day's work if I did not carry home from 20 to 40 dollars every evening. Consequently the burden falls heaviest, if not *entirely*, upon the middling people among us; for the poor (who have always lived hand to mouth, i.e., depended on one day's labor to supply the wants of another) will be supported by the beneficence of the colonies; and the rich, who have lived upon their incomes either as landlords or usurers, will still have the same benefit from their wealth, for if one tenant is [unable] to pay the annual rent, there is always another ready, *that is able*, to supply his place, and some among the moneylenders will rather be benefited by our calamities. . . .

Such are the inevitable consequences resulting from a stoppage of trade; . . . the branch of the distillery of rum alone, at the smallest computation, is allowed to be a loss of 6000 pounds lawful money a week to the town . . . the manufacturers of that article in [the neighboring towns of] Mystic, Watertown, Salem, Haverhill, and Newbury [occupy] the whole of the trade, and it's a chance . . . whether it will ever revert to us again. The constant intercourse of heavy loaded carriages passing between this place and Salem has so worn the road, in addition to the many uphills and down, that those carriers and wagoners who prided themselves in keeping *their* horses fat and in good case, are obliged to submit to the mortification of being able to count *their* ribs without the assistance of [spectacles] or the sense of feeling, such is the fatigue they undergo! If so now, what will it be in the fall and winter, when every step will immerse 'em a foot or two deep in mud and mire.

II. The Great Era of City Building

When George Washington took the oath of office as first President in 1790, less than 5 per cent of the American people lived in towns. Seventy years later, Abraham Lincoln presided over a country where almost 20 per cent of the population lived in cities. In the intervening years the United States was subtly transformed from a simple rural society with a handful of important centers into a complex national community with major cities in every section. Indeed, the four decades between 1820 and 1860 witnessed the most rapid rate of urbanization that the country would ever know.

Everywhere the central fact of American development was the expansion of its cities. Long-established towns boomed: Philadelphia grew from 28,522 in 1790 to 565,529 in 1860. New York surged to over 800,000 on the eve of the Civil War. In the Ohio Valley and along the Great Lakes new towns sprang up to gather the growing trade of areas only recently wilderness. Pittsburgh, Cincinnati, Louisville, and St. Louis were built on inland rivers and grew fat on the commerce of the Mississippi system; Buffalo, Cleveland, Detroit, and Chicago became the entrepots of a booming lake trade. Nor were the South and the Far West excluded from this first urban explosion. Although the development of southern cities seemed slow by northern standards, their rate of growth exceeded that of most other places in the world. In the Far West, San Francisco became the nation's most spectacular "instant city" when its population leaped from roughly 2000 to 50,000 in the ten years following the discovery of gold in California.

Though cities were beset with internal problems resulting from rapid growth, they engaged in intense competition with each other. Most urban leaders of the time believed that a bright future was dependent on continued growth. If a city did not grow, it would stagnate and die. And the key to expansion lay in commerce. Each sought to strengthen its mercantile position in its own region and clinch additional markets in newly settled areas. Cincinnati and Louisville fought over the southern trade that moved north to the Ohio

Valley. Chicago and St. Louis contested for the immense hinterland west past the Mississippi. But the fiercest was the rivalry of the urban giants of the Atlantic Coast — New York, Philadelphia, Baltimore, and Boston — for trade in the grain and livestock of the Middle West.

By 1860 new commercial centers were firmly established and the historic city was struggling to contain its growing numbers. Congestion mounted, municipal services were strained, and social institutions developed in response to urban needs. Jefferson would perhaps have recognized these cities, but his worst fears would have been realized. Yet despite the difficulties of urban life, it seemed that when people had the option, more and more of them chose to cast their lot with America's new towns. ■

Population Growth of Representative Cities, 1800–1860

	1800	1820	1840	1860
Boston	24,937	43,298	93,383	177,840
Chicago	——	——	4470	112,172
Cincinnati	——	9642	46,338	161,044
Cleveland	——	606	6071	43,417
Detroit	——	1422	9102	45,619
New Orleans	——	27,176	102,193	168,675
New York*	60,515	123,706	312,710	813,669
Philadelphia	41,220	63,802	93,665	565,529
Pittsburgh	1565	7248	21,115	49,221
St. Louis	——	——	16,469	160,773
Washington	3210	13,247	23,364	61,122

* Borough of Manhattan only

Note the spectacular increases in the population of New York and Philadelphia between 1840 and 1860, when the tide of immigration was running high.

1. A Splendid Capital¹

✦ Pierre L'Enfant

The members of the Constitutional Convention of 1787 had decided that the new nation should have a new capital. After several years of Congressional bickering, the question of location was settled in 1790 by a compromise. In exchange for southern support for the fiscal policy of Alexander Hamilton, Secretary of the Treasury, the capital was to be placed in the South. The following year President Washington personally selected a site on the Potomac River not far from his plantation, Mount Vernon. Pierre L'Enfant, a French citizen and volunteer in the Revolutionary army, was hired to help with the surveying. Within a few months, Major L'Enfant presented President Washington with the most ambitious city plan in American, if not in world, history. The excerpt below has been drawn from L'Enfant's report and contains the core of his ideas.

In 1800 the official building period was over, and President John Adams, his staff, and the Congress moved from Philadelphia to the new city. Just as the government outlined in the Constitution came to be molded and changed by time, men, and events, so it was with the capital, which grew slowly and not always in ways its creator had envisioned. ■

SIR:

. . . Having determined some principal points to which I wished to make the others subordinate, I made the distribution regular with every street at right angles, north and south, east and west, and afterwards opened some in different directions, as avenues to and from every principal place, wishing thereby not merely to contrast with the general regularity, nor to afford a greater variety of seats with pleasant prospects . . . but principally to connect each part of the city . . . and by making them thus seemingly connected promote a rapid settlement over the whole extent. . . . [They will] become the means for a rapid intercourse with all parts of the city, to which they will serve as does the main artery in the animal body, which

¹ Slightly adapted from Elizabeth S. Kite, *Historical Documents, Institut Français de Washington, Cahier III, L'Enfant and Washington, 1791–1792* (Baltimore: Johns Hopkins Press, 1929), pp. 52–58. Reprinted by permission.

diffuses life through the smaller vessels and inspires vigor and activity throughout the whole frame.

These avenues I made broad, so as to admit of their being planted with trees leaving eighty feet for a carriage way, thirty feet on each side for a walk under a double row of trees, and allowing ten feet between the trees and the houses. . . .

With respect to the point upon which it is expedient first to begin the main establishment . . . I believe the question may be easily solved . . . [by] embracing in one view the whole extent from the Eastern Branch[2] to Georgetown[3] and from the banks of the Potomac to the mountains. . . . In considering impartially the whole extent, viewing it as that of the intended city, it will appear that to promote a rapid settlement throughout, across the Tiber[4] above the tide water is the most eligible one for an offset of the establishment which . . . .* should be begun at various points equidistant from the center. [This is] not merely because settlements of this sort are likely to diffuse an equality of advantages over the whole territory allotted . . . but because each of these settlements by a natural jealousy will most tend to stimulate establishments on each of the opposed extremes. . . . A canal is easily opened from the Eastern Branch across those primary settlements of the city to issue at the mouth of the Tiber into the Potomac, giving entrance to the boats from the falls of that river into the Eastern Branch harbor, which will undoubtedly facilitate a conveyance . . . of the utmost convenience to all trading people. . . .

After a minute search for other eligible situations, I may assert without apprehension of appearing prejudiced in favor of a first opinion, that I could not discover one in all respects so advantageous . . .* for erecting the Federal House[5] . . . [as]* the western end of Jenkin's Heights [which] stands really as a pedestal waiting for a superstructure. . . .

The other position of a different nature offers a local equality, answerable for a Presidential palace,[6] better calculated for a com-

[2] **Eastern Branch:** the Anacostia River which flows from Hyattsville, Maryland, through the southern part of Washington. It was considered to be the "eastern branch" of the Potomac.

[3] **Georgetown:** an already existing city northwest of the site. It was annexed to Washington in 1878 and is today a well-preserved residential area.

[4] **Tiber:** a small stream on a site called Rome by its original owner; it has since disappeared.

[5] **Federal House:** the capitol building.

[6] **Presidential palace:** this was called the Executive Mansion in 1818, and officially renamed the White House in 1902.

* Ellipsis in original source.

modious house and which may be rendered majestic and agreeable. This position which very justly attracted your attention when first viewing the ground . . . [is] upon the west side and near the mouth of the Tiber on the height dividing the Burnes and the Pierce plantations.

The spot I assigned I chose somewhat more in the wood and off the creek than when you stood in the partition line . . .* two considerations determined me: first, to lessen the distance to the Federal House, and secondly, to obtain a more extensive view down the Potomac, with a prospect of the whole harbor and town of Alexandria [in Virginia]; also to connect with more harmony the public walks and avenue of the Congress House with the garden park and other improvements around the palace, which, standing upon this high ridge . . . would overlook the vast esplanade in the center of which, and at the point of intersection of the sight from each of the Houses, would be the most advantageous place for an equestrian statue.[7] . . .

Fixed as expressed on the [plan], the distance from the Congressional House will not be too great . . . as . . . no message to nor from the President is to be made without a sort of decorum which will doubtless point out the propriety of [a] committee waiting on him in [a] carriage should his palace be even contiguous to Congress.

To make . . . the distance less to other officers, I placed the three grand Departments of State contiguous to the principal palace; and on the way leading to the Congressional House, the gardens of the one together with the park and other improvements . . . are connected with the public walk and avenue to the Congress House in a manner as must form a whole as grand as it will be agreeable and convenient for the whole city . . . and all along side of which may be placed playhouses, rooms of assembly, academies, and all sorts of places as may be attractive to the learned and afford diversions to the idle.

I am with respectful submission,
Your most humble and obedient servant,
P. C. L'ENFANT

[7] **equestrian statue:** the Continental Congress in 1783 had called for the building of a monument to George Washington. The proposed statue never appeared. Instead, some hundred years later, the tall obelisk of the Washington Monument was completed at the far end of the Mall. For a detailed story about this incredible delay, see "George Washington's Monument," in *American Heritage*, December, 1968.
* Ellipsis in original source.

2. New City on the Frontier[1]

✤ *Francis Baily*

The creation of Washington was an enterprise in city planning on the grand scale. More typical was the experience of those who moved west and tried to re-create the environment they had come from. For models they used the seaboard cities, adapting their designs to the conditions of the inland region. "Penn's plan" was among those most often copied, and as a result Philadelphia subtly but strongly influenced American urban development. Francis Baily, an Englishman traveling through America in 1796 and 1797, recorded the speed of the transformation from forest to town in Waynesville, Ohio, and the optimism and aspirations of its people. ■

I shall now attempt to give you an idea of the little town which my friend has laid out here. Its situation is on the brow of the second bank, which at this place is not many feet from the edge of the river, which flows with a gentle current and in a beautiful meandering course at the foot of the town. The second bank is here formed like a semicircle, the projecting part of which faces the river, which preserves a similar course. In the front of this spot he has fixed his own habitation, and he intends throwing several of the front lots into gardens, so that the view of the river may not be obstructed from the houses in the rear. The opposite shore consists of a beautiful rich bottom, extending a great way into the country.

The town (it is to be called Waynesville, in honor of General [Mad Anthony] Wayne [American Revolutionary general]) he has laid out at right angles, with a square in the middle, which he told me, with a degree of exulting pride, he intended for a court house, or for some public building for the meeting of the legislature. . . . He has already fallen into the flattering idea which every founder of a new settlement entertains, that his town will at some future time be the seat of government. He also described to me, and walked over, the ground where he intended to make his gardens, his summerhouse, his

[1] Francis Baily, *Journal of a Tour in Unsettled Parts of North America in 1796 and 1797* (London: Baily Brothers, 1856), pp. 215–216.

fishpond, his orchard, etc. [A]nticipating a few years, [he] showed me where there was to be a serpentine walk,[2] then a seat, then a shady bower; and, in the heat of his imagination, I believe he was as happy as if he saw them all before him. Whereas for myself, not being so interested in it, I could behold nothing but a wild uncultivated country, full of lofty trees and prickly shrubs; and when he showed me his fishponds and his serpentine walks, I could only discover a little standing water and a few deertracks.

After being here a few days, I observed this wilderness begin to assume a very different appearance . . . after having built my friend a house, the settlers had set about their own plantations, and in a short time I saw quite a little town rise from the desert . . . in several places gardens were actually laid out and the walks formed. I could not but be pleased at this early fruit of their industry, and seemed to have a secret inclination to stay and cultivate the ground with them. I wished very much to anticipate a few years and take a prospective of the future prosperity of this little colony — when promiscuous[3] society and uncouth habits had given way to more refined and polished manners and when the first class of settlers had moved off and a more civilized race had succeeded. Then to have sat down upon the bench at the evening sun and told one's children how we raised this flourishing settlement from the howling wilderness; to have run through the different scenes and difficulties which we encountered in endeavoring to accomplish our end; and still to have looked forward to a more remote period, when this work of our hand might become renowned either for its splendor or for the prowess of its inhabitants — I say, to have dwelt upon these points would have afforded the mind the highest satisfaction and pleasure, and would have sufficiently compensated for those other difficulties we met with in the first process of our undertaking.

[2] **serpentine walk:** a winding path, often walled.
[3] **promiscuous:** here, casually or indiscriminately mixed.

3. The Best of Everything

Success in establishing new towns depended largely on the ability to lure new residents. Proprietors advertised widely, claiming that their sites offered the best in water, soil, climate, and

*commercial opportunities. But the most aggressive promotional
effort sometimes came to naught. The proposed town of Havannah, located in northern Alabama, an area of heavy speculation
in land purchase, probably died a-borning, for it does not appear
on any modern map of the state. Given here is the highly optimistic description of Havannah's possibilities, as prepared by its
trustees in 1818.*

*Some of the advertising extolling the virtues of new towns was
so exaggerated that many people grew skeptical and cynical. The
second selection, a parody of such descriptions, ran in the Au-
gusta, Georgia, Chronicle and was widely circulated throughout
the West. As successful satire blending reality and fancy in proportion, it provided both amusement and a new perspective on
a common experience. Skunksburg was at once the epitome and
the nightmare of early American "new towns."* ■

A. NOTHING DOWN, FOUR YEARS TO PAY[1]

The undersigned trustees for the proprietors of the site where the
town of Havannah is to be laid off give this public notice that lots
in the above-mentioned town will be offered for sale on the premises
on the 26th and 27th days of October next.

Havannah is situated in Lauderdale County, Alabama Territory,
on the north side of the Tennessee River, immediately above Colberts
reserve within nine miles of the town of Florence and about eight
miles distant from Colberts ferry.

The town of Havannah is included in that section of the country
which was recently sold at Huntsville when 42 townships brought to
the government the unprecedented sum of five million dollars. The
simple fact that within this district land sold for purposes of agriculture from 30 to 78 dollars per acre furnishes an incontestable evidence
of the fertility of the soil and the value of its productions. The
climate too is of an agreeable temperature, subject neither to the
excessive heats of the South nor the chilling blasts of the North;
yet the fruits and growth of the latter arrive at greater perfection here
and the best profitable species of agriculture of the former are produced in the most luxuriant abundance.

[1] From the Durrett Collection, Miscellaneous Papers, in the University of
Chicago Manuscript Collections.

Of all the sites for towns in the late sales, the town of Havannah has incomparably the highest claim to precedence in a commercial point of view.

Considering the situation of this place, as it respects its commercial advantages, the rising importance of the north side of the Tennessee River within the limits of this Territory, and the remarkably rich settlements in the adjacent counties . . . of Tennessee, all of which must necessarily depend upon this point as being the head of navigation on the Tennessee for steamboats, barges, and keel boats [and] for their supply of foreign articles, we say, taking these local advantages into consideration, many persons who are to be extensively engaged in mercantile and agricultural pursuits by their repeated solicitations have induced the proprietors to lay off a town on this site.

The purchaser of cotton, the staple of this section of country, will find it emphatically to his interest to locate himself at Havannah where he can ship his purchases at any season of the year, which will arrive in market several months earlier than the cotton from Madison County or any place above the Muscle Shoals. Thus this place embraces important advantages both in the export and import trade.

Havannah is situated at a point on the Tennessee River which is the nearest possible route from the most populous settlements in Kentucky and Tennessee to Mississippi, the southern parts of Alabama Territory, and West Florida. It may be . . . remarked that a ferry will be established here by which the river can be crossed with as much ease as at any other point whatever — situated immediately at the lower end of an island and known by the name of Long Island. No convenient plan for crossing is offered after you leave the military ferry till you reach this point.

Much has been said about the value of lands east of Lauderdale, in Limestone and Madison Counties. But when we reflect that the productions in the vicinity of Havannah will anticipate the other in market by several months, and they are in a degree dependent upon this place for their foreign supplies, the undersigned confidently believe that the situation will attract the attention of discerning, enterprising men.

Havannah has the advantage of being supplied with pure and wholesome spring water which cannot be surpassed by any in the western country. The situation of the town is high, with a fine view of this majestic river and the variegated scenery of a picturesque surrounding country.

Persons disposed to invest a share of their capital in town property after a careful examination of the map of the southern country will readily discover the propriety of the selection of this place for a town which is near the head of navigation, on a large majestic river, furnishing the greatest facilities to the commercial and agricultural pursuits of a country equalled by none in America for the fertility of its soil and value of its productions. An agreeable and healthy point possessing these advantages cannot fail of speedily rising . . . to importance. Every facility will be offered to mechanics who wish to settle in a new place where the population is increasing with unheard-of rapidity and whose wants must be many and urgent. . . .

Terms of sale, one third in one year, one third in three years, and the remaining third in four years from the sale.

E. J. BAILEY
GEORGE COLTER
HUGH CAMPBELL } TRUSTEES
SAML. RAGSDALE
JOSEPH FARMER

June 25, 1818

B. SEVENTEEN BANKS WITH ASYLUMS ATTACHED[2]

This charming place, better known as Log-Hall, heretofore the residence of Fiddler Billy, is situated in Wilks County, not far from the junction of Pickett's main spring branch and a western fork, called the Slough, which runs in the rainy season and washes the confines of Farnsworth's lower hog pens. This noble stream, by use of *proper* and *sufficient* means, may be made navigable to the sea. It abounds in delicate minnows, a variety of terrapins, and its frogs, which in size, voice, and movement are inferior to none. . . . A noble bluff of 18 inches commands the harbor, and affords a most advantageous situation for defensive military works. This bluff slopes off into nearly a level, diversified only by the gentle undulations of surface, as will

---

[2] From *Liberty Hall* (Cincinnati), October 1, 1819.

give a sufficient elevation for the principal public edifices. Commodious and picturesque positions will be therefore reserved for the exchange and city hall, a church, one gymnastic and one polytechnic foundation, one Olympic and two dramatic theaters, a equestrian circus, an observatory, two marine and two foundling hospitals, and in the most commercial part of the city will be a reservation for seventeen banks, to each of which may be attached a lunatic hospital. . . .

The future advantage of this situation in now impossible to calculate; but already it is an emporium of all the watermelons, ground peas, . . . and all the brooms, chickens, and baskets that are bought and sold among the before-mentioned places in the course of commerce. To mercantile men, however, a mere statement of its geographical position is deemed sufficient without comment. It stands on the middle ground between Baltimore and Orleans, Charleston and Nickajack, Savannah and Coweta, Knoxville and St. Mary's, Salisbury and Cusseta, and between Little Heil on the Altamaha, and Telfico block house. A line of velocipede stages will be immediately established from Skunksburg straight through the O-ke-fin-o-cau Swamp to the southernmost point of the Florida peninsula; and as soon as a canal shall be cut through the Rocky Mountains, there will be direct communication with the Columbia River, and thence to the Pacific Ocean. Then opens a theater of trade bounded only by the universe! . . .

> ANDREW AIRCASTLE
> THEORY M'VISION
> L. MOONLIGHT, JR., & CO.
> PROPRIETORS

4. Factory Town

Before 1812 the development of industry in the United States proceeded at a slow pace. Great Britain was the leading industrial power in the world with a seeming monopoly on the manufacture of textiles and textile machinery and on advanced processes for the production of coal and iron. The British Parliament tried to keep trade secrets at home by forbidding the export of information on new machines and the emigration of skilled workers.

Two men who got around this prohibition were Samuel Slater and Francis Lowell. Slater was a Scotsman who had learned his trade from Richard Arkwright, inventor of the spinning machine used in his great Lancashire cotton mill. Slater kept all the intricate construction details in his head and in 1791 in Pawtucket, Rhode Island, set up the first power-driven textile factory in the United States. Lowell, a wealthy Bostonian visiting in England, observed the English system and absorbed a tremendous amount of technical information. In 1815 in Waltham, Massachusetts, he established a new kind of factory, in which all parts of the clothmaking process took place under one roof.

The rapid growth of manufacturing in the early nineteenth century meant that communities sprang up around the mills. Typical were those which developed as a result of the New England textile industry. One of the best-known was Lowell, Massachusetts, named after the innovator described above, and as famous for the high quality of its early women operatives as for its flannel and gingham. ■

A. ORIGINS[1]

✦ The Lowell Journal

About fifteen years ago, the [present] territory of Lowell, being about four square miles and bearing upon it 15,000 inhabitants, was owned by a few honest farmers, who obtained subsistence for themselves and families by the cultivation of this comparatively barren spot and the fish they caught in the Merrimack and Concord Rivers. It comprised the northeasterly part of Chelmsford and [was] bounded easterly by the Concord River, which separated it from Tewksbury, and northerly by the Merrimack, that divided it from Dracut; and from the fact of its situation at the confluence of these rivers was called Chelmsford Neck. . . .

Thus for centuries it lay with vast resources, which we now see developed, slumbering in its bosom, unsuspected and unknown. But the spirit of enterprise and improvement came . . . and turned this

[1] From *The Lowell Journal*, quoted in George S. White, *Memoir of Samuel Slater* (Philadelphia, 1836), pp. 252–253.

seeming wilderness . . . into a busy, enterprising, and prosperous city.

In 1819, Kirk Boott, Esq., a wealthy merchant of Boston, in the [dress] of a hunter, explored this place. He discovered its resources, and immediately, in company with several other rich merchants of that city, purchased the land and water privileges. They were incorporated by the name of the "Proprietors of the Locks and Canals on Merrimack River," and commenced operations by digging a canal from the Pawtucket Falls easterly one mile and a half, where it emptied into the Concord River. This canal is sixty feet wide and carries in depth eight feet of water. This is their grand canal; lateral branches are cut, which carry the water to the several manufacturing mills, and then discharge into the Merrimack or Concord Rivers. They then erected a large brick machine shop and commenced building machinery. This company sells out the privileges to manufacturing companies, digs the canal, erects the mills, and builds the machinery, and puts the whole in operation; they do it cheaper than anybody else would do it; and these are the only terms on which they will sell the privileges. . . . A part of their lands they have sold out to individuals at an enormous advance on the original price. Land for which they paid twenty or thirty dollars per acre they have sold for one dollar per square foot.[2] They have still a considerable portion of it on hand and unsold. Kirk Boott, Esq., is their agent.

Lowell . . . was incorporated in 1823 into a town distinct from Chelmsford and received its name from Francis C. Lowell, Esq., who early introduced manufactures into this country. There are now 25 factories in operation, and there yet remain unoccupied privileges for nearly as many more. When these shall be taken up, as they in all probability will, they will probably afford means of subsistence to another 15,000 inhabitants, making in the whole 30,000.[3]

A new canal is now being dug, which will furnish sites for about a dozen mills of the size already built. A company has recently been incorporated by the name of "Boott Cotton Mills," which have purchased four of these sites, and upon them are immediately to erect four large brick mills. The railroad from this place to Boston is now complete. . . . It is said to be more permanently built than any other in the country.

[2] This would amount to over $40,000 an acre.

[3] Lowell's population rose to 95,000 in 1900 and reached a peak of 113,000 in 1920. With the decline of the New England textile industry after that date, the number of inhabitants decreased substantially.

B. THE PEOPLE WHO CAME[4]

✦ *Harriet H. Robinson*

In 1831 Lowell was little more than a factory village. Several corporations were started, and the cotton mills belonging to them were building. Help was in great demand; and stories were told all over the country of the new factory town, and the high wages that were offered to all classes of working people — stories that reached the ears of mechanics' and farmers' sons and gave new life to lonely and dependent women in distant towns and farmhouses. Into this Yankee El Dorado, these needy people began to pour by the various modes of travel known to those slow old days. The stagecoach and the canal boat came every day, always filled with new recruits for this army of useful people. The mechanic and the machinist came, each with his homemade chest of tools, and oftentimes his wife and little ones. The widow came with her little flock and her scanty housekeeping goods to open a boarding house or variety store, and so provided a home for her fatherless children. Many farmers' daughters came to earn money to complete their wedding outfit or buy the bride's share of housekeeping articles. . . .

In 1832 the factory population of Lowell was divided into four classes. The agents of the corporations were the aristocrats, not because of their wealth, but on account of the office they held. . . .

The agents usually lived in large houses, not too near the boarding-houses [of the operatives], surrounded by beautiful gardens which seemed like paradise to some of the homesick girls who, as they came from their work in the noisy mill, could look with longing eyes into the sometimes open gate in the high fence, and be reminded afresh of their pleasant country homes. . . .

The second class were the overseers, a sort of gentry, ambitious mill-hands who had worked up from the lowest grade of factory labor. They usually lived in the end-tenements of the blocks, the short connected rows of houses in which the operatives were boarded. . . .

---

[4] Harriet H. Robinson, *Loom and Spindle* (New York: Thomas Y. Crowell & Company, 1898), pp. 62–63, 13–15.

The third class were the operatives, and were all spoken of as "girls" or "men." . . .

The fourth class, lords of the spade and shovel, by whose constant labor the building of the great factories was made possible, and whose children soon became valuable operatives, lived first on what was called the "Acre." Here, clustered around a small stone Catholic church, were hundreds of little shanties, in which they dwelt with their wives and numerous children. Among them were sometimes found disorder and riot, for they had brought with them from the "Old Country" [Ireland] their feuds and quarrels.

5. Land Fever in Chicago[1]

✦ Harriet Martineau

Land speculation seemed and often was totally irrational. Some new towns failed, others stayed small, and a few grew at a fantastic rate. Chicago had obvious advantages to start with, not the least of which was its location on the Great Lakes and near the Mississippi Valley. It too experienced a wave of speculative fever in which some individuals, such as William B. Ogden, first mayor of the city, amassed fortunes. Property he bought in 1845 for fifteen thousand dollars was worth ten million twenty years later.

In 1834, Harriet Martineau, an English writer of stories and essays, came to America to observe and record her impressions. Her two-year journey took her as far south as New Orleans and as far west as Chicago. Here she describes the "rage for speculation" which gripped the infant city. Miss Martineau never expected that Chicago would become America's "second city." ■

I never saw a busier place than Chicago was at the time of our arrival [1836]. The streets were crowded with land speculators hurrying from one sale to another. A Negro, dressed up in scarlet, bearing

[1] Harriet Martineau, *Society in America* (New York: Sanders and Otley, 1837), Vol. I, pp. 259–262.

a scarlet flag, and riding a white horse with housings of scarlet, announced the times of sale. At every street corner where he stopped, the crowd flocked around him, and it seemed as if some prevalent mania infected the whole people. The rage for speculation might fairly be so regarded. As the gentlemen of our party walked the streets, storekeepers hailed them from their doors, with offers of farms and all manner of land lots, advising them to speculate before the price of land rose higher. A young lawyer of my acquaintance there had realized $500 per day the five preceding days by merely making out titles to land. Another friend had realized in two years ten times as much money as he had before fixed upon as a competence for life.

Of course, this rapid moneymaking is a merely temporary evil. A bursting of the bubble must come soon. The absurdity of the speculation is so striking that the wonder is that the fever should have attained such a height as I witnessed. The immediate occasion of the bustle which prevailed the week we were at Chicago was the sale of lots, to the value of two millions of dollars, along the course of a projected canal; and of another set immediately behind these. Persons not intending to [gamble] and not infected with mania would endeavor to form some reasonable conjecture as to the ultimate value of the lots by calculating the cost of the canal, the risks from accident, from the possible competition from other places, etc., and, finally, the possible profits, under the most favorable circumstances, within so many years [after] purchase. Such a calculation would serve as some sort of guide as to the amount of purchase-money to be risked. . . .

Wild land on the banks of a canal, not even marked out, was selling at Chicago for more than rich land, well improved, in the finest part of the valley of the Mohawk, on the banks of a canal which is already the medium of an almost inestimable amount of traffic. If sharpers and gamblers were to be the sufferers by the impending crash at Chicago, no one would feel much concerned, but they, unfortunately, are the people who encourage the delusion in order to profit by it. Many a high-spirited but inexperienced young man, many a simple settler would be ruined for the advantage of knaves.

Others, besides lawyers and speculators by trade, make a fortune in such extraordinary times. A poor man in Chicago had a pre-emption right to some land, for which he paid in the morning $150. In the afternoon he hold it to a friend of mine for $5000. A poor

Frenchman, married to a squaw, had a suit pending when I was there
. . . for the right of purchasing some land by the lake for $100, which
would immediately become worth one million.

There was much gaiety going on at Chicago, as well as business.
On the evening of our arrival, a fancy fair took place. As I was too
much fatigued to go, the ladies sent me a bouquet of prairie flowers.
There is some allowable pride in the place about its society. It is a
remarkable thing to meet such an assemblage of educated, refined,
and wealthy persons as may be found there, living in small, inconvenient houses on the edge of a wild prairie. There is a mixing, of
course. I heard of a family of half-breeds setting up a carriage and
wearing fine jewelry. When the present intoxication of prosperity
passes away, some of the inhabitants will go back to the eastward;
there will be an accession of settlers from the mechanic classes; good
houses will have been built for the richer families; and the singularity
of the place will subside. It will be like all the other new and thriving
lake and river ports of America. Meantime I am glad to have seen
it in its strange early days.

6. Sailing Day in New York¹

✤ *Basil Hall*

*The steamboat played a primary role in the dynamic growth
of New York City. One historian has argued that the rise of
New York as a seaport can be attributed to the extension of
steamboat service to the city's hinterland (inland from the
coast); to the establishment of the "cotton triangle" which made
New York the focal point of trade between Europe and the
South; and to the appearance of the packet, a heavy-sailed forerunner of the ocean liner and freighter. These three developments secured New York's hold on the nation's business, and
the grip was later tightened by the completion of the Erie Canal.
Captain Basil Hall, a British naval officer, toured North America
in 1827 and 1828, and described the activity generated by the*

¹ Captain Basil Hall, R.N., *Travels in North America in the Years 1827 and
1828,* 3rd edition in 3 vols. (Edinburgh: Printed for Robert Cadell, 1830), II,
207–211.

packets, the cosmopolitan character they lent the port, and their role in expanding and regularizing communications between Europe and the New World. ■

At one end of the deck stood a very lively set of personages chattering away at a most prodigious rate, as if the fate of mightiest monarchies, to say nothing of republics, depended on their volubility. This group consisted of a complete company of French players with all their lap dogs, black servants, helmets, swords, and draperies — the tinsel and glitter of their gay profession. They had been acting for some time at New York, and were now shifting the scene to New Orleans, as the [malaria] season had gone past. Our ears could also catch, at the same moment, the mingled sounds of no less than five different languages, French, Spanish, German, Italian, and English, all running on without the parties having the least apparent consciousness that there was anything remarkable [about it]. . . .

Every mortal on board the ships which we visited was engaged with his own particular business. The captain, the mate, the crew were severally employed in heaving up the anchor, hoisting the luggage in, or in making sail, while the poor bewildered passengers wandered about, ignorant where to go. . . . The pilot roared and swore to the master that if more haste were not made, the tide would be lost. The captain, of course, handed over these reproaches, with interest, to the officers, who bestowed them, with suitable variations, on the seamen, and these again, though in a lower key, growled and muttered their [curses] upon the poor newcomers. The hens lay cackling and sprawling in bunches of a dozen each, tied by the legs, while the pigs ran madly about under the influence of a shower of kicks, squealing in concert with the fizzing of the steam from the waste pipe of the engine.

. . . On the first day of every month throughout the year, a number of packet ships sail from this grand focus of American commerce to various parts of the world, and as they all start about the same hour, no small bustle is the necessary consequence. Exactly as the clock strikes ten, a steamboat with the passengers for the different packets leaves the wharf, close to a beautiful public promenade called the Battery . . . The crowd on the shore was immense. Troops of friends, assembled to take leave, were jostled by tradesmen, hotelkeepers, and hackney coachmen urging the payment of their accounts and by news-men disposing of papers wet from the printing press, squeezing amongst carts, wagons, and wheelbarrows filled with luggage. Through this crowd of idle and busy folks we elbowed our way with some dif-ficulty and at last found ourselves on the deck of the steamer. Here a new description of confusion presented itself. There were no fewer, the captain assured us, than 160 passengers on board his boat at that moment, destined for different packets, each of whom . . . [might have] at least one parting friend; the crush, therefore, may be imag-ined!

At length we put off and paddled alongside of two packets for Havre [France], two for New Orleans, and one [each] for . . . Charleston, London, and Liverpool. Every set of passengers was accompanied by a huge mountain of chests, portmanteaus, bags, writing-desks, birdcages, bandboxes, cradles, and the whole family of greatcoats, boat-cloaks, umbrellas, and parasols. The captains of the several packets were of course on board the steamer, in charge of their monstrous letter bags, while close under their lee came the watch-maker with a regiment of chronometers, which he guarded and coddled with as much care as if they had been his children. . . . Slender clerks belonging to the different mercantile houses flitted about with bundles of letters, bills of lading, and so forth. . . .

7. The Process of Urbanization[1]

✦ Fortescue Cuming

Fortescue Cuming, a little-known Scotch traveller, passed through Pittsburgh in the winter of 1807. However dismal he found the muddy streets, his description of a young western city is significant for its indication of the speed of the urbanization process. Cuming reported all the things one expects to find in

[1] Fortescue Cuming, *Sketches of a Tour to the Western Country Through the States of Ohio and Kentucky; A Voyage Down the Ohio and Mississippi Rivers; and a Trip Through the Mississippi Territory and a Part of West Florida. Commenced at Philadelphia in the Winter of 1807 and Concluded in 1809* (Pittsburgh: Cramer, Spear & Eichbaum, 1810) in Reuben Gold Thwaites, ed., *Early Western Travels 1748–1846* (Cleveland: The Arthur H. Clark Company, 1904), Vol. IV, pp. 76–87.

cities: cultural activities, diversity of population, the beginnings of
social stratification, and even air pollution. Emphasis on business
and politics was characteristic of these new American towns. ▪

The appearance of Pittsburgh in the winter is by no means pleasing,
notwithstanding its fine situation, as none of the streets being paved
except Market Street, they are so extremely [muddy] that it is impossible to walk them without wading over the ankle, except during
frosty weather, which rarely continues many days successively from
[the town's] lying so low and being so well sheltered by the surrounding hills. This [situation], though unpleasant now, is in reality in
favor of the place, as when the streets are all paved, that inconvenience will be [removed] and the advantage of shelter from the bleak
wintry winds will still remain, without its being followed by an exclusion of fresh air during the summer. . . . [T]he rivers at that season
act as ventilators, a refreshing breeze always drawing up or down one
of them.

Another cause of the unprepossessing appearance of Pittsburgh
proceeds from the effect of one of the most useful conveniences and
necessaries of life, which it enjoys in a pre-eminent degree, namely,
fuel, . . . as fine coal as any in the world, in such plenty, so easily produced, and so near town that it is delivered in wagons drawn by four
horses at the doors of the inhabitants, at the rate of five cents per
bushel.

A load of forty bushels, which costs only two dollars, will keep two
fires in a house a month, and in consequence there are few houses,
even amongst the poorest of the inhabitants, where at least two fires
are not used — one for cooking and another for the family to sit at.
This great consumption of a coal abounding in sulfur and its smoke
condensing into a vast quantity of [soot] gives the outside of the
houses a dirty and disagreeable appearance — even more so than in
most populous towns of Great Britain, where a proportionately great
quantity of coal is used. [This] must be caused by a difference of
quality, which appears in the grate to be in favor of the coal of this
country. . . .

Music and Drama

Several musical amateurs are associated here under the title of the
Apollonian Society. I visited it by invitation at the house of Mr. F.

Amelung, the acting president, and was most agreeably surprised to hear a concert of instrumental music performed by about a dozen gentlemen of the town, with a degree of taste and execution which I could not have expected in so remote a place. . . .

The Apollonian Society is principally indebted for its formation to the labors of Mr. S. H. Dearborn, a New England man, who came here about a year ago to exercise the profession of a portrait painter. Being a very versatile genius and having some knowledge of and taste for music, he soon discovered all the respectable people who were harmoniously inclined and succeeded in associating them into a regular society, which meets one evening every week. It consists not only of those who can take parts, but also of many of the most respectable inhabitants of the town who do not play but who become members for the sake of admission for themselves and families to the periodic concerts.

There are also two dramatic societies in Pittsburgh, one composed of the students of law and the other of respectable mechanics. They occasionally unite with each other in order to cast the pieces to be performed with more effect. The theater is in the great room of the upper story of the court house, which from its size and having several other . . . apartments which serve for greenroom,[2] dressing rooms, etc., is very well adapted to that purpose. It is neatly fitted up under the direction of Mr. Dearborn, whose mechanical genius has rendered him a useful associate of the disciples of Thespis[3]. . . . On the whole . . . the dramatic societies exhibit in a very respectable manner a rational entertainment to the inhabitants of Pittsburgh about once monthly through the winter. They have hitherto confined themselves to the comic walk, but I have no doubt that if they appear in the buskin[4] they will do equal credit to tragedy. . . .

Religion and Politics

There are five societies of Christians, which have each an established minister. Mr. Steele, the pastor of one of the Presbyterian societies, possesses all that liberality of sentiment and Christian charity inculcated by the divine founder of his religion, and dignifies the pulpit by his clear and pleasing exposition of the scriptures. . . . There

---

[2] **greenroom:** a retreat for actors and actresses when they are not required on stage during a performance.
[3] **Thespis:** a Greek poet of the sixth century B.C., reputedly the first actor.
[4] **buskin:** the high shoe worn by Greek tragic actors; hence, tragedy.

are here several Roman Catholics, Methodists, and Anabaptists, who have as yet no established place of worship, but who occasionally meet to profit by the exhortations of some of their spiritual directors who travel this way. On the whole, the religious sects appear to be more free here than in most places I have visited from those illiberal and anti-Christian prejudices, which render Christianity the scoff of even the ignorant Indians, whom we term savages.

But though difference of religious opinions does not cause any animosity here, politics have reduced society to a most deplorable state. There are two parties, which style themselves Federal republicans, and Democratic republicans, and call each other Federalists and Democrats. . . . [T]heir opinions . . . are argued with more warmth and are productive of more rancor and violence in Pittsburgh than perhaps in any other part of America. There are very few neutrals, as it requires a bold independence of sentiment to prevent a person from attaching himself to one or the other party. . . . [B]esides, to a man who has not resources for the employment of time within himself, the alternative of not being of one or the other party is insupportable, as he is shunned equally by both and in this populous town lives, with respect to society, as though he were in a desert. This may be one cause that Pittsburgh is not celebrated for its hospitality. [A]nother (which is equally applicable to most new[ly] settled towns) is that it is inhabited by people who have fixed here for the express purpose of making money. This employs the whole of their time and attention, when they are not occupied by politics, and leaves no leisure to devote to the duties of hospitality.

Social Snobbery

Another cause, which one would scarcely suspect, is pride. Those who from the [accidental] circumstance of having settled here at an early period and . . . became possessed of landed property when . . . it was obtained in the most easy manner, for a mere trifle, now find themselves rich suddenly from its rapid increase in value. Those who came after them had not the same opportunities and of course were not so fortunate. Wealth acquired suddenly generally operates on the ignorant to make them wish to seem as if they had always been in the same situation. . . . [I]n affecting the manners and appearance of the great, they always overact their part, and assume airs of superiority even over the really well-born and well-bred part of the community who have been reduced from a more affluent situation . . . or who have not been so fortunate as themselves in acquiring what stands the possessor in lieu of descent and all the virtues and accomplishments. This accounts for the pride which generally pervades the fortunate first settlers, but it is carried to such extravagant excess that I have been credibly informed that some of the females of this class have styled themselves and their families the Well Born, to distinguish them from those not quite so wealthy. . . . This is all [a] matter of ridicule and amusement to a person possessed of the least philosophy.

There is also a very numerous class which assumes a certain air of superiority throughout this whole country: I mean the lawyers. They (even their students and pupils) arrogate to themselves the title or epithet of "esquire," which the uninformed mass of the people allow them; and as, by intrigue, they generally fill all the respectable offices in the government as well as the legislature, they assume to themselves a consequence to which they are in no other way entitled.

8. Forging a Water System[1]

✤ Asa Greene

The new cities of the nation were flourishing, but unprecedented increase in population magnified old problems and created new ones. Perhaps most crucial was the securing of an adequate water supply. Taken for granted and used lavishly by today's city-dwellers, water was anxiously sought by people living with the constant threat of fire and epidemic. New York became the first big city in history to have an ample supply of pure water when the Croton system was opened in 1842. Later the city moved a hundred miles out into the Catskill Mountains in its search for additional sources. Croton, much enlarged, is still part of the New York City system.

Asa Greene, New York physician and author, in 1837 published a book on New York which included the following information on the city's plans for improving the water supply. ■

[1] Asa Greene, A *Glance at New York* (New York: A. Greene, 1837), pp. 179–186.

The cry of the citizens of New York for water — "pure and wholesome water" — has been . . . unceasing. There is not perhaps in the Union a city more destitute of the blessing of good water than New York.

The present supply, such as it is, comes from three sources, to wit: the town pumps, the Manhattan Company, and Knapp's Spring. To this we should add a fourth source, namely, the clouds, from which the chief supply for washing is obtained.

The town pumps are conveniently situated at the corners of the streets, everywhere throughout the city, so that no person who is athirst need perish for want of water, if he will take the trouble of walking the length of a square. If he stand in need of physic at the same time, the pump will furnish that also — without money. . . . Besides the virtue derived from the neighboring sinks, the pump-water is also impregnated with certain saline properties, which render it peculiarly efficacious in certain complaints.

Little less so is that — if we may judge from its peculiar hue and taste — which comes from the Collect and is called Manhattan water. This is ready pumped up to the people's hands by the Manhattan Banking Company, which was chartered many years ago for the purpose of supplying the city with "pure and wholesome water." Not that people get it gratis, as they do the town pump beverage. But they can have it brought to their houses in pipes, on application to the Manhattan Company, and paying the regular price. The pumping up of this water from the depths of the Collect is an expensive affair. It requires the constant employment of a powerful steam engine, and the constant operation of a still more powerful banking company, which . . . is provided with a perpetual charter to issue bank bills and discount notes. By perpetual, meaning, of course, as long as they shall keep the great steam pump in operation. With such an inducement to keep their stream of "pure and wholesome" constantly running, it is not likely that this source will soon fail. But "pure and wholesome" as it is, by the express terms of the charter, the people generally prefer that from the town pumps, except for the purposes of washing, and for that most people use rain water.

The third source, namely Knapp's Spring, furnishes the only tolerable water in the city. This is conveyed about the streets in hogsheads and sold, we believe, at a penny a gallon. Small as this price seems, their supply of spring water costs some of the larger hotels more than 300 dollars per annum. The hotels, boarding houses, and respectable private families make use of this water for tea, coffee, and ordinary drink. The poor all resort to the town pump.

Such is, such has been, and such is likely to be for some years to come, the condition of New York, in regard to the indispensable article of water.[2] . . . Various projects have from time to time been started, examined, discussed, debated, and finally thrown aside as impractical until very recently, when it was resolved, after a scientific survey of the river and the ground, and duly calculating the expense, to bring hither the waters of the Croton. For this purpose an act has been obtained from the legislature; and if the money can be raised, the water will probably be forthcoming, sometime within the life-lease of the present generation.

That part of the Croton River from whence the water is to be taken is about 44 miles in a northerly direction from the City Hall. The water is to be conveyed by a covered aqueduct of strong mason work to a rise of land on the island [of Manhattan] called Murray Hill; from whence, by the force of its own gravity, it will distribute itself through all the streets and avenues of the city. The length of pipe required for the distribution is estimated at 167 miles.

The amount of water which the Croton will furnish is set down at 30 million gallons daily, in the driest times; and 50 million daily, in times of ordinary plenty. In the former case, the supply for each inhabitant, old and young, of our present population, would be 100 gallons a day, in the latter 166⅔ gallons for the same time, a supply altogether sufficient, it is believed, to satisfy the desires of the most laborious water-drinker the city can afford, besides leaving a surplus for all the convenient purposes of making tea, coffee, cleansing the outer man, and extinguishing fires.

The Croton water is found by chemical analysis to be exceedingly pure, and such as will prove highly agreeable to the tastes of all hydro-epicures.[3] . . . Thus free from impurities the Croton water will be a

---

[2] What we have said above of the New York supply of water relates only to that for the domestic and ordinary uses of our citizens. The supply for the extinguishing of fires is derived chiefly from the Reservoir at the corner of Thirteenth Street and the Bowery. This water is forced up by steam and distributed to the various parts of the city, where hydrants are erected at every corner. This scheme of a supply against fires is of very recent date and is found of immense use; for which we give our worthy corporation all due praise.

[3] **hydro-epicures:** those who fancied themselves as experts in judging the quality of water.

great inducement to personal cleanliness. Having it, as they will, running pure in their very bedrooms, the citizens will find it an agreeable pastime, instead of a disgusting labor, to wash themselves of a morning. The Philadelphians who visit New York shall not then have occasion to make invidious comparisons, as they now do, between their delightful Schuylkill water and the vile slops wherewith our bedrooms are furnished.

All this, and more, we expect from the Croton water, when it gets to New York. But that *when,* we fear, is a considerable way off. The expense will be enormous — no less, by estimate, than 5.5 million dollars. The labor will be immense. And large bodies, like our corporation, proverbially move slowly. Some years therefore must elapse before we shall be able to quench our thirst and lave our limbs in the pure waters of the Croton.[4]

This delay is to be regretted on many accounts, and very particularly as it will afford an excuse to many persons for continuing the use of strong drink. The water is now so bad, they plead, that it is absolutely necessary to qualify it with a drop of ardent spirits to render it [drinkable].

[4] The Croton system began functioning five years after this was written.

9. Fire in New York[1]

✤ *Basil Hall*

Although organized firefighting was not new to nineteenth century America, little technical advance had been made in equipment or method since colonial days.

One night in 1827 while in New York City, Captain Basil Hall watched with interest the techniques of some volunteer engine companies. Hall was dismayed by the confusion displayed, but what he witnessed was actually less chaotic than firefighting in other cities where there were no superintendents to direct traffic and where competition between volunteer companies often led to "fire riots" and pitched battles in the streets.

[1] Captain Basil Hall, R.N., *Travels in North America in the Years 1827 and 1828,* 3rd edition in 3 vols. (Edinburgh: Printed for Robert Cadell, 1830), I, pp. 19–23.

Hall's observations, excerpted below, include a suggestion that New York import from Scotland a hose tower for use in reaching fires high in buildings. ■

At two o'clock in the morning of the 20th of May, I was awakened by loud cries of "Fire! Fire!" and started out of bed, half dreaming that we were still at sea and the packet [boat] in flames. In a few minutes the deep rumbling sound of the engines was heard, mingled in a most alarming way with the cheers of the firemen, the loud rapping of the watchmen at the doors and window-shutters of the sleeping citizens, and various other symptoms of momentous danger and the necessity of hot haste.

So much had been said to me of the activity and skill of the New York firemen that I was anxious to see them in actual operation, and . . . having dressed myself quickly, I ran downstairs. Before I reached the outer door, however, the noise had wellnigh ceased, the engines were trundling slowly back again, and the people grumbling, not without reason, at having been dragged out of bed to no purpose. . . .

I was scarcely well asleep again before a second and far more furious alarm brought all the world to the windows. The church bells were clanging violently on all hands, and the ear could readily catch, every now and then, a fresh sound chiming in with the uproar with much musical discord. . . .

On opening the street door, I saw in the east a tall column of black smoke, curling and writhing across the cold morning sky. . . .

On the top of the City Hall, one of the finest of the numerous public buildings which adorn New York, a fire warden or watchman is constantly stationed, whose duty when the alarm is given is to hoist a lantern at the extremity of a long arm attached to the steeple and to direct it towards the fire as a sort of beacon to instruct the engines what course to steer. There was something singularly striking in this contrivance, which looked as if a great giant with a blood-red finger had been posted in the midst of the city to warn the citizens of their danger.

I succeeded by quick running in getting abreast of a fire engine. . . . [A]lthough it was a very ponderous affair, it was dragged along so smartly by its crew of some six-and-twenty men, aided by a whole legion of boys, all bawling as loud as they could, that I found it difficult to keep up with them. On reaching the focus of attraction, the crowd of curious persons like myself began to thicken while the engines came dashing in amongst us from every avenue in the most gallant and businesslike style.

Four houses, built entirely of wood, were on fire from top to bottom and sending up a flame that would have defied a thousand engines. But nothing could exceed the dauntless spirit with which the attempt was made. In the midst of a prodigious noise and confusion, the engines were placed along the streets in a line, at the distance of about 200 feet from one another and reaching to the bank of the East River. . . . The suction hose of the last engine in the line . . . being plunged into the river, the water was drawn up and then forced along a leathern hose or pipe to the next engine and so on till at the tenth link in this curious chain it came within range of the fire. As more engines arrived, they were marshalled by the superintendent into a new string. . . .

I moved about amongst the blazing houses till driven back by the police, who labored hard to clear the ground for the firemen alone. On retiring reluctantly from this interesting scene, I caught a glimpse of a third jet of water playing away from the back part of the fire. . . . [O]n going around to that quarter, [I] discovered that these energetic people had formed a third series, consisting of seven engines reaching to a different bend of the river. . . .

The chief thing to find fault with on this occasion were the needless shouts and other uproarious noises, which obviously helped to exhaust the men at the engines, and the needless forwardness, or it may be called foolhardiness, with which they entered houses on fire or climbed upon them by means of ladders when it must have been apparent to the least skillful persons that their exertions were utterly hopeless. A small amount of discipline, of which, by the way, there was not a particle, might have corrected the noise, and the other evil, I think, might have been removed by a machine recently invented in Edinburgh and found to be efficacious on like occasions.

At the request of a committee of the Fire Department, I afterwards explained this simple and excellent device. It consists of a lofty triangle, as it is called, formed by three poles joined at top, and carrying a socket through which passes the nozzle or spout of a pipe connected with an engine below. By means of guys, or directing lines, this spout may be raised, lowered, or turned to the right or left. By means also of a proper adjustment of the legs, two of which may be brought close to the wall of the burning house and the third pushed either backwards or forwards, a solid stream of water can be directed, in its unbroken state. . . . [I]t may [also] be spouted into a room on fire, not only without danger to the firemen but with much greater precision and effect than by ordinary methods. . . .

The committee listened very attentively to my lecture and inspected the drawings made to illustrate what was said. But I had the mortification, five months afterwards, to see three fine houses burned to the ground, two of which might have been saved, as an old fireman assured me on the spot, had this contrivance been introduced.

10. Crime in the Streets

In 1837 Asa Greene wrote: "A great city may be considered as the mother — the 'nursing mother' — of rogues. A great city affords them [nourishment]; and they do so much credit to their keeping as to 'grow by what they feed on.' They not only find [nourishment] in a great city, but they also find security. They hide themselves in the crowd. They find holes and lurking places, where they lie . . . until the cry of thief is over, when they come boldly forth and prowl as before."

Before the appearance of organized police forces in the 1830's, city officials did not have adequate means for controlling disorderly elements. Overworked constables carried the burden of law enforcement. As early as 1812, swindling had become an easy way to earn a living. One rather elaborate "con game" is described here by New Yorker Charles Christian. Nor were city-dwellers the only targets: Christian also describes the problem in the suburbs. The second document is an address by Philadelphia's mayor, William Milnor, to the city councils requesting additional police to cope with rising crime in a growing city. ■

A. SHARP PRACTICES[1]

♣ Charles Christian

An Old, Old Game

There is a horde of low gamblers, vagabonds, and agents for passing
off counterfeit notes that prowl about the suburbs of the city, markets,
and wharfs. Their standing prey are seamen and countrymen; their
arts are infinite and suited to every occasion, one of which, as it is
frequently employed, I shall state. One of the gang will drop a bill
close to a person whom they have previously fixed upon to plunder,
and pick it up as if he had found it. Then another of them will come
up, as if accidentally and a stranger. When he hears how near the
bystander was to the money when found (who, commonly, is wishing
and wondering why he himself did not see it, and he so near)
promptly gives his opinion that "this honest man is entitled by rule
to one half." To this the first sharper seemingly objects, but at length
yielding to reason he generously concludes to "divide what fortune
threw in the way."

It is then proposed to get the bill (which is always counterfeit, lest
the person should change it from his own money on the spot)
changed, and have a drink. The victim invites the second sharper,
who in his opinion so generously took his part, to join them. In ten
minutes they are all seated in the back room of some tavern brothel,
where they are joined by the rest of the gang. Liquor is brought in,
generally hot, strong toddy, in ten minutes more cards or dice are
on the table, and in less than an hour the simple and unfortunate
poor fellow is fleeced of his money and watch.

It would fill a volume to relate the technique practiced on those
occasions. If cunning fails, force is employed and the plot winds up
with the villains running off, leaving the poor wretch unable to follow, either by intoxication or by blows. The landlady (a personification of one of the Furies) then enters to act her part, loudly de-
claiming against "the noise made in her house," and demands the
reckoning of the sufferer. She soon closes her performance by telling
him that "he is a liar and a sharper and came there with them other

---

[1] Adapted from A Citizen [Charles Christian], *A Brief Treatise on the Police
of the City of New York* (New York: Southwick and Pelsue, 1812), pp. 21–22,
29.

fellows, who ran off, to bilk her house, but if he ever does so again she will send him to bridewell."[2] After which pithy and salutary threat, a bully thrusts him into the street, and the gang re-enter at the back door to divide the spoils and give the landlady her proportion.

Suburban Crime

. . . The suburbs of this city are annoyed, in a much greater degree than the center, by the brutal effusions of vulgar and intemperate persons, common disturbers of the peace, and are, almost exclusively, the retreat of sharpers, passers of counterfeit money, pickpockets, and other villains that have their dens in those parts of town. It would be a great advantage to the public in general, and manifestly so to the citizens residing in the upper parts of the city, if the police office was established in that quarter, say at the watch-house at the head of Chatham Street, for those who have no respect for society or the laws fear their agents [the police].

B. THE ANSWER: MORE PATROLMEN [3]

✤ *William Milnor*

MAYOR'S OFFICE
January 28, 1830

To the Select and Common Councils
Gentlemen:

The numerous acts of violence and outrage upon the persons and property of our peaceable citizens, and the boldness with which many of those acts are committed at an early hour in the evening, are sure indications that we are infested at this time by an unusual number of villains of the boldest and most daring character. To put a stop to those outrages as far as lies in my power, I have ordered the silent watchmen to patrol the streets from the hour of seven in the evening. I have also directed the two high constables to patrol the streets during the evening with such of the city constables as they can procure to assist them. It must be obvious, however, that these means (and

---

[2] **bridewell:** a prison or house of correction.
[3] *The Register of Pennsylvania*, Samuel Hayard, ed., Vol. V, No. 6, February 6, 1830 (Philadelphia), p. 87.

they conceived to be all that are within the control of the Mayor) are entirely inadequate in the present emergency. It is therefore respectfully suggested to Councils whether it would not be expedient to authorize the appointment of an additional number of police officers for a limited time, to be placed under the direction of the Mayor, and to provide a suitable compensation for their services. This or any other plan that may have suggested itself to Councils shall receive my hearty co-operation.

Respectfully,

WILLIAM MILNOR, MAYOR

11. The Control of Disease[1]

Yellow fever and smallpox, the scourges of the seventeenth and eighteenth centuries, were overshadowed by cholera in the nineteenth. The country experienced epidemics in 1832–1834 and 1848–1849, and each year between 1849 and 1854 cholera appeared in some part of the United States. The causes and cures were unknown; most people, including doctors, looked on the epidemics as heaven-sent punishment for man's transgressions. But the frequency of the occurrences finally forced cities to take practical steps. The 1849 report of the Boston Committee of Internal Health indicates how well organized were that group's efforts to cope with cholera. The report is also impressive because of its wide-ranging attack on conditions fostering disease: filth, poor sanitation and ventilation, overcrowding, and the greed of land speculators and slum landlords. The members of the committee urged the City of Boston to ask the state legislature for strict laws which would enable it to crack down on those responsible for shocking abuses in areas where the poor were forced to live. ■

Organization of the Board of Health

The old arrangement of joint committees of the [Boston] City Council having been found practically inconvenient and cumbersome,

[1] *Report of the Committee of Internal Health of the Asiatic Cholera, together with a Report of the City Physician on the Cholera Hospital* (Boston, 1849), pp. 4–16.

the Board of Health, consisting of the Mayor and Aldermen, undertook the sole charge and responsibility of all future measures in reference to this matter. For greater convenience, the city was divided into districts, each of which was placed under the particular care of a member of the Board, with power to obtain from the Police and Internal Health Departments as large a force as should be necessary for the effective and thorough cleansing of his district. All nuisances, not removable in a summary way, were reported to the Board, which passed the necessary orders and carried them into effect through this Committee.

The Board commenced their labors by republishing the report of the Consulting Physicians in the public journals, and leaving printed notices at each house in the city, requesting the inhabitants to thoroughly cleanse their houses, yards, privies, and drains, and deposit all decayed vegetable and animal matter, and other deleterious substances in the streets opposite their dwellings, on certain specified days. The requisition was very generally complied with, and a large number of carts were at once employed to carry off what had thus been collected. The police, under the City Marshal, were then detached, in squads proportioned to the size of the respective districts, to carefully inspect, from garret to cellar, every building in the city; to order and see to the removal of every offensive substance which could readily be removed; and to report all cases of important or permanent nuisance to this committee.

In consequence of these efforts, the city was soon in a greater state of cleanliness, it is believed, than it ever had been since its foundation; but, in order that the labor which had been expended might not be lost, the police were again detailed in squads to visit, in daily rounds, every part of their respective districts, and carts were assigned to them for the immediate removal of any offensive substance which they might find. Every street was swept, and the house dirt and offal were carried off from each dwelling, twice a week, through the Health Department; and, in the exposed localities, these precautionary labors were performed daily, under the direction of the police.

Preparations for the Cholera Epidemic

On the approach of the cholera, several additional measures were undertaken. Printed notices were published in the journals and posted up in various places, containing directions as to regimen, diet, clothing, and the treatment to be pursued on the discovery of premonitory symptoms. The police were directed to see that houses and cellars, in exposed places, were whitewashed. Large quantities of disinfecting substances were purchased and freely distributed wherever they were required.

For the relief of the poorer classes, the Board fitted up a large building on Fort Hill, formerly a gun house, as a cholera hospital, and placed it in the charge of this committee. A medical staff, under the direction of Dr. Clark, the City Physician, and all necessary nurses and attendants were speedily provided, and the whole establishment was ready for the reception of patients before its use was required. As a further measure, your Committee, with the consent of the Board and the approval of the Consulting Physicians, appointed special physicians for each ward, who were required to visit and prescribe for cholera patients at their own dwellings, and be at their service, both day and night, with power to procure nurses and medicine.

From the above account, it will be seen that the city was well prepared for the cholera before its arrival; and, though the precautionary measures which had been taken did not prevent the anticipated attack, there is every reason to believe that they were effective in checking its progress and diminishing its virulence. As is well known, most persons, throughout the city, were more or less affected by the cholera atmosphere; but few cases of the actual disease, and still fewer deaths, occurred in any of the more dry and airy portions of the metropolis.

Responsibility for Clean Streets

Before closing their report, your Committee deem it their duty to call the special attention of the Board of Health, and their successors in office, to the present unhealthy condition of many of the streets, in the lower parts of the city. In all these localities, there are many streets, courts, and lanes which are exceedingly contracted, ill ventilated, and dirty, without any proper grade and with no, or very insufficient, sewerage. This state of things is mainly owing to the fact of their having been originally laid out by private speculators, whose only object was to make a profitable investment for themselves, and who paid but very slight attention to the health or comfort of those who have to reside upon them. But in some cases, it arises from the great increase of population, which renders the space and accommodation, originally provided for a limited number of residents, wholly insufficient for the proper supply of the present necessities. In certain localities, as on the South Cove, the marshy and newmade ground has settled, and the imperfect sewerage which was originally provided has become nearly useless.

The great body of the streets alluded to are private ways, over which the city exercises no special care or custody; and the policy, hitherto pursued by it, has been to refuse to accept them until they are graded and put in good order by the abutters. It may be questioned whether this policy is a sound one. The public interest would seem to require that the Board of Health should have the power to cause all streets and ways to be laid out, of a suitable width, and to be properly graded and provided with ample sewerage, constructed and laid down in the best manner, before any buildings are erected upon them. And, in case of neglect or refusal to comply with their requisitions, they should be authorized to proceed by their own agents; and the adjacent territory should be held answerable for the payment of the necessary expenses.

Remedy: Crack Down on Landlords

The Committee would gladly have been excused from the task of setting before you the above most painful details, but it has been forced upon them by a sense of duty and the hope and belief that, for the large portion of the evils complained of, some adequate remedial measures can and ought to be found by the city. Great public considerations seem to them to demand, that every dwelling house should be provided with sinks, drains, and privies, that are adapted, in size, number, and construction, to the number of individuals who shall occupy it; that the owners should be compelled by law to construct them, under the direction of the Board of Health; and, in case of neglect or refusal, that the estate itself should be held liable for the payment of all expenses which may be incurred by the City in making such provision. A just regard to the health and comfort of the poorer classes, as well as to the rights of tenants, who are unable to prosecute them, would also make it reasonable that every landlord should be required to fit his building properly to the purposes for which it is to be used, in respect to light, air, and necessary conveniences; and that some provision of law should be made by which the number of tenants should be apportioned to its size and general arrangements. And, especially is it important that some legal power, sanctioned by penalties sufficiently stringent, should be obtained to prevent entirely the occupation of underground cellars as dwelling houses.

Your committee submit the above subjects to the serious consideration of the Board of Health, and they recommend that an early application be made to the legislature for such additional powers, as may be needed to abate the evils complained of.

12. Books for the Working Boy[1]

✦ Asa Greene

Libraries have been a part of urban culture for thousands of years, but until recent centuries they were usually sponsored by universities or wealthy individuals and restricted to scholars and specialists. In 1731 in Philadelphia, Benjamin Franklin and a few friends established the Library Company, a forerunner of many such "society libraries." These were usually small, supported by subscription, dues, and donations, and serving particular groups. The New York associations described in the following selection would be classified as "society libraries." Out of them came the public-library movement. The first truly public library of consequence, municipally controlled and tax supported, was opened in Boston in 1854. ■

The citizens of New York have evidently not forgotten that "knowledge is power," as any man may convince himself who will take the trouble to glance at the various libraries in this city. We do not speak of private collections of books, nor of those owned by particular individuals and loaned out for public use [called] circulating libraries. We shall only take notice of some of the principal collections belonging to public associations.

The New York Society Library

The first of these in point of age, as well as in number of volumes, is the New York Society Library. It was founded while we were yet in the colonial state, and 21 years before the commencement of the revolution, namely in 1754. It began with about 700 volumes. The

[1] Asa Greene, *A Glance at New York* (New York: A. Greene, 1837), pp. 221–230.

price of a share was $12.50, subject to an annual tax of $1.50. In 1772, during the administration of Governor Tryon, the society was incorporated. It was just beginning to flourish — to increase in numbers and to add to its stock of books — when the war broke out; and while the British had possession of New York, the principal part of the books were scattered or destroyed. The project, however, was revived soon after the peace, and the library is now among the most valuable in the character, as well as the number, of its books to be found in the United States. It contains more than 25,000 volumes. The price of a share is now $25, and the annual tax $4.

The Mercantile Library Association

The next, in number of volumes, is the clerks' library, a collection belonging to the merchants' clerks, united together under the name of the Mercantile Library Association. This library was founded in the year 1821 by the union of a few clerks who thought they could devote their leisure hours more profitably, if not more agreeably, to books than to the theaters, ballrooms, and other fashionable amusements. They began by uniting their own collections with such books as they could get together by way of donation. Thus a few hundred volumes were collected, which have since been increased in number, chiefly by means of the subscriptions of members and by an annual tax, until they now amount to more than 13,500, enabling the Mercantile Library to rank as the tenth in point of numbers in the United States.

The increase in 1836 was 1845 volumes, and the number of members added during the same year was 867. The whole number of members is now about 3500. The initiation fee is $1, and the annual tax $2, payable by quarterly instalments of 50 cents each. To the library is added a reading room, furnished with all the most valuable periodical literature of the day.

Merchants are allowed all the privileges of the library and the reading room by paying an annual subscription of $5. And so far they are considered members but they are not allowed the privilege of voting. . . .

Connected with the association of clerks is the Clinton Hall Association, a corporate body composed of some of the first merchants in the city, united for the laudable purpose of aiding the clerks in their efforts for intellectual improvement. Clinton Hall, in which there are the library, reading, and lecture rooms, is the property of this association. As the use of these rooms is granted rent free, the income of the stores and such other parts of the building as are let out on rent all goes to the Mercantile Library to increase its stock of books. This source, as soon as some arrears of expense for building are paid, will, we are assured, amount to little less than $5000, which with the income from subscriptions and assessments of members, will give to the Mercantile Library Association an income of more than $10,000 a year, all of which, laid out in books, will cause their collection to increase more rapidly than perhaps any other library in the United States.

The Apprentices' Library

Next to the Mercantile Library in number of volumes, and not inferior to it in point of usefulness, is the Apprentices' Library. It was founded in the year 1820, and has now upwards of 12,000 volumes. This library is the property of the General Society of Mechanics and Tradesmen, a benevolent association formed in 1784, 36 years before the establishment of the library. The initiation fee, for members of this society, is $10, and $12 more, paid in four annual instalments of $3 each, or $20, paid in the beginning, constitutes a man a life member.

The books of this library are loaned to merchants' apprentices, for whose use alone it is intended, free of all expense, their masters engaging to become responsible for the safe return of the books. Nothing could be more noble and generous than this provision of the mechanics' and tradesmen's societies. Of all persons in the world, apprentices are apt to be the most destitute of books, when left to their own resources. How great then the importance, how benevolent the object, of an institution which provides a remedy for so great a want.

Apprentices are inclined to read — at least a large proportion of them are so — if the means are furnished them, as anyone may be convinced who will step into their library of an evening (the only time it is open). Here he will behold the pleasing sight of hundreds of boys, from twelve years old and upwards, in humble apparel, but all eager to obtain books and warm in their desire for intellectual improvement.

Other New York Libraries

There are several other public libraries in the city, the largest of which is that belonging to the New York Historical Society, founded in 1809 and containing upwards of 10,000 volumes. That of the American Institute, established in 1828, contains about 3000 volumes; and that of the Law Institute, founded in the same year, upwards of 2000.

The Mechanics' Institute, founded in 1831, has a library of about 1200 volumes. One work belonging to this collection cost $800. It is Denon's great work on Egypt, consisting of 24 large folio volumes, illustrated with a great number of very expensive engravings. The other works belonging to this library are mostly valuable scientific and literary works, particularly calculated for the association to which they belong. This institute has an annual course of lectures on various subjects connected with improvement in science and the mechanic arts.

These are the principal public libraries in New York, and all are of exceeding value and importance, both in the materials of which they are composed and the objects to which they are devoted. But in this latter respect — as will be gathered from what we have said above — there are none of them we think of such high importance as those of the apprentices and the clerks. . . . These afford reading and improvement to those who could not well obtain them by other means, besides furnishing an inducement to the avoidance of evil company and to the cultivation of habits of correct thought and useful study.

13. New York Ascendant[1]

✦ *John A. Dix*

Urban rivalries were crucial to national development. Everywhere cities fought to acquire the widest possible marketing areas and in so doing spurred technological change and brought civilization to the wilderness. Supplying goods cheaply and quickly to as many buyers as possible led to the opening of extensive internal transport systems.

Among the first and most important of these was New York's Erie Canal. John A. Dix, lawyer and Democratic politician, saw

[1] John A. Dix, *Sketch of the Resources of the City of New-York* (New York: G. & C. Carvill, 1827), pp. 48–49, 53–57, 65–66.

the canal as only one step — but an important one — for New York's domination of the nation's resources and commerce. Characteristic of this urban imperialism was the way in which projects such as the Ohio Canal, begun for the benefit of others, were always seen as operating in one's own favor. ■

The system of internal communication by canals, which the state of New York adopted a few years ago, . . . has given an impulse to the industry of her citizens, of which no foresight can properly estimate the results. A country of vast extent and inexhaustible fertility has been penetrated to its center, and its products brought, by the virtual annihilation of distance, . . . to the very skirts of the city. On the other hand, the products of foreign countries accumulated within the city by the operations of commerce and exchange are distributed with the same ease to the various parts of the state . . . Consistently with its design, the system can only be viewed in connection with the particular interests of the city and as subordinate to the commercial prosperity, which it is destined so powerfully to stimulate. . . .

When the practicability of the Erie Canal became fully established and experiment had shown that the profits on the capital employed would be greater than those of ordinary investments, similar improvements were projected in other states. Two canals of great importance to the city of New York have been marked out and are already in a train of execution. The first of these is the Ohio Canal, intended to unite the waters of the Ohio River with those of Lake Erie. This communication may be considered as an extension of the Erie Canal and will render the city of New York the market for the agricultural products of a large portion of Ohio, Indiana, and Illinois.

It may not be improper in this place to observe that a scheme has been formed of cutting a canal from Albany to Boston, for the purpose of extending to New England the benefits of the industry and resources of the interior of New York. . . . [I]t has been supposed by some that this new communication, by opening another market, would divert from the city of New York a large portion of the products of the West and make Boston the market for the exchange of those products with imports from foreign countries. But even according to this calculation, the difference exhibited in favor of the New York market would inevitably exclude from the Boston market every article produced in the interior of the state of New York or in the western states and designed for export. It is to be remembered also that when once a city has acquired an established character as the great commercial emporium of a country, . . . the course of trade becomes settled by flowing regularly in the same channel, permanent investments of capital are made, and the foreign as well as the inland commerce of the country takes a direction which nothing but the development of extraordinary superiorities of position in some other place can change.

The present superiority of New York over every other city in point of local facilities for the prosecution of foreign and internal trade is indisputable. . . . [I]t is only necessary to glance at her physical relations with the different sections of the country to see that no other position can gain an ascendancy over her, for there is no other position which is endowed with equal advantages. The city which approaches most nearly to New York in local facilities for the operations of foreign commerce is New Orleans. This city occupies the terminating point of the only natural channel through which the products of the southwestern states seek a passage to the ocean and where inland must be exchanged for external navigation. But her advantages of position with regard to internal communication are counteracted in some degree by disadvantages of climate; and the approach to the city from the ocean with all the improvements that art can devise will never cease to be inconvenient and [slow]. The immense power of production which the western states possess in fertility of soil and in facilities for the application of labor to manufacturing purposes is destined to rank them among the most industrious and productive sections of the country. But it may be fairly calculated that the immense regions which the Columbus Canal will open to Lake Erie, including a large portion of Ohio, Indiana, and Illinois, will become tributary to New York, from the greater ease and economy of sending their products to her, as well as from her superiority as a market.

From a review of the statements relative to the progress of the several canal communications which are to have their termination at the city of New York and the productive powers which they are destined to bring into operation, it is apparent that no position in this country, perhaps in the world, unites so many facilities for becoming permanently great and prosperous.

14. An Empire for Philadelphia

Although New York City took on the whole country, most urban rivalries were limited to competition between two cities for the same territory. For more than eighty years, from before 1780 to 1860, Philadelphia and Baltimore struggled for commercial control of Pennsylvania's Susquehanna Valley. At one point in the battle, Philadelphia tried to circumvent Baltimore by building a canal connecting the Chesapeake and Delaware bays.

In the first selection given below, Samuel Breck, a transplanted New Englander, sets the terms of the struggle from the Philadelphia viewpoint and finds the prospects bright for his city's eventual domination of the nation's trade. In the second selection, Thomas Cope of the board of directors of the canal expresses high hopes for an undertaking which was to fail because of mechanical and financial difficulties. ■

A. REALIZING PENN'S DREAM[1]

✤ Samuel Breck

Foreign commerce during the golden days of neutrality and a monopoly of the best share of western trade have heaped together in this small district so vast a treasure. But our foreign commerce is less extensive and less gainful now, and rivals in the North and South are about to deprive us of our home trade. We must defeat their efforts; we must maintain, protect, and increase these riches. We can and will baffle the attempts of our neighbors. We have a *motive* in the defense of our property; we have the *means* in that *property* itself; and nature points out to us the road — a road broad, fair, safe, and interminable! If we follow it, we shall insure to ourselves, without the possibility of rivalship from any quarter, the most brilliant career and highest destiny. We may command at one and the same

[1] Samuel Breck, *A Sketch of Internal Improvements* (1818 pamphlet), pp. 80–81, quoted in James Weston Livingood, *The Philadelphia-Baltimore Trade Rivalry, 1780–1860* (Harrisburg: The Pennsylvania Historical and Museum Commission, 1947) p. 19.

time the trade of the Great Lakes, of the Ohio, half the Mississippi, the whole of the Missouri, these parts of Pennsylvania, and one third of New York; and in such event, an event [about] to be realized, we shall see the expectations of the great founder of our city fulfilled. We shall behold storehouses and commercial streets lining the banks of the Schuylkill and receding east until they meet those of the Delaware, and thus cover the vast area marked out by Penn as the ground plot of his city of brotherly love.

B. A SECOND TRY[2]

♣ Thomas Cope

Fellow-citizens: We are this day assembled on a deeply interesting occasion.

More than half a century has elapsed since the idea of connecting the waters of the Chesapeake and Delaware bays by means of a canal was cherished by some of our calculating and enlightened forefathers.

About twenty years ago, the work actually commenced. It proved abortive, from causes on which it is not necessary at this time to [speak at length]. But to whatever circumstances the failure may be ascribed, it could not be expected that a subject of such vast import to the states of Pennsylvania, Maryland, and Delaware, a subject, indeed, of so much interest to the nation at large, would ever be abandoned.

This day gives birth to a new era in the history of our country. This day commences a link in the chain of that great system of inland navigation which is eventually to unite Georgia with Maine and to bind more firmly together the extremes of this mighty republic.

When we contemplate the fruitful districts which are laved by the waters of the great Chesapeake Bay and its numerous tributary rivers to the south — the majestic Delaware, on whose green bank so much of human happiness is to be found, together with the countless fertile valleys which are embraced on the north and the west by the . . . [branches] of our own Susquehanna — in no country, perhaps of the world, certainly in no part of these United States, can a canal be

2 *Niles' Weekly Register*, Vol. 26, Supplement to No. 2, May 15, 1824 (Baltimore: Franklin Press), p. 180.

(*Continued on page 84*)

Philadelphia has been a center of American political and cultural life for nearly three centuries. The painting (top left) shows the city's most famous citizen, Benjamin Franklin (center, standing) at the opening in 1731 of the colonies' first subscription library, which he helped found. Left is Independence Hall where the Declaration was signed July 4, 1776. Below is a section of elegant Chestnut Street in the 19th century. Above right is a drawing of a busy street corner at the time of the American Centennial Exhibition of 1876. Philadelphia has been chosen as the major site of the nation's bicentennial observance of the signing of the Declaration of Independence, taking place in 1976.

found which by so short a line unites greater advantages or connects more . . . flourishing regions.

Are our near neighbors, the respectable inhabitants of Baltimore, using means to participate with us in the rich harvest of their own fields? So much the better; I sincerely wish them success in all their laudable undertakings. Rivalry of this character, conducted on liberal and honorable principles, is creditable to both parties, will be serviceable . . . to each, and prove highly beneficial to the country. There is room enough and will be produce enough for us all. The farmer will be profited by the enhanced value of his lands and the new market opened for whatever he may have to sell, and the citizen by the additional quality and variety which will be conveyed to his doors. Some of us may yet live to witness the fountains of Lake Erie and the Allegheny River intermingling with the tide of the Delaware; and to see the treasures of the earth and the rich fruits of human industry flow by means of canals from the Ohio, the Mississippi, and the Missouri to our wharves in Philadelphia.

But, in all our undertakings, let us not forget to implore the favor and protection of that supreme, all-wise, irresistible power which can in a breath lay waste the proudest labors and monuments of man and without whose blessing our best-formed schemes and efforts will be vain and inglorious.

15. St. Louis vs. Chicago

Later in the century the Midwest was the scene of another struggle between rival cities. St. Louis battled to maintain a strong commercial position based on river traffic, in the face of Chicago's spectacular growth as a rail center. The tragedy of St. Louis was its abject dependence on the Mississippi. City leaders feared that the construction of bridges across the river would seriously impede navigation and destroy the commercial value of the port.

The positions of the two cities are sketched in the first two documents given below, one from the minutes of the St. Louis Chamber of Commerce (1860) and the other from a Chicago newspaper of 1859. In the third selection, dated 1865, a St. Louis booster, Henry Cobb, compares the plight of his city to that of Samson in the Biblical story, the giant brought low by the tempting Delilah (Chicago), the tool of the Philistines (the eastern capitalists and railroad tycoons). ■

A. NO MORE RAILROAD BRIDGES![1]

The railroads reaching the east bank of the Mississippi and above Quincy [Illinois] are clamoring for bridges, but the firm stand taken by St. Louis has deterred them from doing anything more than making their nominal commencement which was rendered necessary to save their state charters. If we are beaten in this suit or abandon it, two years will not pass over our heads before we shall see the Mississippi bridged in at least three additional places and perhaps more. A half dozen bridges in the rapid current and changing channel of this river would render navigation extremely hazardous, if not impracticable, and the commercial position of St. Louis, which is now the pride and boast of her citizens, would be counted among the things that were.

The city always has been and must necessarily remain dependent upon her rivers for the bulk of her trade, and it well becomes her to watch with a jealous eye all attempts to encroach thereon. We do not propose to decry the importance of railroads, nor shut our eyes to the immense benefit they have been to the country. [B]ut we cannot consent that our noble rivers should be obstructed just when and where it may suit the interests of those corporations, and we are quite sure that our position will be sustained by the highest judicial authority in the land.

B. "MANIFEST DESTINY"[2]

As well may St. Louis attempt to dam up the Mississippi as to prevent the bridging of that river at half a score of points where the

[1] Saint Louis Chamber of Commerce, *Fifth Annual Report* (1860), quoted in Wyatt W. Belcher, *The Economic Rivalry Between St. Louis and Chicago, 1850–1880* (New York: Columbia University Press, 1947), p. 65.

[2] *Weekly Chicago Press and Tribune*, March 10, 1859, quoted in Belcher, *op. cit.*, p. 64.

necessities will soon demand it. . . . We tell St. Louis once for all that not Chicago but the genius of the age demands the bridging of the Mississippi and the Missouri, and the removal of every obstacle to the great central railway of the continent. It must soon bind the states of the Atlantic and the Pacific in one brotherhood forever. Instead, therefore, of opposing this decree of "manifest destiny," we again commend to the serious attention of St. Louis the project of building a bridge at her own doors, and now and hereafter Chicago offers her best wishes to her anxious sister and asks only a fair field and an honorable struggle for the prize of commercial supremacy — the position of the great central city of the continent.

C. ST. LOUIS CRIPPLED[3]

But alas! St. Louis that used to be a Samson of strength and a ruling master of the commercial domain from the Allegheny to the Rocky Mountains . . . has fallen a sleepy victim into the lap of the artful Delilah that is cunningly watching in the garden city on Lake Michigan.

Chicago, the tool of the Philistines in the East who were jealous of the strength of St. Louis; Chicago, the Delilah, has been furnished with money by the lords of eastern capital for shaving St. Louis of his strength in cutting off, by means of iron railways, the trade of his rivers in which his strength lay, and delivered him a seduced captive into the hands of the enemy.

Not only is the trade of the Upper Mississippi River, from St. Paul to Hannibal in Missouri, cut off from St. Louis by Chicago, but also the trade of the Missouri River from St. Joseph to Omaha, and even the Rocky Mountains. [N]ot only is the trade of the Lower Mississippi in winter cut off by the same hand, using the Illinois Central Railway, but even the trade of the Ohio River at Pittsburgh is this day being clipped by the Fort Wayne and Chicago Railway. . . .

The Chicago capitalists are bridging the Mississippi River at Quincy and even the Missouri River at Kansas City, and propose to draw off the trade not only of our Missouri Road, but also the Southwest, even daringly striking at the center of our state. . . .

[3] *Missouri Republican*, October 4, 1865, quoted in Belcher, *op. cit.*, pp. 160–161.

Then might it be said to St. Louis, "The Philistines be upon thee, Samson!" and St. Louis might wake up and shake himself but find that his strength was gone, that he was bound by the enemy in fetters stronger than brass.

16. Slavery in the Cities

The word "slavery" usually brings to mind a decidedly rural image: black men and women bent at the waist picking cotton, or hoisting baskets filled with it up on their shoulders. But this harsh institution was urban as well. In southern cities slavery developed characteristics quite different from those prevailing on the plantation.

The selections that follow deal with different aspects of urban slavery. In the 1830's Joseph Ingraham, New England author of historical romances (sample title: Scarlet Feather, *or the* Young Chief of the Abenaquies, *a Romance of the Wilderness of Maine), visited New Orleans and Natchez, Mississippi, where he noted the differences between city slaves (and free Negroes) and their rural counterparts. He describes the "hiring out" system, which tended to modify and weaken the tyrannous master-slave relationship. In the 1850's, the* New York Times *commissioned Frederick Law Olmsted, designer of Central Park, to write a series of articles on the Cotton Kingdom. Given here is Olmsted's classic explanation for the decline of urban slavery. The third selection, by John S. C. Abbott, a resident of Maine who traveled in the South in 1859, deals with the disappearance of the Negro population.* ■

A. A "MUTUALLY ADVANTAGEOUS" SYSTEM[1]

✦ Joseph H. Ingraham

There are properly three distinct classes of slaves in the South. The first, and most intelligent, is composed of the domestic slaves, or "servants," as they are properly termed, of the planters. . . .

---

[1] Joseph H. Ingraham, *The South-West, by a Yankee*, 2 vols. (New York: Harper & Brothers, 1835), II, p. 249–254.

The second class is composed of town slaves; [it] not only includes domestic slaves, in the families of citizens, but also all Negro mechanics, draymen, hostlers, laborers, hucksters, and washerwomen, and the . . . multitude of every other occupation who fill the streets of a busy city — for slaves are trained to every kind of manual labor. The blacksmith, cabinetmaker, carpenter, builder, wheelwright, all have one or more slaves laboring at their trades. The Negro is a third arm to every working man who can possibly save enough to purchase one. . . . Even free Negroes cannot do without them; some of them own several, to whom they are the severest masters.

"To whom do you belong?" I once inquired of a Negro whom I had employed. "There's my master," he replied, pointing to a steady old Negro who had purchased himself, then his wife, and subsequently his three children, by his own manual exertions and persevering industry. . . .

Many of the Negroes who swarm in the cities are what is called "hired servants." They belong to planters, or others, who, finding them qualified for some occupation in which they cannot afford to employ them, hire them to citizens as mechanics, cooks, waiters, nurses, etc., and receive the monthly wages for their services. Some steady slaves are permitted to "hire their own time"; that is, to go into town and earn what they can, as porters, laborers, gardeners, or in other ways, and pay a stipulated sum weekly to their owners, which will be regulated according to the supposed value of the slave's labor. Masters, however, who are sufficiently indulgent to allow them to "hire their time," are seldom rigorous in rating their labor very high.

But whether the slave earns less or more than the specified sum, he must always pay that, and neither more nor less than that, to his master at the close of each week, as the condition of this privilege. Few fail in making up the sum; and generally they earn more, if industrious, which is expended in little luxuries, or laid by in an old rag among the rafters of their houses, till a sufficient sum is thus accumulated to purchase their freedom. This they are seldom refused, and if a small amount is wanting to reach their value, the master makes it up out of his own purse, or, rather, takes no notice of the deficiency. I have never known a planter to refuse to aid, by peculiar indulgences, any of his steady and well-disposed slaves, who desired to purchase their freedom. On the contrary, they often endeavor to excite emulation in them to the attainment of this end. The custom of allowing slaves to "hire their time," insuring the master a certain sum weekly and the slave a small surplus, is mutually advantageous to both.

The majority of town servants are those who are hired to families by planters, or by those living in town who own more than they have employment for, or who can make more by hiring them than by keeping them at home. Some families, who possess not an acre of land but own many slaves, hire them out to different individuals, the wages constituting their only income, which is often very large. There are indeed few families, however wealthy, whose incomes are not increased by the wages of hired slaves, and there are many poor people who own one or two slaves, whose hire enables them to live comfortably. From three to five dollars a week is the hire of a female, and 75 cents or a dollar a day for a male. Thus, contrary to the opinion [in] the North, families may have good servants, and yet not own one, if they are unable to buy. . . .

The city slaves are distinguished, as a class, by superior intelligence, acuteness, and deeper moral degradation. A great proportion of them are hired, and, free from restraint in a great degree, compared with their situations under their own masters or in the country, they soon become corrupted by the vices of the city, and in associating indiscriminately with each other and the refuse of the white population. Soon the vices of the city, divested of their refinement, become their own unmasked. Although they may once have ranked under the first class, and possessed the characteristics which designate the decent, well-behaved domestic of the planter, they soon lose their identity. There are of course exceptions. . . . Some of these exceptions, of a highly meritorious character, have come within my knowledge.

The third and lowest class consists of those slaves who are termed "field hands."

B. RICHMOND NEGROES[2]

✦ *Frederick Law Olmsted*

There was no indication of their [Richmond Negroes] belonging to a subject race, but that they invariably gave the way to the white

[2] Frederick Law Olmsted, *A Journey in the Seaboard Slave States*, (New York: Mason Brothers, 1859), pp. 28–29.

people they met. Once, when two of them, engaged in conversation and looking at each other, had not noticed his approach, I saw a Virginia gentleman lift his cane and push a woman aside with it. In the evening I saw three rowdies, arm in arm, taking the whole of the sidewalk, hustle a black man off it, giving him a blow as they passed that sent him staggering into the middle of the street. As he recovered himself he began to call out to, and threaten them. Perhaps he saw me stop and thought I should support him, as I was certainly inclined to.

"Can't you find anything else to do than to be knocking quiet people round! You jus' come back here and I'll teach you how to behave. Knock people round! Don't care if I does hab to go to der watch-house."

They passed on without noticing him further, only laughing jeeringly, and he continued:

"You come back here and I'll make you laugh; you is just three white nigger cowards, dat's what *you* be."

I observe in the newspapers complaints of growing insolence and insubordination among the Negroes, arising, it is thought, from too many privileges being permitted them by their masters and from too merciful administration of the police laws with regard to them. Except in this instance, however, I have seen not the slightest evidence of any independent manliness on the part of the Negroes toward the whites. As far as I have yet observed, they are treated very kindly and even generously as servants, but their manner to white people is invariably either sullen, jocose, or fawning.

C. BACK TO THE PLANTATION[3]

✦ *John S. C. Abbott*

Sunday, December 11 [1859]. This is the great market day in the French quarter in New Orleans. As I was anxious to witness the novel scene, which brings in a large number of plantation Negroes with their little ventures for sale, I went down at an early hour of the morning to market. The whole scene is most decidedly French, and re-

[3] John S. C. Abbott, *North and South: Or Impressions Received During a Trip to Cuba and the South* (New York: Abbey and Abbot, 1860), pp. 73–74.

minds one of Paris. Still I saw very many less plantation Negroes than I had expected to see, and very many less than I would have seen a few years ago. Nothing has surprised me more in New Orleans than the small number of the colored population. When the *DeSoto* was made fast to the levee, the wide and extended plateau was thronged with laborers, but they were nearly all Germans or Irish. Rarely could I see a dark skin. It was the same in the streets as we drove through them. Upon speaking of this to a very intelligent gentleman, he observed that the slaves were becoming so exceedingly profitable upon the plantations that large numbers of them had been sold from the city for that purpose; and that also it was found not well to have them associated with free laborers, as they acquired bad notions and restless habits.

Clearly it must be so. The cities, especially the commercial ones, will soon be drained, and the powerful tendency now must be to gather the slaves upon the remote plantations, where they can be excluded from popular view and no longer be agitated by the sights and the sounds of freedom. There are many secluded plantations now where there are from 500 to 1000 slaves. They are never permitted to leave the plantation — never. And no one is permitted to visit them from another plantation — not one. Thus they are buried from the world and toil in darkness from the cradle to the grave. . . .

. *Part Two*

The Urbanization of America: 1860 to the Present

Part Two: Introduction

The "historic city" was characterized by compactness. It had to be small because it was a "walking city." People went to work, to shop, to visit, and to play on foot. Some of the wealthy lived outside the municipal limits and commuted to their businesses by carriage, but most people, rich and poor, walked. Hence they lived closer together than they ever would again. To be sure, the affluent appropriated the high land and the most desirable locations and the poor huddled in shacks along the waterfront or tucked into alleys and lanes. Yet no great spaces separated mansions from hovels. In addition, commercial and manufacturing facilities were mixed with housing. In small retail shops, owner or clerks lived above the store, and tanneries, meatpacking plants, and breweries were often within sight — and smell — of the most elegant residences. Railroads and freight yards cut through the heart of the city, the tracks often moving along major streets. The compactness of the "historic city" created a mixture of land uses which would be generally unknown in the twentieth century.

The Transportation Revolution

Into this restricted urban center was introduced one of the most revolutionary agents of modern society. Called an omnibus, it provided an alternative, though not always a comfortable one, to walking. Operating first in New York in 1829, the system was quickly adopted in other large cities. Soon the omnibus was placed on tracks to become the horsedrawn streetcar. Then the cable car was invented, followed by the electric trolley, the elevated and underground railways, and finally the automobile. (*See Section III, selection 1, and Section IV, selection 9.*)

Mass transportation broke the confinement of the "historic city" and created the conditions necessary for the "modern city" to develop. For now it was possible for residents to work downtown and yet live quite removed from it. A person walks at about three miles an hour;

the horsedrawn streetcar went about six miles an hour. When electricity replaced horses, the rate of speed of mass transportation was doubled. And, of course, the elevated and subway carried passengers at an even faster pace, to which the automobile added still another dimension.

The "historic city" has been confined to a few square miles. But with the ease of movement brought by mass transit, American towns quickly spread outside their old limits and covered the surrounding country. Land that lay within an hour's commuting time to the job was opened up to settlement. Municipal boundaries were everywhere greatly extended, and even suburban development grew up beyond the city line. In 1876, St. Louis more than tripled its territory; in 1889, Chicago annexed 126 square miles. By 1920, most places had reached their present geographic limits; by 1970, over half of the people in metropolitan areas lived in suburban villages and towns. (*See Section III, selection 2.*)

The second consequence of the introduction of mass transit was the sorting out of people within the city. As soon as the new forms of transportation made it possible to live at the edge of the city and work downtown, the wealthy began to move away from the central area. Soon the familiar social geography of the modern city appeared — with the rich at the outer edges and the poor huddled in the inner section. There were, of course, exceptions to this pattern, but it prevailed in most large cities by the end of the nineteenth century.

The third consequence stemming from the transportation revolution was an accelerating mobility in the entire urban structure. Everyone was in movement — not only those already in the city who continually changed residences, but also those coming in from the outside. In addition, industrial facilities were moved away from high-priced downtown land. Commercial location, of course, still favored the central district. Yet as cities grew and expanded, business too began to move out to serve outlying neighborhoods. Thus, change and instability became the central characteristics of the American metropolis. City planners later complained that the growth was disorderly; local officials found it difficult to control the process; church and civic leaders struggled to maintain community in old neighborhoods. But the decisions of thousands, indeed tens of thousands, of citizens created the shape and social texture of the modern city.

The Great People Boom

This urban expansion came about because the immense flow of immigration commenced during the period when mass transit made possible the accommodation of large numbers. A few statistics can convey the magnitude of the change. New York's population jumped from 515,500 in 1850 to 3,437,000 in 1900 and to over 7,800,000 in 1950. Figures for Chicago were at least as startling: 29,900; 1,690,000; and 3,621,000. Nor was the increase confined to bigger places. Omaha, not even founded in 1850, reached 102,555 at the beginning of the century, and moved over the 250,000 mark in 1950. The South joined the sweepstakes with Miami's residents numbering 1681 by 1900 and 249,276 fifty years later. And Los Angeles broke most records when its population soared from 102,479 in 1900 to 1,970,358 in 1950.

But the most visible effect of the first urban explosion was the transformation of the central part of the city. Although immigrants and their children accounted for most of the rapidly growing urban population, the American countryside also contributed. Rural areas had always sent sons and daughters to the city, but hard times on the farms after the Civil War accelerated the historic process. From the wheatlands of the plains, from the cotton Black Belt, from the cornfields of the Midwest, from the declining agricultural backlands of New England, the surplus population, mostly young, headed for the burgeoning cities and towns. The characteristic beginning of the popular novel found the hero or victim buying a one-way ticket to New York or Chicago. (*See Section III, selection 7C.*)

Most of these newcomers arrived with few or no resources. They settled in the central city and took what housing they could get. Some occupied small apartments carved out of mansions left behind by the wealthy; others jammed into makeshift conversions of large commercial facilities; still others sheltered in tenements erected especially to meet the rudimentary requirements of low-income families. With congestion came all the resultant problems — disease, delinquency, vice, crime, and hopelessness. In every city, these densely populated sections were marked as trouble spots by local authorities. (*See Section III, selection 3.*)

A Political System for the Inner City

This new urban structure produced its own political institutions, for the process of growth had created a divided city. The newcomers, strangers in a new environment, afflicted with congestion, irregular jobs, and persistent poverty, struggled to find some kind of social organization or identity. None of their old institutions seemed wholly relevant to their predicament, but they utilized what they could — the church, for example — and through voluntary associations met some of their needs. Still they remained economically weak and socially insecure.

Though their very numbers were in most cases a curse — the job market was flooded, the breadwinner had too many mouths to feed — in politics this liability could be turned into an asset. Their combined strength could accomplish what none could do alone. Soon the political "boss" and the "machine" rose to organize this potential. Feeding on the vulnerability of the neighborhoods and the hostility of those outside them, the boss system became a distinctive feature of American politics. It succeeded because it was rooted in the realities of block life — the clubhouse, the saloon, the cheap theaters, and the street. The boss helped recent arrivals to find housing and jobs, mediated with public authorities, helped families through bad times, and somehow gave newcomers a sense of belonging. To be sure, the cost was high in laws bent and broken, officials corrupted, funds embezzled, and the franchise sullied. Essentially, however, the boss system was simply the political expression of inner-city life. (*See Section III, selection 5.*)

Movement Up and Out

As slum-dwellers found an economic footing, some of them moved away from the central city to outlying residential areas. Irish, Germans, and Scandinavians, who had come in the first wave, began the flow, and people originally from Eastern Europe followed. By the 1920's many sons and daughters lived far from the scenes of their parents' struggle. But others remained in the inner city, investing the neighborhoods with a kind of warmth and stability and welcoming new arrivals from the old country. This process of concentration and dispersal characterized all the groups which had settled in the city with the important exceptions of blacks and Spanish-speaking immigrants.

Those who moved out found conditions very different on the tree-shaded streets of the residential areas ringing the city. They lived in detached houses on large lots or in two- or three-story apartment dwellings. Men took the trolley to work; women dominated the daytime society of schools, churches, shopping, and clubs. Political organization in the white-collar districts was as much an expression of these neighborhoods as the boss system was of the congested center. "Reform" associations sprang up to protect and advance the concerns of the middle-class constituents of outlying wards. Thus the characteristic instrument of reform was the "Committee of One Hundred" or the "Committee of Seventy-five," etc. Since neighborhoods were scattered and interests diverse, unlike the more compact and socially unified center, the outer regions found the broadly based committee more appropriate than the "boss."

The Impact of the Automobile

Both inner city and outer fringes were profoundly influenced by the introduction of the automobile. At first a monopoly of the rich, by the twenties it had become a middle-class necessity and after World War II essential to blue-collar workers as well. Though designed for individual use, the vehicle was easily converted into the bus, and soon this form of mass transportation began to push the trolley off the street. Communities outside municipal limits were now freed from dependence upon commuting rail lines. New suburbs sprang up all around the cities, and those already in existence expanded. Near Cleveland, the population of Shaker Heights increased tenfold between 1920 and 1930. Beverly Hills, near Los Angeles, jumped from 674 to 17,429. In the same decade, Westchester County, New York, added 176,511 to its previous total of 344,436. (*See Section IV, selection 8.*)

The Great Depression

For three decades into the twentieth century, metropolitan growth sustained the economic development of the nation as a whole. Prosperity, broken by occasional reversals, characterized the nation between 1900 and the Great Depression of the 1930's. But it was essentially an urban prosperity; the countryside did not share in the "good times." Most of the economic activity flowed from the cities where housing construction, the building of new schools, streets, and sewers, industrial expansion, and population growth provided the primary impetus to national prosperity.

It all came to an end in 1929 with the stock market crash. Since prosperity had been largely urban based, the Depression had a severe impact on the cities. As unemployment rates rose to over 25 per cent, the relief resources of local governments soon were exhausted and authorities called on Washington for help. The Hoover administration moved reluctantly and cautiously. By 1935 conditions had worsened so much that President Roosevelt initiated massive assistance plans. New Deal programs dealt largely with human salvage: relief payments; creation of jobs; measures to promote individual and family security. The Public Works Administration began construction of public buildings and facilities. Yet despite the unprecedented involvement of the federal government in their affairs, the cities remained stagnant through most of the 1930's. (*See Section IV, selection 9.*)

Indeed, the revival of urban economies did not come until World War II intervened. The cities were the major beneficiaries of military spending, which began even before Pearl Harbor. Jobs became plentiful, relief rolls dropped quickly, and industrial construction boomed. To be sure, new troubles accompanied the economic upswing. The influx of black workers heightened racial tensions that sporadically spilled over into violence; the conversion of automobile factories to military production put a great strain on urban mass-transit systems; and scarcity of materials prevented even the adequate maintenance of public facilities.

The Metropolitan Age

The postwar period saw the urban age become the metropolitan age. The census of 1920 had indicated that for the first time more Americans lived in "urban places" than in "rural places." This fact symbolized statistically the supremacy of the city over the countryside. In 1970 the census showed that for the first time more people lived in the suburbs than within city limits. The nation had entered the era of the metropolis. Beginning almost with the peace treaty following World War II, American urbanites headed for the suburbs in larger numbers than they ever had before. Housing shortages in the cities, federal subsidies for residential building through veterans' programs, and general prosperity combined to impel a whole generation to seek homes in suburbia. (*See Section V, selections 1 and 2.*)

For over two decades, this movement was the most powerful influence on metropolitan growth. Developers flocked to vacant or sparsely used land around every city; great numbers of houses were quickly built, often on small plots, with little concern for design or individuality. Shopping centers, schools, and churches rose — the process of "instant community" produced new towns all around old municipal boundaries. As people and commercial activity moved out, so did manufacturing. In the 1950's and the 1960's most cities were losing factories and jobs to the suburbs, especially to those developed along the new expressways.

Evaluation of Postwar Achievements

The surge to the suburbs drained the city of some of its vitality by taking away most of its high- and middle-income residents along with new commercial and industrial activity. Even without this flight, municipal governments would have seemed to be heading for trouble. Their basic facilities, built at the end of the century, needed renewal or replacement; very little new housing had been constructed since 1929; World War II had brought another wave of in-migration of low-salaried workers; downtown commercial activity was threatened by the new suburban shopping centers. Experts were predicting a gloomy future for American cities.

But the experts were wrong. The next years witnessed an extraordinary burst of municipal movement. With the help of federal money, cities cleared out some of their worst slums; neighborhoods that seemed to be headed for the scrap heap were renewed; the resurgence of life in central business districts was embodied in new downtown skylines; modern civic centers took the place of antiquated facilities. A group of new mayors provided a kind of energetic leadership missing since the early years of the century. Both private and public investment in the cities suggested that no matter what the "experts" might predict there were still great wells of strength in American urban life. (*See Section V, selection 8.*)

Critics, however, were not wholly disarmed by the surge of activity. Many complained that renewal programs, however successful they might appear in regenerating a neighborhood, resulted in wide-scale displacement of the poor, and especially of the black poor. Others asserted that inducements, such as tax rebates, offered to private builders constituted an improper subsidy for businessmen of considerable means. Still others contended that new programs, whether renewal or expressway construction, destroyed the fabric of communities. And opponents of public housing noted that almost all new building reinforced social segregation instead of reducing it. To be sure, some of this criticism was unwarranted and self-serving, yet by 1970 most observers agreed that no matter how substantial the achievements of the postwar decades, city governments would not do it the same way again. The surgery had been successful but the pain and the cost were needlessly high. (*See Section V, selection 4.*)

Actually, the objective problems of American cities were not so staggering as many believed. In the 1950's and 1960's, for example, large amounts of substandard housing were removed; during the War on Poverty, despite its shortcomings a million people a year moved above the poverty line; urban schools spent more money, hired better-trained teachers, used more elaborate techniques, and carried more pupils through more years than ever before; and the level of municipal service, either in terms of personnel or performance, was generally better than it had been fifty years before. (*See Section V, selection 10.*)

The Sources of the Urban Crisis

Yet the crisis in American cities is real and profound. Indeed, it is not too much to say that it constitutes the most serious threat to the nation's existence since the argument over slavery led to civil war over a hundred years ago. The symptoms are everywhere evident. In the late sixties, countless cities witnessed bloody and costly riots; black ghettos which did not explode seethed and festered; city governments found resources inadequate even if they had solutions. The source of the difficulty lies in two new divisive forces within the metropolis which were not present on a large scale before. The first is the division between city and suburb, and the second is the division between black and white.

The split between city and suburb is, of course, as old as the cities themselves, but extraordinary postwar suburban growth altered the balance between the old municipality and the newer communities. The process fragmented the metropolis. Though problems spread across political jurisdictions, authority to deal with them was divided among dozens of small local governments. A good pollution ordinance, for example, was useless so long as the areas surrounding the city originating it did not cooperate. Local zoning regulations blocked low-income families and blacks from moving out of the central city. As the "urban crisis" deepened, it was clear that political divisions made a coordinated assault on its causes impossible.

The problem of race was even more threatening. Blacks had always lived in American cities, but the extraordinary exodus from farms into both northern and southern cities created a whole new set of conditions. At first it was assumed that Negro newcomers would experience the same reception that had greeted immigrants from abroad. They would be forced to gather in the least desirable section, occupy the worst housing, perform menial jobs, go to inadequate schools, and live in great insecurity. But after a time they would become aware of their numbers, find a political identity, accumulate resources, and move out of the slums. This is the way it happened for previous immigrant groups, but it is not the way it happened for the blacks. They concentrated in the center, but as time went on they did not disperse throughout the metropolis. Rather Negro neighborhoods simply spread out block by block. The word "ghetto" had been used to describe a section of a city where a group of immigrants, most often Jews, was confined; but the new black ghetto was different from the earlier ones.

In the old immigrant ghetto, life was made tolerable by the knowledge that people escaped. Every family saw some of its members or neighbors or friends move into better areas of town. Yet the blacks, especially the young ones, were aware that no matter what they did, chances of clearing the barrier were very slight. Many said, "What's the use of trying?" In the 1960's, programs directed toward the ghetto often foundered because of lack of motivation. And, more ominously, the hopeless and the frustrated from time to time struck back in violence and rioting. (*See Section V, selection 5.*)

Response to the Crisis

The urban scene was not without some hopeful signs, however. The split between city and suburb, although still serious, was somewhat reduced by attempts to come to grips with metropolitan problems. In Nashville, Tennessee, for example, five counties joined to make a single governmental unit. In other places, cooperative efforts to cope with pollution, water supply, and transportation have brought cities and suburbs together to seek solutions for their common dilemmas. Planners increasingly take the whole metropolitan area as the subject of their concern. Suburban residents, faced with soaring taxes, mounting crime rates, and increasingly complex problems were beginning to discover that they could not live alone and that only efforts coordinated with those of other suburbs and nearby cities could protect the quality of life that historically had made their communities attractive. (*See Section V, selection 7.*)

The race question, however, provided less reason for optimism. To be sure, more and more blacks moved out of poverty every year, and the ranks of the Negro middle class continued to grow. The election of black mayors in Cleveland and Gary, Indiana,[1] indicated that Negroes were beginning to use their concentrated urban population as leverage for political power, as other inner-city groups had done. Yet black unemployment remained twice as high as white; city schools still had not provided an appropriate education for rapidly rising numbers of black students; and promotions within large corporations remained more difficult for Negroes than for whites. And, most importantly, the walls of the ghetto still stood. Though civil-rights gains in the 1960's were greater than in any previous decade, the metropolis faced the 1970's with understandable uncertainty and anxiety.

[1] In 1967, Carl B. Stokes became mayor of Cleveland and Richard G. Hatcher mayor of Gary.

III. The New City

With the introduction of mass transportation, the historic city began to undergo changes which would transform it into the modern city. While the already established commuter railroad remained a factor in the suburbanizing process, it was new systems such as the cable car and the electric train which stimulated the growth of communities closer to downtown and along the new routes of street traffic. Most of the expansion between 1860 and 1900 took place within enlarged city limits.

As the middle class was moving out from the center, immigrants from foreign lands and rural America were flooding in. Their great numbers together with their unfamiliarity with urban life intensified all the historic problems of the city — congestion, disease, poverty, crime. In response to the plight of the newcomers, a new kind of political structure emerged. This was the era of the ward boss, the machine, the manipulation of voting blocs, often along ethnic lines, and, undeniably, of municipal corruption on a grand scale.

The new urban population also provided a source of cheap labor which, together with the revolution in transportation, advances in technology, and the availability of raw materials, spurred the growth of great industries in such cities as Pittsburgh, Detroit, and Cleveland. Into the factories poured the men, women, and children of the new city.

As industrialization increased and the cities boomed, they came to be the magnet and market for all kinds of talent and the target of critics and reformers. Newspapers and other periodicals flourished; city art museums and orchestras were established; entertainment became a mass commodity. But undesirable forms of recreation drained the meager income of many families. The cities themselves were condemned by moralists as corrupters of youth and destroyers of religion and taste, while others defended them as offering unparalleled opportunity for cultural advance and individual growth. ∎

Population Growth of "New Cities," 1860–1900

	1860	1880	1900
Chicago	112,172	503,185	1,698,575
Cleveland	43,417	160,146	381,768
Detroit	45,619	116,340	285,704
Pittsburgh	49,221	156,589	321,616
San Francisco	56,802	233,959	342,782

Chicago	7%
Cleveland	11%
Detroit	16%
Pittsburgh	15%
San Francisco	17%

1860 population as percentage of 1900 figure

By 1900 cities founded after the Revolution were boasting large populations and booming economies.

1. Mechanized Mobility

The coming of mass transit was generally welcomed as a beneficial development, but there were complaints that its equipment obstructed streets and roads, and that it would ruin the peace of outlying areas. For good or ill, mass transportation spurred and shaped the development of the new American city. "Downtown" more and more became the place for business and industry, and those who had the option chose to reside on the outer edges and ultimately in separate communities. Thus was born the conflict in life styles, attitudes, and needs between people remaining in the inner city and those who "fled" to the suburbs, a conflict which was to intensify in the twentieth century.

The group of selections which follows deals with the transition from horse-powered transportation to the elevated street railway. ■

A. THE HORSE RAILROAD[1]

♣ *Sidney George Fisher*

The highly detailed personal diary of Sidney George Fisher contains much information of interest to urban historians. Fisher's account of the impact of horse-powered rail transportation on the city of Philadelphia suggests the development and problems that would be associated with the introduction of mass transit. ■

February, 1859

These passenger cars, as they are called, but which are street railroads with horse power, and which have suddenly sprung into extensive use, are a great convenience. Though little more than a year old, they have already almost displaced the heavy, jolting, slow, and uncomfortable omnibus and are destined soon to banish it and hacks almost entirely. They are roomy, their motion smooth and easy, they are clean, well cushioned, and handsome, low to the ground so that it is convenient to get in or out, and are driven at a rapid pace. They offer great facilities in traversing the city, now grown so large that the distances are very considerable from place to place. They traverse the city in its length and breadth and save time and expense. They are all crowded, too much so, indeed, often for comfort. Already are built and in use lines on 2nd and 3rd, 5th and 6th, 9th and 10th, Race and Vine, Market, Spruce, and Pine Streets. Tracks are now laying for one in Arch Street and many more are projected.

They will also soon stretch out to the neighboring villages, thus merging them in the town. The beneficial effect of this will be to enable everyone to have a suburban villa or country home, to spread the city over a vast space, with all the advantages of compactness and the advantages, moreover, of pure air, gardens, and rural pleasures. Before long, town life, life in close streets and alleys, will be confined

[1] Slightly adapted from *A Philadelphia Perspective: The Diary of Sidney George Fisher Covering the Years 1834–1871*, ed. by Nicholas B. Wainwright (Philadelphia: Copyright 1967 by the Historical Society of Pennsylvania), pp. 316, 327–328, 521–522. Reprinted by permission.

to a few occupations, and cities will be mere collections of shops, warehouses, factories, and places of business. There is only one objection to them: they obstruct the streets for carriages; the rails make driving very inconvenient and unpleasant. But the few keep carriages, the many ride in the cars, and they are now so comfortable that the most fastidious may endure them.

Six Months Later

. . . He [George Blight] took me through one or two streets between his place and Germantown, which I had not seen for many years and which are now lined with cottages and villas, surrounded by neat grounds, trees, shrubbery, and flowers, many of them costly and handsome, all comfortable and pretty. They are the result of railroads which enable anyone to enjoy the pleasures of country life and at the same time attend to business in town. . . . The advantages are so obvious that this villa and cottage life has become quite a passion and is producing a complete revolution in our habits. It is dispersing the people of the city over the surrounding country, introducing thus among them ventilation, cleanliness, space, healthful pursuits, and the influences of natural beauty, the want of which are the sources of so much evil, moral and physical, in large towns.

The passenger cars, as they are absurdly called, or horse railroads have given a great impulse to this movement. They are scarcely more than two years old, yet they have become a vast system already. They occupy nearly all the principal streets and traverse the city in every direction and are rapidly extending into the country. They are crowded with passengers and pay large dividends. They operate in two ways to disperse the population over the country, by making the streets inconvenient for all other vehicles and by offering cheap means of reaching the country. It is very unpleasant to drive the streets now because of the rails, so that private carriages have become useless while the cars, comfortable and easy, offer to those who live in the country a pleasant way of going to town at all hours and in any weather at trifling expense. . . . One consequence of this is the immense improvement of the country and rise in the value of property. In Germantown, they have now gas and water from water works in every house. Shops and mechanics follow the rich population of the villas, and soon every luxury of a city can be had in the neighborhood. . . . The same process is going on in every direction around the city.

Seven Years Later

Went to town in the morning. As I had a pretty long list of errands, took the carriage and, notwithstanding the badly paved streets and the nuisance of the rails by which they are encumbered, found it much more comfortable than getting in and out of cars and walking. . . . These horse railroads are an immense convenience, but are so managed as to be at the same time a serious evil and a proof of the grossly corrupt character of our city government, which has abdicated its power over the highways in favor of corporations whose interest it is to make them as bad as possible for a twofold reason — to save expense and to force everyone to use their cars. These corporations care only to make money. They are responsible to no one, owe no duty to the public, and are beyond its control. They contract indeed to keep the streets in order, but for obvious reasons this contract cannot be enforced in the courts, for there must be innumerable suits for innumerable breaches of it, and what is everybody's business is nobody's. . . . So the companies do as they please and the people submit to high fares, crowded cars, and almost impassable and often dangerous streets and roads. Indeed the majority care nothing about the matter. They are accommodated and do not regard the annoyance of the minority who use carriages or who object to a crowded car.

B. THE CABLE CAR[2]

✦ John Anderson Miller

In San Francisco in 1837, Andrew Hallidie introduced the cable or "grip" car, the first technological innovation in mass transit. The body was much the same as that of the horse car, and it too rode on rails, but the horses were replaced by a continuously running cable laid under the streets. To go forward the cable was gripped; to stop, it was released and brakes were applied. The opening of the Chicago City Railway in 1882 gave this method its biggest boost, and soon cable cars became a familiar part of the urban scene. ■

· [2] From the book *Fares, Please! From Horse Cars to Streamliners* by John Anderson Miller, pp. 36–39, 49–50. Copyright © 1941 by John Anderson Miller. Published by D. Appleton Century Co., 70 Fifth Avenue, New York.

Hallidie knew that for some time the coal-cars had been hauled by cable on the English colliery railways, and he thought "Why not do this job the same way?" His plan was to have a stationary steam engine operate an endless wire rope on rollers in a conduit below the pavement. A gripping clamp on the car, extending downward through a slot in the pavement, would take hold or let go of the moving cable at the will of a "gripman." Brakes, similar to those on horse cars, would be provided on the vehicle to bring it to a stop after the grip on the cable had been released.

This was a brand new idea in city transportation, but Hallidie got permission to try it, and Clay Street hill was selected for the experiment. At one place the hill rose 300 feet in half a mile, a grade of more than 12 per cent....

The chill gray dawn of August 1, 1873, saw a small group of people gathered on the brow of Clay Street hill to witness the daring demonstration of Andrew Hallidie's invention. One good look down the steep slope into the cold waters of the bay convinced the appointed "gripman" that he had not been cut out for the role of hero — or martyr. He resigned then and there. Hallidie promptly rose to the occasion. Taking the grip himself, he ran the car down the hill and brought it up again....

San Francisco's "big four" lived on the top of fashionable Nob Hill in those days: the quiet dreamer, Leland Stanford; the energetic builder, Charles Crocker; the long-headed lawyer, Mark Hopkins; and the shrewd financier, Collis P. Huntington. After having built the Central Pacific Railroad, and obtained a virtual monopoly on railroading in California, they became interested in the business of providing local transportation.

On June 14, 1876, a franchise was granted to the "big four" for a cable line on California Street. Henry Root, the engineer, estimated the cost of building the road at $350,000. On hearing this estimate Mark Hopkins said emphatically that it was too much money ever to get back in five-cent fares. Governor Stanford, however, paid no attention to Hopkins' pessimism and went right ahead with the construction of the line. Before long the cars were scurrying up and down between the top of Nob Hill and the Embarcadero. Property values doubled overnight — the beginning of a real-estate boom that lasted for years....

San Francisco was the first city in the world to have a cable railway, but it was Chicago that gave this form of transportation its greatest impetus. The far-flung system of the Chicago City Railway, which commenced operation in 1882, was the sensation of the day. Horse-car managers from all over the country came to inspect it and went home to tell what they had seen. . . .

The cable cars proved their prowess in winter. They were excellent snow fighters. On more than one occasion when all the steam railroads entering the city of Chicago were tied up for hours by a heavy snowfall, the cable cars were running as usual and their tracks afforded the only path of travel for pedestrians and teams. It is said, in fact, that the City Railway never lost a single trip from snow, frost, or ice upon the track.

. . . By 1890 there were about 500 miles of cable-railway track in the United States and some 5000 cars. Altogether these lines carried about 400 million passengers a year. . . . At no time, however, were there cable systems in more than 15 or 16 cities in the United States.

C. THE ELECTRIC TRAIN[3]

✣ John Anderson Miller

The following selection describes the origins of the Capital City Railway of Montgomery, Alabama, first city-wide system of electric transportation. ■

Pigs and cows held the greatest interest for nearly everyone attending the Toronto Agricultural Fair in the summer of 1885. They were a farming people. But James A. Gaboury's interest was elsewhere. His eye spied a car running back and forth on a short piece of railway track without any visible means of propulsion other than a small wire overhead; after spotting this car he had no interest in anything else.

"What have you got here?" he asked the young man who was collecting five cents a ride for trips on this railway.

"It's an electric car," the young man answered, "but I don't know anything about it except how to run it. The inventor is uptown at the hotel."

Now this Mr. Gaboury was an engineer and promoter who had been active in building street railways in a number of cities in the

[3] *Ibid.,* pp. 54–57.

southern part of the United States. These lines were operated by mule-power, as was customary in the South in those days, but Gaboury realized that animal traction had many limitations as a means of providing transportation service. He had heard about various experiments with electricity, but none of them seemed to amount to much.

He was excited by the thought that the inventor of what appeared to be a practical means of electric propulsion was in town, and went straight up to the hotel to look for him. There he found Charles J. Van Depoele, a Belgian sculptor who had come over to the United States some years before and had since been experimenting with the use of electricity in various ways. Gaboury started to question him about the railway at the fair grounds.

"Can you haul people as cheaply with electricity as I can haul them with mules?" he asked.

"Much cheaper," Van Depoele replied.

"Then why haven't you put your electric cars in American cities, if they are so practical?"

"I have hawked the idea over the whole Middle West," said Van Depoele. "I have given demonstrations in several cities, but I can't get the financial backers of the streetcar systems interested in the idea. They have all turned me down, and I've been forced to give demonstrations at exhibitions and fairs to earn enough money to get along."

"I'm the man you have been looking for, then," exclaimed Gaboury. "I own the controlling interest in the streetcar system in Montgomery, Alabama, and I'll finance a trial of your idea there."

Van Depoele and Gaboury talked until long after midnight. Before the discussion ended it had been decided that Van Depoele should follow Gaboury to Montgomery as quickly as possible and work out a plan for electrifying the Capital City Street Railway.

When word of this scheme reached the minority stockholders of the railway, some of them raised a howl about the "fool way" Gaboury was proposing to spend the company's money. He paid no attention to them, however, and went right ahead with the project. On November 2, 1885, the company asked the City Council for permission to operate its cars by electricity. Some delay followed, but the permission was granted early in January, 1886.

Construction work proceeded rapidly. But the end of March the system was practically complete, so Gaboury and Van Depoele made a trial trip in secret one night between 12 and 1 A.M. Everything went well. The car moved smoothly and quickly over the moonlit track. Trial trips continued for the next several weeks, always at night when most people were asleep, lest some slight mishap should undermine public confidence in the new venture.

Finally the company was ready to start regular service. On April 15, 1886, the Montgomery *Advertiser* announced:

> The Capital City Railway Company had the two new cars out and running by the electric motor system last night. One of the cars had never run before, but both went like a charm and made the round trip without a hitch or bobble.
>
> The electric street railway in Montgomery is a success. Both the cars on the Court Street line will be operated by the motor system today, beginning at ten o'clock this morning. Heretofore, no attempt has been made to run the cars on the "Lightning Route" in the daytime, as the running was only to test the system. Some unexpected delay has been met in getting the new machinery in working order. . . .

The cars used for electric operation were essentially the same as those used previously for animal traction. Each had a single motor mounted on the front platform. Power was transmitted to the wheels by a steel chain. At first the electrical energy for the motor was obtained through a small two-wheel carriage, called a "monkey," running on an electrified overhead wire and connected to the car by a flexible cable. The wheels of the overhead carriage were arranged somewhat like a pair of pulleys in tandem. Endless trouble resulted from this arrangement, especially at turnouts where cars passed each other, as no satisfactory means could be devised to permit the "monkeys" to pass. Instead, the flexible cables had to be detached from the cars and the "monkeys" exchanged. In doing this the motormen often received severe shocks. Finally an arrangement was worked out whereby a pole extending upward from the roof of the car pressed a rolling contact against the underside of the wire.

So successful was the Court Street line that electrification was gradually extended until the system had eighteen cars running on fifteen miles of track. Montgomery thus became the first place in the world to have a city-wide system of electric transportation, since none of the lines placed in operation in other cities up to that time had attempted to give a complete service.

Following the electrification, Montgomery experienced a great boom in general business. Real estate increased in value so rapidly "as to astonish the old natives who predicted the failure of the attempt to run the mule cars by lightning."

D. THE ELEVATED RAILWAY[4]

The greatest advantage of the elevated lay in the fact that it went over the street and the traffic. In 1895 Chicago opened the Metropolitan West Side Elevated. Eighteen miles long, it was the first rapid-transit electric railway in the United States. For more than thirty years, elevated railways, popularly known as "els," were the major means of mass transportation in American cities. The reporter for the Chicago Tribune *who covered the maiden voyage of the Metropolitan was clearly aware of the effects this installation would have on his city's character and growth.* ■

The first train to carry other persons than officials made its first trip yesterday over the Metropolitan Elevated road. The northwest branch of the road is complete to Wicker Park, and to this pretty suburb the special train was run. Within a few weeks the cars may go their full course in the same general direction to Logan Square and Humboldt Park. The first part of yesterday's passage was straight west to Forty-eighth Street on the main line. A return trip was made to the Paulina Street junction, and then the motorman gave the handle a twist and the four cars were whirled away northwest at the rate of thirty-five miles an hour. Next week . . . the Metropolitan road will open its lines for traffic for the distance and in the direction taken by the trial train yesterday.

A number of the road's officials met twenty-five newspaper men on the platform of the Canal Street station at two o'clock. The members of the party strung themselves through four new cars of the Pullman[5] product. Thirty people to four cars gave every man a window seat with no one to ride backward. Two conductors in uniforms as new as the cars shouted "All aboard!" For the first time in the history of the line, a motorman turned on the power and the train started west smoothly, rapidly, and with no accompaniment of smoke, steam, or smell.

The street demonstrations which marked the moving of the first

---

[4] *Chicago Tribune*, April 18, 1895, p. 12.
[5] **Pullman**: George M. Pullman was the originator and manufacturer of railroad passenger vehicles, such as parlor cars and sleeping cars.

train over the Alley "L" road three years ago were present. The small boys cheered at every cross street, and the fences between held their share of the youngsters. The teamsters stopped their horses and looked up, and from every rear balcony of the well-populated flats a dustcloth or two were waved.

As far as Paulina Street the road has four tracks. To that point express trains will be run. They will have each way a clear track. Beyond Paulina Street on all the three branches of the road . . . running to Douglas Street there are double tracks. Just before reaching this general turning-off point there is an apparently intricate but in reality simple interlocking switch system, which is managed from an attractive little house perched between tracks.

Yesterday's train shot over the switch system, rounded the "control cottage," and swept by the big power station with never a halt in the gait. It was so fast and free from jolt that those on board barely had time to tire of a vista of back windows and shed roofs before the country opened and the wind came whistling across a big patch of prairie. Over to the right lay Garfield Park, while stretching its length along the skyline was the rival road, the Lake Street "L."

The effect of running a rapid transit proposition into new territory is strikingly shown in the country pierced by the Metropolitan. Great stretches of prairie are now city lots, and buildings are going up at a rate that rivals the running of the trains.

2. Outward Bound

The advent of mass transit changed not only the physical shape of the city but also its social configuration. With geographical expansion the population began a kind of "sorting out" process. Those whose type of employment and financial situation permitted often chose to live outside the city.

The two excerpts which follow deal with different types of residential communities lying in the "frontier between city and country." The first, "Charlesbridge" (actually Cambridge, Massachusetts), described by the novelist William Dean Howells in his Suburban Sketches *(1871), was an older, settled town, which already possessed some ethnic diversity and a little indus-*

try. *The effects of mass transit on "Charlesbridge" were felt mainly in the rise of the commuter population. The second community, Morgan Park, was a brand-new "dormitory suburb." Its promotional literature, excerpted below, stressed advantages which would appeal to middle-class home buyers, such as "desirable families," "good schools," and the absence of saloons.* ■

A. CHARLESBRIDGE[1]

♣ William Dean Howells

It was on a morning of the lovely New England May that we left the horse car, and, spreading our umbrellas, walked down the street to our new home in Charlesbridge....

... It was [a] very quiet [place]; we called one another to the window if a large dog went by our door; and whole days passed without the movement of any wheels but the butcher's upon our street, which flourished in ragweed and buttercups and daisies. . . . The neighborhood was in all things a frontier between city and country. The horse cars, the type of such civilization — full of imposture, discomfort, and sublime possibility — as we yet possess, went by the head of our street, and might, perhaps, be available to one skilled in calculating the movements of comets; while two minutes' walk would take us into a wood so wild and thick that no roof was visible through the trees. We learned, like innocent pastoral people of the golden age, to know the several voices of the cows pastured in the vacant lots, and like engine-drivers of the iron age, to distinguish the different whistles of the locomotives passing on the neighborhood railroad. The trains shook the house as they thundered along, and at night were a kind of company, while by day we had the society of innumerable birds. . . . All round us carpenters were at work building new houses.

Our street was not drained nor graded; no municipal car ever came to carry away our ashes; there was not [water] within half a mile to save us from fire, nor more than the one thousandth part of a policeman to protect us from theft. Yet, as I paid a heavy tax, I

[1] William Dean Howells, *Suburban Sketches* (New York: Hurd and Houghton, 1871), pp. 11, 13–14, 60–61, 47, 22.

somehow felt that we enjoyed the benefits of city government, and never looked upon Charlesbridge as in any way undesirable for residence. . . .

. . . I sometimes go on a pedestrian tour, which is of no great extent in itself, and which I moreover modify by keeping always within sound of the horse-car bells, or easy reach of some steamcar station.

As I sally forth upon Benicia Street, the whole suburb of Charlesbridge stretches about me. . . . A little farther on I come to the boarding house built at the railroad side for the French Canadians, who have by this time succeeded the Hebrews in the toil of the brickyards. . . . I take my way up through the brickyards towards the Irish settlement on the north, passing under the long sheds that shelter the kilns. . . . As I leave Dublin [the Irish settlement], the houses grow larger and handsomer; and as I draw near the Avenue, the mansardroofs look down upon me with their dormer windows, and welcome me back to the American community.

At that hour [11:00 A.M.] the organ grinder and I are the only persons of our sex in the whole suburban population; all other husbands and fathers having eaten their breakfasts at seven o'clock and stood up in the early horse cars to Boston, whence they will return, with aching backs and quivering calves, half-pendant by leathern straps from the roofs of the same luxurious conveyances, in the evening.

Many of the vacant lots abutting upon Benicia and the intersecting streets flourished up during the four years we knew it into fresh-painted wooden houses, and the time came to be when one might have looked in vain for the abandoned hoopskirts which used to decorate the desirable building sites. The lessening pasturage also reduced the herds which formerly fed in the vicinity, and at last we caught the tinkle of the cowbells only as the cattle were driven past to remoter meadows. And one autumn afternoon two laborers, hired by the city, came and threw up an earthwork on the opposite side of the street, which they said was a sidewalk and would add to the value of property in the neighborhood.

B. MORGAN PARK[2]

Morgan Park is a village of about 2800 inhabitants, incorporated under the laws of the state. It is by all odds the choicest of Chicago's suburbs. It is not an "experiment" but a thoroughly established, progressive village, and while it is chiefly a residence place, we have markets, shops, stores, etc., equal to those of any other village.

It counts among its residents some of the best businessmen of Chicago, and is blessed with having, generally, the right kind of citizens.

It is not only a temperance village, but saloons are *prohibited by law*. Thus, the one curse with which most localities have to contend is here unknown, and our children grow up surrounded only by good influences, . . . our families can go upon the street or walk upon our beautiful groves without the fear of insult or dread of meeting intoxicated persons.

Each season witnesses the erection of new homes and the addition of desirable families to our population. There are many reasons why Morgan Park is much superior to other localities for the purpose of a home. It is near enough to Chicago and sufficiently far removed to afford all the blessings of a suburban home with all the conveniences and advantages of the city, far from all its objectionable features. As there are no bridges to cross to reach Morgan Park, it makes the most accessible suburb around Chicago. Morgan Park is thirteen miles southwest of the Court House and adjoins the city on the north and on the east.

The west, or "Ridge," portion of the beautiful suburb being [at] an elevation of nearly 100 feet above Lake Michigan places us above our neighbors on every side, giving us land easily drained. From the government observatory of the Ridge the view in all directions is grand. . . . and upon a clear day the business portion can be clearly seen with a glass. Turning to the west, beyond our village limits, we behold the most beautiful cemetery grounds — Mount Greenwood, Olivet, and Hope — to be found anywhere in the whole country, while still beyond, the trees of the natural forests and the skies seem to meet. One cannot look upon this scene without wonder and astonishment

[2] *Morgan Park Views*, compiled by C. P. and F. P. Silva, Morgan Park Real Estate, 1899.

(*Continued on page 120*)

There was nothing new in moving people by horse and wagon, but the revolution in mass transportation began early in the 19th century when tracks were laid for the horse cars (above in Fort Wayne, Ind.). Next a moving cable driven by a steam engine was used for the cable-car system (below in Pittsburgh).

Electricity added a new dimension of power and speed. It was used to propel cars over the street on elevated railways (above in Chicago) or in ground-level "trolleys" (below in Long Island City, N.Y.). Many a city-dweller rode a succession of lines to reach a shore or lake vacation spot.

that the great mass of the people of Chicago have so long remained in ignorance of the unequalled inducements this village holds out to those seeking homes such as they can never possess in the city. . . .

. . . Morgan Park speaks for itself . . . . The beauties of nature . . . together with the many examples of up-to-date architecture, as well public as private, afford . . . evidence that naught is set down in exaggeration. 'Twere likewise most difficult to overstate the educational, social, hygenic, and moral attractiveness of this fair suburban community. . . . "Semimountainous" as compared with the surrounding prairies, is a term not infrequently used in Chicago newspapers in referring to the oak-crested, cerulean-skied heights of the Blue Island plateau, and the loveliest peak in the chain is Morgan Park.

Nowhere in all the country can desirable lands be purchased as cheaply as here, but this cannot in the nature of things remain so very long. Opportunities come and go. Hope and fear, rejoicing and vain regrets are as common now as ever before, but there need be no fear that those who locate in Morgan Park will ever regret their choice. Regrets will be left to those who only recognize their opportunities after they have passed on beyond all hope of recall.

3. Standing Room Only[1]

✤ Jacob Riis

As the prospering middle class moved to the suburbs, the inner cities were left to the "other half." In the 1870's and 1880's a rural depression caused many farm people to seek work in the cities just when a flood of immigrants was pouring in from overseas. The urban poor, especially in the older places of the East, were often forced to live under frightful conditions. Builders hastily threw up the multiple-unit dwellings known as tenements. In New York these sometimes took the form of the infamous "dumbbell," a narrow, eight-story building into which 32 families could be crammed.

Jacob Riis, himself an immigrant from Denmark, was a police

[1] Jacob Riis, *How the Other Half Lives* (New York: Charles Scribner's Sons, 1890), pp. 55–57, 61–62, 64–68.

reporter for the New York Tribune *and later for the* Evening
Sun. *His compassionate studies of the slums brought him fame
and helped to spark reform efforts. Although racial and ethnic
stereotyping mar Riis's work, he is the chronicler par excellence
of Manhattan's Lower East Side in 1890. Here he describes the
most squalid, disease-ridden of New York's slums.* ■

"The Bend"

Where Mulberry Street crooks like an elbow within hail of the old
depravity of the Five Points[2] is "the Bend," foul core of New York's
slums. . . . There is but one "Bend" in the world, and it is enough. The
city authorities, moved by the angry protests of ten years of sanitary
reform, have decided that it is too much and must come down. Another Paradise Park will take its place and let in sunlight and air to
work such transformation as at the Five Points, around the corner
of the next block. Never was change more urgently needed. Around
"the Bend" cluster the bulk of the tenements that are stamped as
altogether bad, even by the optimists of the Health Department.
Incessant raids cannot keep down the crowds that make them their
home. In the scores of back alleys, of stable lanes and hidden byways,
of which the rent collector alone can keep track, they share such
shelter as the ramshackle structures afford with every kind of abomi-
nation rifled from the dumps and ashbarrels of the city . . . .

. . . The whole district is a maze of narrow, often unsuspected
passageways — necessarily, for there is scarce a lot that has not two,
three, or four tenements upon it, swarming with unwholesome
crowds. What a birds-eye view of "the Bend" would be like is a
matter of bewildering conjecture. Its everyday appearance, as seen
from the corner of Bayard Street on a sunny day, is one of the sights
of New York.

Bayard Street is the high road to Jewtown across the Bowery,
picketed from end to end with the outposts of Israel. Hebrew faces,
Hebrew signs . . . attend the curious wanderer to the very corner of
Mulberry Street. But the moment he turns the corner the scene
changes abruptly. Before him lies spread out what might better be
the marketplace in some town in southern Italy than a street in New

---

[2] **the Five Points:** a section notorious for crime and squalor, condemned by
many nineteenth century reformers.

York — all but the houses; they are still the same old tenements of the unromantic type. . . . The interest centers not in them, but in the crowd they shelter . . . . When the sun shines, the entire population seeks the street, carrying on its household work, its bargaining, its love-making on street or sidewalk, or idling there when it has nothing better to do. . . .

In this block between Bayard, Park, Mulberry, and Baxter Streets, "the Bend" proper, the late Tenement House Commission counted 155 deaths of children [those under five] in a specimen year (1882). Their percentage of the total mortality in the block was 68.28 while for the whole city the proportion was only 46.20. The infant mortality in any city or place compared with the whole number of deaths is justly considered a good barometer of its general sanitary condition. Here in this tenement, No. 59½, next to Bandits' Roost, fourteen persons died that year, and eleven of them were children; in No. 61 eleven, and eight of them not five years old. . . .

Bottle Alley is around the corner in Baxter Street, but it is a fair specimen of its kind, wherever found. Look into any of these houses, everywhere the same piles of malodorous bones and musty paper, all of which the sanitary police flatter themselves they have banished to the dumps and the warehouses. Here is a "flat"[3] of "parlor" and two pitch-dark coops called bedrooms. Truly the bed is all there is room for. The family teakettle is on the stove, doing duty for the time being as a washboiler. . . . One, two, three beds are there, if the old boxes and heaps of foul straw can be called by that name; a broken stove with a crazy pipe from which the smoke leaks at every joint, a table of rough boards propped upon boxes, piles of rubbish in the corner. The closeness and smell are appalling. How many people sleep here? The woman with the red bandanna shakes her head sullenly, but the bare-legged girl with the bright face counts on her fingers — five, six! . . .

Half a dozen blocks up Mulberry Street there is a ragpickers' settlement, a sort of overflow from "the Bend." . . . Something like forty families are packed into five old two-story and attic houses that were built to hold five, and out in the yards additional crowds are, or were until very recently, accommodated in sheds built of all sorts of old boards and used as drying racks. . . . I found them empty when I visited the settlement while writing this. The last two tenants had just left. Their fate was characteristic. The "old man" who lived in the

---

[3] "flat": today the term "apartment" is more often used.

corner coop, with barely room to crouch beside the stove . . . had been taken to the "crazy house," and the woman who was his neighbor and had lived in her shed for years had simply disappeared. . . I found that for one front room and two "bedrooms" in the shameful old wrecks of buildings the tenant was paying ten dollars a month, for the back room and one bedroom, nine dollars, and for the attic rooms, according to size, from $3.75 to $5.50 . . . .

. . . What squalor and degradation inhabit these dens the health officers know. Through the long summer days their carts patrol "the Bend," scattering disinfectants in streets and lanes, in sinks and cellars and hidden hovels . . . . From midnight till far into the small hours of the morning the policeman's thundering rap on closed doors is heard . . . on his rounds gathering evidence of illegal overcrowding. . . . [One place] was photographed by flashlight on just such a visit. In a room not thirteen feet either way slept twelve men and women, two or three in bunks set in a sort of alcove, the rest on the floor. A kerosene lamp burned dimly in the fearful atmosphere, probably to guide other and later arrivals to their "beds," for it was only just past midnight. A baby's fretful wail came from an adjoining hall room, where, in the semidarkness, three recumbent figures could be made out.

The Sweaters

The tenements grow taller, and the gaps in their ranks close up rapidly as we cross the Bowery, and leaving Chinatown and the Italians behind, invade the Hebrew quarter. Baxter Street, with its interminable rows of old-clothes shops and its brigades of pullers-in . . . . Bayard Street, with its synagogues and its crowds, gave us a foretaste of it. No need of asking where we are. . . .

It is said that nowhere in the world are so many people crowded together on a square mile as here . . . even the alley is crowded out. Through dark hallways and filthy cellars, crowded as is every foot of the street with dirty children, the settlements in the rear are reached. Life here means the hardest kind of work almost from the cradle. The homes of the Hebrew quarter are its workshops also. You are made fully aware of [economic conditions] before you have traveled the length of a single block in any of these East Side streets by the whir of a thousand sewing machines, worked at high pressure from earliest dawn till mind and muscle give out together. Every member of the family, from the youngest to the oldest, bears a hand, shut in the qualmy rooms, where meals are cooked and clothing washed and dried

besides, the livelong day. It is not unusual to find a dozen persons —
men, women, and children — at work in a single small room. The
fact accounts for the contrast that strikes with wonder the observer
who comes across from "the Bend." Over there the entire population
seems possessed of an uncontrollable impulse to get out into the
street; here all its energies appear to be bent upon keeping in and
away from it. Not that the streets are deserted. The overflow from
these tenements is enough to make a crowd anywhere. The children
alone would do it. Not old enough to work and no room to play,
that is their story. . . . Typhus fever and smallpox are bred here . . . .
Filth diseases both, they sprout naturally among the hordes that bring
the germs with them from across the sea, and whose first instinct is
to hide their sick lest the authorities carry them off to the hospital
to be slaughtered, as they firmly believe. The health officers are on
constant and sharp outlook for hidden fever nests. Considering that
half of the readymade clothes that are sold in the big stores, if not a
good deal more than half, are made in these tenement rooms, this is
not excessive caution. It has happened more than once that a child
recovering from smallpox, and in the most contagious stage of the
disease, has been found crawling among heaps of half-finished clothing that the next day would be offered for sale on the counter of a
Broadway store; or that a typhus fever patient has been discovered
in a room whence perhaps a hundred coats had been sent home that
week, each one with the wearer's death warrant, unseen and unsuspected, basted in the lining.

4. Industrialization

*In the post-Civil War years America industrialized. Much of
the heavy manufacturing took place in the country's urban centers where manpower, capital, and transportation facilities were
available.*

*Cleveland was one of the cities which experienced an economic
boom. In 1892 the Cleveland Board of Trade published a report
describing the city's industrial growth over the preceding decade.
The rapidity of the process is detailed in the first excerpt that
follows; it includes the comments of Robert P. Porter, Superintendent of the Census Office. The relatively sophisticated statistics reflect an increasingly rational approach demanded by large-*

scale operations. The other side of burgeoning industrial development — the unrelenting filth and ugliness that too often accompanied it — is amply documented in the second selection, a description of Pittsburgh by soldier and explorer Willard Glazier in his Peculiarities of American Cities *(1883).* ∎

A. CLEVELAND'S BOOM[1]

In the manufacture of heavy forgings, wire nails, nuts and bolts, carriage and wagon hardware, vapor stoves, sewing machines, steel-tired car wheels, and heavy street-railway machinery, Cleveland leads all cities of this country. These are only a few of the most important productive industries allied to the great furnace and rolling mill interests, and prominence is given to them simply for the purpose of calling attention to the fact that the city is distinctively headquarters in these lines. Here are located also the greatest shoddy[2] mills in America; a plant for the manufacture of sewing machine woodwork that has no equal in the world; a steel-bridge works that is represented in massive structures spanning rivers and valleys over the entire continent; and an electric-light carbon works having a capacity of ten million carbons annually, with a market for its product extending to Mexico, South America, China, and Japan. . . .

In ten years you have doubled the number and the value of the product of your establishments. You have nearly trebled the capital invested in manufactures, multiplied the total number employed two and a half times, and you are paying out annually in wages more than three times as much as you did in 1880. We have carefully filed away in Washington a schedule sworn to by the special agent as a true and faithful statement of the condition of every one of the 2300 manufacturing establishments of this city. These statements are cold, clear, official statements of facts, and not warmly colored, exaggerated offerings to the altar of local pride. They show exactly what you have done the last ten years, and it affords me great pleasure to congratulate you on the tremendous showing, for such it is. It places Cleveland in the front rank as one of the great manufacturing

[1] Cleveland Board of Trade, *Annual Report of the Trade and Commerce of Cleveland* (Cleveland: The Cleveland Printing and Publishing Co.), pp. 68, 70–72, 79–80.
[2] shoddy: fiber made from woolen waste.

cities of the Union. I hope it will encourage your enterprising merchants and manufacturers and financiers to renewed efforts for the decade you have already entered upon with such great prestige.

I doubt whether a more interesting comparison of your manufacturing industry is possible than that of the difference in cost of material and value of product, for this might be called the enhanced value due to manufacture and really represents what the industry and capital of your city has accomplished. In 1880, this enhanced value amounted to $16,974,313, while in 1890 it amounted to $40,-745,701, an increase of about 150 per cent.

Comparative Statement of Totals Under General Heads of Inquiry: 1880 and 1890.

	1880	1890
Number industries reported	136	181
Number establishments reporting	1,055	2,300
Capital (a)	$ 19,430,989	$ 56,826,496
Hands employed	21,724	48,771
Wages paid	$ 8,502,935	$ 27,596,408
Cost of materials used	$ 31,629,737	$ 58,763,062
Miscellaneous expenses (b)		4,690,406
Value of product	$ 48,604,050	$104,199,169
Municipal Data—Population	160,146	261,353
" " Assessed valuation	$ 70,548,104	$ 99,614,055
" " Municipal debt (c)	$ 6,467,046	$ 6,143,206

a. The value of hired property is not included for 1890, because it was not reported in 1880.

b. No inquiry in 1880 relating to "miscellaneous expenses."

c. The amount stated represents the "net debt" or the total amount of municipal debt less sinking fund.

B. PITTSBURGH IN THE GLOOM[3]

♣ *Willard Glazier*

A Smoky, Dismal Place

By all means make your first approach to Pittsburgh in the night time, and you will behold a spectacle which has not a parallel on this

[3] Willard Glazier, *Peculiarites of American Cities* (Philadelphia: Hubbard Brothers, 1886), pp. 332–341.

continent. Darkness gives the city and its surroundings a picturesqueness which they wholly lack by daylight. It lies low down in a hollow of encompassing hills, gleaming with a thousand points of light, which are reflected from the rivers, whose waters glimmer, it may be, in the faint moonlight, and catch and reflect the shadows as well. Around the city's edge, and on the sides of the hills which encircle it like a gloomy amphitheater, their outlines rising dark against the sky, through numberless apertures, fiery lights stream forth, looking angrily and fiercely up toward the heavens, while over all these settles a heavy pall of smoke. It is as though one had reached the outer edge of the infernal regions and saw before him the great furnace of [hell] with all the lids lifted. The scene is so strange and weird that it will live in the memory forever. One pictures, as he beholds it, the tortured spirits writhing in agony, their sinewy limbs convulsed, and the very air oppressive with pain and rage.

Failing a night approach, the traveler should reach the Iron City on a dismal day in autumn, when the air is heavy with moisture, and the very atmosphere looks dark. All romance has disappeared. In this nineteenth century the gods of mythology find no place in daylight. There is only a very busy city shrouded in gloom. The buildings, whatever their original material and color, are smoked to a uniform, dirty drab; their smoke sinks and, mingling with the moisture in the air, becomes of a consistency which may almost be felt as well as seen. Under a drab sky, twilight hangs over the town, and the gas lights, which are left burning at midday, shine out of the murkiness with a dull, reddish glare. Then is Pittsburgh herself. Such days as these are her especial boast, and in their frequency and dismalness in all the world she has no rival, save London.

In truth, Pittsburgh is a smoky, dismal city, at her best. At her worst, nothing darker, dingier, or more dispiriting can be imagined. The city is in the heart of the soft coal region; and the smoke from her dwellings, stores, factories, foundries, and steamboats . . . settles in a cloud over the narrow valley in which she is built, until the very sun looks coppery through the sooty haze. According to a circular of the Pittsburgh Board of Trade, about 20 per cent, or one fifth, of all the coal used in the factories and dwellings of the city escapes into the air in the form of smoke. . . . Her inhabitants are all too busy to reflect upon the inconvenience or uncomeliness of this smoke. Work is the object of life with them. It occupies them from morning until night, from the cradle to the grave, except on Sundays, when, for the most part, the furnaces are idle, and the forges are silent. For Pittsburgh, settled by Irish-Scotch Presbyterians, is a great Sunday-keeping day. Save on this day her businessmen do not stop for rest or recreation, nor do they "retire" from business. They die with the harness on, and die, perhaps, all the sooner for having worn it so continuously and so long.

Ravaged Land, Sullied Waters

Pittsburgh is not a beautiful city. That stands to reason, with the heavy pall of smoke which constantly overhangs her. But she lacks beauty in other respects. She is substantially and compactly built, and contains some handsome edifices; but she lacks the architectural magnificence of some of her sister cities; while her suburbs present all that is unsightly and forbidding in appearance, the original beauties of nature having been ruthlessly sacrificed to utility.

Pittsburgh is situated in western Pennsylvania, in a narrow valley at the confluence of the Allegheny and Monongahela rivers, and at the head of the Ohio, and is surrounded by hills rising to the height of four or five hundred feet. These hills once possessed rounded outlines, with sufficient exceptional abruptness to lend them variety and picturesqueness. But they have been leveled down, cut into, sliced off, and ruthlessly marred and mutilated, until not a trace of their original outlines remain. Great black coal cars crawl up and down their sides, and plunge into unexpected and mysterious openings, their sudden disappearance lending, even in daylight, an air of mystery and [black magic] to the region. Railroad tracks gridiron the ground everywhere, debris of all sorts lies in heaps and is scattered over the earth, and huts and hovels are perched here and there, in every available spot. There is no verdure — nothing but mud and coal, the one yellow, the other black. And on the edge of the city are the unpicturesque outlines of factories and foundries, their tall chimneys belching forth columns of inky blackness, which roll and whirl in fantastic shapes, and finally lose themselves in the general murkiness above.

The tranquil Monongahela comes up from the south, alive with barges and tug boats, while the swifter current of the Allegheny bears from the oil regions, at the north, slightly built barges with their freights of crude petroleum. Oil is not infrequently poured upon the troubled waters when one of these barges sinks and its freight, liberated from the open tanks, refuses to sink with it, and spreads itself out on the surface of the stream.

Monster Factories

The crowning glory of Pittsburgh is her monster iron and glass works. One half the glass produced in all the United States comes from Pittsburgh.

In addition to these glass works — which, though they employ thousands of workmen, represent but a fraction of the city's industries — there are rolling mills, foundries, potteries, oil refineries, and factories of machinery. All these works are rendered possible by the coal which abounds in measureless quantities in the immediate neighborhood of the city. All the hills which rise from the river bank of Pittsburgh have a thick stratum of bituminous coal running through them which can be mined without shafts or any of the usual accessories of mining. All that is to be done is to shovel the coal out of the hillside, convey it to cars or by means of an inclined plane to the factory or foundry door, and dump it, ready for the convenience of the Pittsburgh manufactures.

The monster iron works of Pittsburgh consume large quantities of this coal, and it is the abundance and convenience of the latter material which have made the former possible. No other city begins to compare with Pittsburgh in the number and variety of her factories.

[One observer], writing of Pittsburgh, says, it has 35 miles of factories in daily operation, twisted up into a compact tangle; all belching forth smoke; all glowing with fire; all swarming with workmen; all echoing with the clank of machinery.

5. The Heyday of Bossism

The distance between the center and the periphery of American cities of the late nineteenth century was not merely geographical. Diverging life styles produced different political structures and social goals. The two Americas, city and suburb, faced each other across a widening gulf.

The congested city gave birth to the "boss" and the "machine." Large numbers of people, many of them newcomers, jammed together, sharing similar conditions and experiences, could, with proper manipulation, become a power base for an ambitious politician. Thus evolved the institution of the ward boss, usually a man of the same nationality and religion as the most important group in his constituency. Maintaining himself by the distribution of patronage — that is, giving public jobs to loyal constituents, the boss claimed with some justification that he served his people as well as himself, in that he functioned as a one-man welfare agency. Municipal reformers argued that bosses grew fat on graft and corruption, that they bled the taxpayers, that their dependence on illegal votes to stay in power invalidated the democratic process, and that they could not cope with serious urban problems such as mass unemployment. ■

A. PLUNKITT ON HIS OPPORTUNITIES[1]

✤ William L. Riordon

It is almost impossible to speak of machine politics without mentioning Tammany Hall, the popular name for the executive committee of the Democratic Party of New York County. Tammany is in fact a very old organization. Founded in 1789 as a national society to represent the middle class against the aristocracy, it chose the name "Sons of St. Tammany" (from Tamamend, a Delaware Indian chief) to ridicule the pretensions of such groups as the societies of St. George and St. Andrew.

By the middle of the nineteenth century, Tammany had come to be synonymous with the Democratic Party of New York City, although the two were supposedly separate. Among its leaders were Richard Croker, identified with the organization from around 1862; William Marcy Tweed, arrested in 1873 for swindling the city treasury; and Charles F. Murphy, prominent at the turn of the century.

These top men relied heavily on lieutenants, or district leaders. George Washington Plunkitt held such an office on Manhattan's Upper West Side. In a series of "very plain talks on very practical politics," delivered from his rostrum, the bootblack stand in the County Courthouse, and recorded by a free-lance journalist, William L. Riordon, Plunkitt outlined the classic path to bossdom as well as the peculiar brand of civic morality practiced by the professionals. ■

[1] Excerpts from *Plunkitt of Tammany Hall* by William Riordon, pp. 3–7, 8, 9–13, 33–34, 109–111. Published 1948 by Alfred A. Knopf, Inc. Reprinted by permission.

Advice for Would-be Politicians

There's thousands of young men in this city who will go to the polls for the first time next November. Among them will be many who have watched the careers of successful men in politics, and who are longin' to make names and fortunes for themselves at the same game. It is to these youths that I want to give advice. First, let me say that I am in a position to give what the courts call expert testimony on the subject. I don't think you can easily find a better example than I am of success in politics. After forty years' experience at the game I am — well, I'm George Washington Plunkitt. Everybody knows what figure I cut in the greatest organization on earth [Tammany Hall], and if you hear people say that I've laid away a million or so since I was a butcher's boy in Washington Market, don't come to me for an indignant denial. I'm pretty comfortable, thank you. . . .

. . . Some young men think they can learn how to be successful in politics from books, and they cram their heads with all sorts of college rot. They couldn't make a bigger mistake. Now, understand me, I ain't sayin' nothin' against colleges. I guess they'll have to exist as long as there's bookworms, and I suppose they do some good in a certain way, but they don't count in politics.

Another mistake: some young men think that the best way to prepare for the political game is to practice speakin' and becomin' orators. That's all wrong. We've got some orators in Tammany Hall, but they're chiefly ornamental. . . . Look at the 36 district leaders of Tammany Hall today. How many of them travel on their tongues? Maybe one or two, and they don't count when business is doin' at Tammany Hall. The men who rule have practiced keepin' their tongues still, not exercisin' them. . . .

Now, I've told you what not to do. I guess I can explain best what to do to succeed in politics by tellin' you what I did. After goin' through the apprenticeship of the business while I was a boy by workin' around the district headquarters and hustlin' about the polls on election day, I set out when I cast my first vote to win fame and money in New York City politics. Did I offer my services to the district leader as a stump-speaker? Not much. The woods are always full of speakers. Did I get up a book on municipal government and show it to the leader? I wasn't such a fool. What I did was to get some marketable goods before goin' to the leaders. What do I mean by marketable goods? Let me tell you: I had a cousin, a young man who didn't take any particular interest in politics. I went to him and said: "Tommy, I'm goin' to be a politician, and I want to get a followin'; can I count on you?" He said: "Sure, George." That's how I started in business. I got a marketable commodity — one vote. Then I went to the district leader and told him I could command two votes on election day, Tommy's and my own. He smiled on me and told me to go ahead. If I had offered him a speech or a bookful of learnin', he would have said, "Oh, forget it!"

That was beginnin' business in a small way, wasn't it? But that is the only way to become a real lastin' statesman. I soon branched out. Two young men in the flat next to mine were school friends. I went to them, just as I went to Tommy, and they agreed to stand by me. Then I had a followin' of three voters and I began to get a bit chesty. Whenever I dropped into district headquarters, everybody shook hands with me, and the leader one day honored me by lightin' a match for my cigar. And so it went on like a snowball rollin' down a hill. I worked the flat-house that I live in from the basement to the top floor, and I got about a dozen young men to follow me. Then I tackled the next house and so on down the block and around the corner. Before long I had sixty men back of me, and formed the George Washington Plunkitt Association.

What did the district leader say then when I called at headquarters? I didn't have to call at headquarters. He came after me and said: "George, what do you want? If you don't see what you want, ask for it. Wouldn't you like to have a job or two in the departments for your friends?" I said: "I'll think it over; I haven't yet decided what the George Washington Plunkitt Association will do in the next campaign." You ought to have seen how I was courted and petted then by the leaders of the rival organizations. I had marketable goods and there was bids for them from all sides, and I was a risin' man in politics. As time went on and my association grew, I thought I would like to go to the Assembly. I just had to hint at what I wanted, and three different organizations offered me the nomination. Afterwards, I went to the board of aldermen, then to the state senate, then became leader of the district, and so on up till I became a statesman. . . .

Honest Graft

Everybody is talkin' these days about Tammany men growin' rich on graft, but nobody thinks of drawin' the distinction between honest graft and dishonest graft. There's all the difference in the world between the two.

There's an honest graft, and I'm an example of how it works. I might sum up the whole thing by sayin': "I seen my opportunities and I took 'em."

Just let me explain by examples. My party's in power in the city, and it's goin' to undertake a lot of public improvements. Well, I'm tipped off, say, that they're goin' to lay out a new park at a certain place.

I see my opportunity and I take it. I go to that place and I buy up all the land I can in the neighborhood. Then the board of this or that makes its plan public, and there is a rush to get my land, which nobody cared particular for before.

Ain't it perfectly honest to charge a good price and make a profit on my investment and foresight? Of course it is. Well, that's honest graft. . . .

For instance, the city is repavin' a street and has several hundred thousand old granite blocks to sell. I am on hand to buy, and I know just what they are worth.

How? Never mind that. I had a sort of monopoly of this business for a while, but once a newspaper tried to do me. It got some outside men to come over from Brooklyn and New Jersey to bid against me.

Was I done? Not much. I went to each of the men and said: "How many of these 250,000 stones do you want?" One said 20,000, and another wanted 15,000, and another wanted 10,000. I said: "All right, let me bid for the lot, and I'll give each of you all you want for nothin'."

They agreed, of course. Then the auctioneer yelled: "How much am I bid for these 250,000 fine pavin' stones?"

"Two dollars and fifty cents," says I.

"Two dollars and fifty cents!" screamed the auctioneer. "Oh, that's a joke! Give me a real bid."

He found the bid was real enough. My rivals stood silent. I got the lot for $2.50 and gave them their share. That's how the attempt to do Plunkitt ended, and that's how all such attempts end.

I've told you how I got rich by honest graft. Now, let me tell you that most politicians who are accused of robbin' the city get rich the same way.

They didn't steal a dollar from the city treasury. They just seen their opportunities and took them.

The books are always all right. The money in the city treasury is all right. Everything is all right. All they can show is that the Tammany heads of departments looked after their friends, within the law, and gave them what opportunities they could to make honest graft. Every good man looks after his friends, and any man who doesn't isn't likely to be popular. If I have a good thing to hand out in private life, I give it to a friend. Why shouldn' I do the same in public life? ...

"Bosses Preserve the Nation"

Look at the bosses of Tammany Hall in the last twenty years. What magnificent men! To them New York City owes pretty much all it is today. John Kelly, Richard Croker, and Charles F. Murphy — what names in American history compares with them, except Washington and Lincoln? They built up the grand Tammany organization, and the organization built up New York. Suppose the city had to depend for the last twenty years on irresponsible concerns like the Citizens' Union [a reform group], where would it be now? You can make a pretty good guess if you recall the Strong and Low administrations when there was no boss, and the heads of departments were at odds all the time with each other, and the Mayor was at odds with the lot of them. They spent so much time in arguin' and making grandstand play that the interests of the city were forgotten. Another administration of that kind would put New York back a quarter of a century.

Then see how beautiful a Tammany city government runs, with a so-called boss directin' the whole shootin' match! The machinery moves so noiseless that you wouldn't think there was any. If there's any differences of opinion, the Tammany leader settles them quietly, and his orders go every time. How nice it is for the people to feel that they can get up in the mornin' without bein' afraid of seein' in the papers that the Commissioner of Water Supply has sandbagged the Dock Commissioner, and that the Mayor and heads of departments have been taken to the police court as witnesses! That's no joke. I remember that, under Strong, some commissioners came very near sandbaggin' one another.

Of course the newspapers like the reform administration. Why? Because these administrations, with their daily rows, furnish as racy news as prize fights or divorce cases. Tammany don't care to get in the papers. It goes right along attendin' to business quietly and only wants to be let alone. That's the reason why the papers are against us.

Some papers complain that the bosses get rich while devotin' their lives to the interests of the city. What of it? If opportunities for turnin' an honest dollar comes their way, why shouldn't they take advantage of them, just as I have done? As I said, . . . there is honest graft and dishonest graft. The bosses go in for the former. There is so much of it in this big town that they would be fools to go in for dishonest graft.

Now, in conclusion, I want to say that I don't own a dishonest dollar. If my worst enemy was given the job of writin' my epitaph when I'm gone, he couldn't do more than write:

"George W. Plunkitt. He Seen His Opportunities, and He Took 'Em."

B. "MOST CORRUPT AND MOST CONTENTED"[3]

✤ Lincoln Steffens

Plunkitt dismissed reformers as "only mornin' glories" while they viewed him and his like with deep dismay. The magazine publisher S. S. McClure hired skilled reporters to gather evidence of wrongdoing in big business and government. The journalist Lincoln Steffens joined McClure's Magazine in 1901 and produced a sensational series of articles on municipal corruption, later published in book form under the title The Shame of the Cities. *Labeled by President Theodore Roosevelt as mere "muckrakers," Steffens and others persisted in exposing conditions they considered deplorable. The following selection from* The Shame of the Cities, *an indictment of the Philadelphia machine, is a typical display of reform indignation.* ■

. . . All our municipal governments are more or less bad, and all our people are optimists. Philadelphia is simply the most corrupt and the most contented. Minneapolis has cleaned up, Pittsburgh has tried

---

[3] Lincoln Steffens, *The Shame of the Cities* (New York: McClure, Phillips & Co., 1904), pp. 195–196, 198–201, 203–205 *passim*.

to, New York fights every other election, Chicago fights all the time. Even St. Louis has begun to stir (since the elections are over), and at the worst was only shameless. . . .

Philadelphia is a city that has had its reforms. Having passed through all the typical stages of corruption, Philadelphia reached the period of miscellaneous loot with a boss for chief thief, under James McManes and the Gas Ring way back in the late sixties and seventies. This is the Tweed stage of corruption from which St. Louis, for example, is just emerging. Philadelphia, in two inspiring popular revolts, attacked the Gas Ring, broke it, and in 1885 achieved that dream of American cities — a good charter. The present condition of Philadelphia, therefore, is not that which precedes, but that which follows reform, and in this distinction lies its startling general significance. What has happened since the . . . charter went into effect in Philadelphia may happen in any American city "after reform is over." . . .

. . . The Philadelphians do not vote; they are disfranchised, and their disfranchisement is one anchor of the foundation of the Philadelphia organization.

This is no figure of speech. The honest citizens of Philadelphia have no more rights at the polls than the Negroes down South. Nor do they fight very hard for this basic privilege. . . .

The machine controls the whole process of voting, and practices fraud at every stage. The assessor's list is the voting list, and the assessor is the machine's man. The assessor pads the list with the names of dead dogs, children, and nonexistent persons. . . . A ring orator in a speech resenting sneers at his ward as "low down" reminded his hearers that that was the ward of Independence Hall, and naming over signers of the Declaration of Independence, he closed his highest flight of eloquence with the statement that "these men, the fathers of American liberty, voted down here once. And," he added, with a catching grin, "they vote here yet." Rudolph Blankenburg,[4] a persistent fighter for the right and the use of the right to vote (and, by the way, an immigrant), sent out just before one election a registered letter to each voter on the rolls of a certain selected division. Sixty-three per cent were returned marked "not at," "removed," "deceased," etc. . . .

The repeating is done boldly, for the machine controls the election officers, often choosing them from among the fraudulent names, and

[4] See pp. 179–181.

when no one appears to serve, assigning the heeler ready for the expected vacancy. The police are forbidden by law to stand within thirty feet of the polls, but they are at the box and they are there to see that the machine's orders are obeyed and that repeaters whom they help to furnish are permitted to vote without "intimidation" on the names they, the police, have supplied. . . . The repeaters go from one polling place to another, voting on slips, and on their return rounds change coats, hats, etc. The business proceeds with very few hitches; there is more jesting than fighting. Violence in the past has had its effect; and it is not often necessary nowadays, but if it is needed the police are there to apply it. Several citizens told me that they had seen the police help to beat citizens or election officers who were trying to do their duty, then arrest the victim. . . .

But many Philadelphians do not try to vote. They leave everything to the machine, and the machine casts their ballots for them. . . . A friend of mine told me he was on the lists in the three wards in which he had successively dwelt. He votes personally in none, but the leader of his present ward tells him how he has been voted. . . . If necessary after all this, the machine counts the vote "right," and there is little use appealing to the courts, since they have held, except in one case, that the ballot box is secret and cannot be opened. The only legal remedy lies in the purging of the assessor's lists, and when the Municipal League had this done in 1899, they reported that there was "wholesale voting on the very names stricken off."

Deprived of self-government, the Philadelphians haven't even self-governing machine government. They have their own boss, but he and his machine are subject to the state ring, and take their orders from the state boss, Matthew S. Quay, who is the proprietor of Pennsylvania and the real ruler of Philadelphia. . . .

. . . The people of Philadelphia are Republicans in a Republican city in a Republican state in a Republican nation, and they are bound ring on ring. The President of the United States and his patronage; the National Cabinet and their patronage; the Congress and the patronage of the senators and the congressmen from Pennsylvania; the governor of the state and the state legislature with their powers and patronage; and all that the mayor and the city councils have of power and patronage — all these bear down upon Philadelphia to keep it in the control of Quay's boss and his little ring. This is the ideal of party organization, and, possibly, is the end toward which our democratic republic is tending. If it is, the end is absolutism. Nothing but a revolution could overthrow this oligarchy,[5] and there is its danger. With no outlet at the polls for public feeling, the machine cannot be taught anything it does not know except at the cost of annihilation.

[5] **oligarchy:** government by a dominant few or clique.

6. New Skylines[1]

✤ Louis H. Sullivan

Faced with increasing land costs and the need for more light in buildings, and aided by technical innovations like the elevator and steel-frame construction, the cities expanded vertically as rapidly as they had grown horizontally. Louis Sullivan was the founder of the "Chicago school" of architecture with its "form follows function" theory of design. He, more than any other architect, gained acceptance for the skyscraper as an essentially modern and American structure. In passages from his enigmatic autobiography, written in the third person, Sullivan conveys the thrill of this achievement. ■

At the age of 25, Louis H. Sullivan became a full-fledged architect before the world, with a reputation starting on its way. . . . He could now, undisturbed, start on the course of practical experimentation he long had in mind, which was to make an architecture that fitted its functions — a realistic architecture based on well-defined utilitarian needs — that all practical demands of utility should be paramount as basis of planning and design; that no architectural dictum, or tradition, or superstition, or habit, should stand in the way. . . . This meant in his courageous mind that he would put to the test a formula he had evolved, through long contemplation of living things, namely that form follows function, which would mean, in practice, that architecture might again become a living art, if this formula were but adhered to.

The building business was again under full swing, and a series of

[1] Louis H. Sullivan, *The Autobiography of an Idea* (New York: W. W. Norton & Company, Inc. Copyright 1922, 1924, 1926 by Press of the American Institute of Architects, Inc.), pp. 257–258, 293, 304, 309, 313 *passim*. Reprinted by permission.

important mercantile structures came into the office, each one of which he treated experimentally, feeling his way toward a basic process, a grammar of his own. The immediate problem was increased daylight, the maximum of daylight. This led him to use slender piers, tending toward a masonry and iron combination, the beginnings of a vertical system. This method upset all precedent, and led Louis's contemporaries to regard him as an iconoclast,[2] a revolutionary, which was true enough — yet into the work was slowly infiltrated a corresponding system of artistic expression, which appeared in these structures as novel, and to some repellent, in its total disregard of accepted notions. . . .

. . . Important work was at hand in other cities as well as in Chicago. The steel-frame form of construction had come into use. It was first applied by Holabird & Roche in the Tacoma Office Building, Chicago; and in St. Louis, it was given first authentic recognition and expression in the exterior treatment of the Wainwright Building, a nine-story office structure, by Louis Sullivan's own hand. He felt at once that the new form of engineering was revolutionary, demanding an equally revolutionary architectural mode. That masonry construction, insofar as tall buildings were concerned, was a thing of the past, to be forgotten, that the mind might be free to face and solve new problems in new functional forms. That the old ideas of superimposition must give way before the sense of vertical continuity. . . .

In Chicago, the progress of the building art from 1880 onward was phenomenal. . . .

The essential scheme of construction, however, was that of solid masonry enclosing-and-supporting walls. The "Montauk" Block had reached the height of nine stories and was regarded with wonder. Then came the Auditorium Building with its immense mass of ten stories, its tower, weighing thirty million pounds, equivalent to twenty stories — a tower of solid masonry carried on a "floating" foundation; a great raft 67 by 100 feet. Meanwhile Burnham and Root had prepared plans for a sixteen-story solid-masonry office building to be called the "Monadnock." As this was to be a big jump from nine stories, construction was postponed until it should be seen whether or not the Auditorium Tower would go to China of its own free will. . . . Then the "Monadnock" went ahead: an amazing cliff of brickwork, rising sheer and stark, with a subtlety of line and surface, a direct singleness of purpose, that gave one the thrill of romance. It

---

[2] **iconoclast:** literally, image-smasher; one who breaks with tradition and convention.

was the first and last word of its kind; a great word in its day, but its day vanished almost overnight, leaving it to stand as a symbol, as a solitary monument, marking the high tide of masonry construction as applied to commercial structures. . . .

Then came the flash of imagination which saw the single thing. The trick was turned, and there swiftly came into being something new under the sun. For the true steel-frame structure stands unique in the flowing of man and his works, a brilliant material example of man's capacity to satisfy his needs through the exercise of his natural powers. . . .

The architects of Chicago welcomed the steel frame and did something with it.

7. The Lure of the City

The new skyline, symbol of power, adventure, and opportunity, emphasized the sharp contrast between city and country. By the thousands the young sons and daughters of farmers and small-town businessmen deserted the family hearth to try their luck in the metropolis.

The city as magnet was a common theme in American fiction of the late nineteenth century. In Horatio Alger's popular rags-to-riches tales, it was the land of opportunity, as in Ragged Dick, *excerpted below. The second selection, from Theodore Dreiser's classic* Sister Carrie, *describes the journey to the city, the shock of first encounter, the fear, and the determination to be part of it all.* ■

A. RAGGED DICK[1]

♣ *Horatio Alger*

"Wake up there, youngster," said a rough voice.

Ragged Dick opened his eyes slowly and stared stupidly in the face of the speaker but did not offer to get up.

[1] Horatio Alger, Jr., *Ragged Dick, or, Street Life in New York with the Boot-Blacks* (Boston: Loring, Publishers, 1868), pp. 9–11, 12, 19, 20, 22, 24–25, 36–37, 45–46, 49, 53, 54.

"Wake up, you young vagabond!" said the man a little impatiently. "I suppose you'd lay there all day if I hadn't called you."

"What time is it?" asked Dick.

"Seven o'clock."

"Seven o'clock! I oughter've been up an hour ago. I know what 'twas made be so precious sleepy. I went to Old Bowery last night and didn't turn in till past twelve." . . .

While this conversation had been going on, Dick had got up. His bedchamber had been a wooden box half full of straw, on which the young bootblack had reposed his weary limbs and slept as soundly as if it had been a bed of down. . . . He jumped out of the box, shook himself, picked out one or two straws that had found their way into the rents in his clothes, and drawing a well-worn cap over his uncombed locks, he was all ready for the business of the day. . . .

Dick's business hours had commenced. He had no office to open. His little blacking-box was ready for use, and he looked sharply in the faces of all who passed, addressing each with "Shine yer boots, sir? . . .

When Dick had got through with his last customer, the City Hall clock indicated eight o'clock. He had been up an hour and hard at work, and naturally began to think of breakfast. He went up to the head of Spruce Street and turned into Nassau. Two blocks further and he reached Ann Street. On this street was a small, cheap restaurant, where for five cents Dick could get a cup of coffee, and for ten cents more, a plate of beefsteak with a plate of bread thrown in. . . .

Dick had scarcely been served when he espied a boy about his own size standing at the door, looking wistfully into the restaurant. This was Johnny Nolan, a boy of fourteen, who was engaged in the same profession as Ragged Dick. . . .

"Had your breakfast, Johnny?" inquired Dick, cutting off a piece of steak.

"No."

'Come in, then. Here's room for you." . . .

Breakfast over, Dick walked up to the desk and settled the bill. Then, followed by Johnny, he went out into the street.

"Where are you going, Johnny?"

"Up to Mr. Taylor's on Spruce Street, to see if he don't want a shine." . . .

". . . Where'd you sleep last night?"

"Up an alley in an old wagon."

"You had a better bed than that in the country, didn't you?"

"Yes, it was as soft as — cotton." ...

"Why didn't you stay?"

"I felt lonely," said Johnny.

Johnny could not exactly explain his feelings, but it is often the case that the young vagabond of the streets, though his food is uncertain and his bed may be any old wagon or barrel that he is lucky enough to find unoccupied when night sets in, gets so attached to his precarious but independent mode of life that he feels discontented in any other. He is accustomed to the noise and bustle and ever-varied life of the streets, and in the quiet scenes of the country misses the excitement in the midst of which he has always dwelt. ...

"Well," said Dick reflectively. "I dunno as I'd like to live in the country. I couldn't go to Tony Pastor's or the Old Bowery. There wouldn't be no place to spend my evenings...."

Dick shouldered his box and walked as far as the Astor House. He took his station on the sidewalk and began to look about him.

Just behind him were two persons — one a gentleman of fifty, the other a boy of thirteen or fourteen. They were speaking together and Dick had no difficulty in hearing what was said.

"I am sorry, Frank, that I can't go about and show you some of the sights of New York, but I shall be full of business today. It is your first visit to the city, too." ...

Now Dick had listened to all this conversation. Being an enterprising young man, he thought he saw a chance for a speculation, and determined to avail himself of it.

Accordingly he stepped up to the two just as Frank's uncle was about leaving, and said, "I know all about the city, sir; I'll show him around if you want me to."

The gentleman looked a little curiously at the ragged figure before him. ...

"I don't know what to say, Frank," he remarked after a while. "It is rather a novel proposal. He isn't exactly the sort of guide I would have picked out for you. Still he looks honest. He has an open face, and I think he can be depended upon." ...

[The Whitneys give Dick some clothes and a chance to wash and comb his hair at their hotel. Then the boys start for Chatham Street where Dick proposed to buy a hat to complete his new outfit.]

In order to reach Chatham Street it was necessary to cross Broadway. This was easier proposed than done. There is always such a throng of omnibuses, drays, carriages, and vehicles of all kinds in the neighborhood of the Astor House that the crossing is formidable to one who is not used to it. Dick made nothing of it, dodging in and out among the horses and wagons with perfect self-possession. Reaching the opposite sidewalk, he looked back and found that Frank had retreated in dismay, and that the width of the street was between them. . . .

Finally Frank got safely over after several narrow escapes, as he considered them. . . .

They were soon in Chatham Street, walking between rows of ready-made-clothing shops, many of which had half their stock in trade exposed on the sidewalk. The proprietors of these establishments stood at the doors watching attentively the passers-by, extending urgent invitations to any who even glanced at the goods to enter.

"Walk in, young gentlemen," said a stout man at the entrance of one shop.

"No, I thank you," replied Dick, "as the fly said to the spider."

"We're selling off at less than cost."

"Of course you be. That's where you makes your money," said Dick. "There ain't nobody of any enterprise that pretends to make a profit on his goods." . . .

A hat and cap store being close at hand, Dick and Frank went in. For 75 cents, which Frank insisted on paying, Dick succeeded in getting quite a neat-looking cap, which corresponded much better with his appearance than the one he had on. The last, not being considered worth keeping, Dick dropped on the sidewalk, from which, on looking back, he saw it picked up by a brother bootblack who appeared to consider it better than his own.

They retraced their steps and went up to Chambers Street to Broadway. . . .

The boys crossed to the west side of Broadway and walked slowly up the street. To Frank it was a very interesting spectacle. Accustomed to the quiet of the country, [he found] something fascinating in the crowds of people thronging the sidewalks and the great variety of vehicles constantly passing and repassing in the street. Then again the shop windows with their multifarious contents interested and amused him, and he was constantly checking Dick to look in at some well-stocked window. . . .

B. A WAIF AMID FORCES[2]

✤ *Theodore Dreiser*

When Caroline Meeber boarded the afternoon train for Chicago, her total outfit consisted of a small trunk, a cheap imitation alligator-skin satchel, a small lunch in a paper box, and a yellow leather snap purse, containing her ticket, a scrap of paper with her sister's address in Van Buren Street, and four dollars in money. It was in August, 1889. She was eighteen years of age, bright, timid, and full of the illusions of ignorance and youth. Whatever touch of regret at parting characterized her thoughts, it was certainly not for advantages now being given up. A gush of tears at her mother's farewell kiss, a touch in her throat when the cars clacked by the flour mill where her father worked by the day, a pathetic sigh as the familiar green environs of the village passed in review, and the threads which bound her so lightly to girlhood and home were irretrievably broken.

To be sure there was always the next station, where one might descend and return. There was the great city, bound more closely by these very trains which came up daily. Columbia City was not so very far away, even once she was in Chicago. What, pray, is a few hours — a few hundred miles? She looked at the little slip bearing her sister's address and wondered. She gazed at the green landscape, now passing in swift review, until her swifter thoughts replaced its impression with vague conjectures of what Chicago might be.

When a girl leaves her home at eighteen, she does one of two things. Either she falls into saving hands and becomes better, or she rapidly assumes the cosmopolitan standard of virtue and becomes worse. Of an intermediate balance, under the circumstances, there is no possibility. The city has its cunning wiles. . . . The gleam of a thousand lights is often as effective as the persuasive light in a wooing and fascinating eye. . . . A blare of sound, a roar of life, a vast array of human hives, appeal to the astonished senses. . . .

A half-equipped little knight [Carrie] was, venturing to reconnoiter the mysterious city and dreaming wild dreams of some vague, far-off supremacy, which would make it prey and subject — the proper penitent, groveling at a woman's slipper. . . .

They were nearing Chicago. Signs were everywhere numerous. Trains flashed by them. Across wide stretches of flat, open prairie they could see lines of telegraph poles stalking across the fields toward the great city. Far away were indications of suburban towns, some big smokestacks towering high in the air.

Frequently there were two-story frame houses standing out in the open fields, without fence or trees, lone outposts of the approaching army of homes.

To the child, the genius with imagination, or the wholly untraveled, the approach to a great city for the first time is a wonderful thing. Particularly if it be evening — that mystic period between the glare and gloom of the world when life is changing from one sphere or condition to another. Ah, the promise of night. What does it not hold for the weary? . . .

. . . In 1889 Chicago had the peculiar qualifications of growth which made such adventuresome pilgrimages even on the part of young girls plausible. Its many and growing commercial opportunities gave it widespread fame, which made of it a giant magnet, drawing to itself, from all quarters, the hopeful and the hopeless — those who had their fortune yet to make and those whose fortunes and affairs had reached a disastrous climax elsewhere. It was a city of over 500,000, with the ambition, the daring, the activity of a metropolis of a million. Its streets and houses were already scattered over an area of 75 square miles. Its population was not so much thriving upon established commerce as upon the industries which prepared for the arrival of others. The sound of the hammer engaged upon the erection of new structures was everywhere heard. Great industries were moving in. The huge railroad corporations which had long before recognized the prospects of the place had seized upon vast tracts of land for transfer and shipping purposes. Streetcar lines had been extended far out into the open country in anticipation of rapid growth. The city had laid miles and miles of streets and sewers through regions where, perhaps, one solitary house stood out alone — a pioneer of populous ways to be. . . .

In the central portion was the vast wholesale and shopping district, to which the uninformed seeker for work usually drifted. It was a characteristic of Chicago then, and one not generally shared by other cities, that individual firms of any pretensions occupied individual buildings. The presence of ample ground made this possible. It gave an imposing appearance to most of the wholesale houses, whose offices were upon the ground floor and in plain view of the street. The large plates of window glass, now so common, were then rapidly coming into use, and gave to the ground floor offices a distinguished and prosperous look. The casual wanderer could see as he passed a polished array of office fixtures, much frosted glass, clerks hard at work, and genteel businessmen in "nobby" suits and clean linen lounging about or sitting in groups. Polished brass or nickel signs at the square stone entrances announced the firm and the nature of the business in rather neat and reserved terms. The entire metropolitan center possessed a high and mighty air calculated to overawe and abash the common applicant and to make the gulf between poverty and success seem both wide and deep.

Into this important commercial region the timid Carrie went. She walked east along Van Buren Street through a region of lessening importance, until it deteriorated into a mass of shanties and coal yards, and finally verged upon the river. She walked bravely forward, led by an honest desire to find employment and delayed at every step by the interest of the unfolding scene, and a sense of helplessness amid so much evidence of power and force which she did not understand. . . .

It was so with the vast railroad yards, with the crowded array of vessels she saw at the river, and the huge factories over the way, lining the water's edge. . . . The great streets were wall-lined mysteries to her; the vast offices, strange mazes which concerned far-off individuals of importance. She could think of people connected with them as counting money, dressing magnificently, and riding in carriages. It was all wonderful, all vast, all far removed, and she sank in spirit inwardly and fluttered feebly at the heart as she thought of entering any one of these mighty concerns and asking for something to do — something that she could do — anything.

8. The Literary Life in San Francisco¹

✤ Mark Twain

From earliest times the city has been a place where people of mutual interests could meet and influence each other, and where talent of all kinds could be noticed and encouraged. When San Francisco was young, barely out of its gold rush days, it became the center for a group of writers who helped create a uniquely American literature. In his autobiography, excerpted below, Mark Twain looked back upon the period in the 1860's when he, Bret Harte, Ambrose Bierce,² and others were associated. ■

After leaving Nevada I was a reporter on the *Morning Call* of San Francisco. I was more than that — I was *the* reporter. There was no other. There was enough work for one and a little over, but not enough for two — according to Mr. Barnes's idea, and he was the proprietor, and therefore better situated to know about it than other people.

By nine in the morning I had to be at the police court for an hour and make a brief history of the squabbles of the night before. . . . Each day's evidence was substantially a duplicate of the evidence of the day before, therefore the daily performance was killingly monotonous and wearisome. So far as I could see there was only one man connected with it who found anything like a compensating interest in it, and that was the court interpreter. He was an Englishman who was glibly familiar with 56 Chinese dialects. . . . Next we visited the higher courts and made notes of the decisions which had been rendered the day before. All of the courts came under the head of "regulars." They were sources of reportorial information which never failed. During the rest of the day we raked the town from end to end, gathering such material as we might, wherewith to fill our required column — and if there were no fires to report we started some.

¹ Abridged from pp. 119–120, 123–125 in *The Autobiography of Mark Twain,* edited by Charles Neider. Copyright © 1959 by the Mark Twain Company. Copyright © 1959 by Charles Neider. Reprinted by permission of Harper & Row, Publishers.

² **Ambrose Bierce:** though not as well known as Bret Harte, Ambrose Bierce is highly regarded as a short-story writer. He disappeared in Mexico in 1913.

At night we visited the six theaters, one after the other, seven nights in the week, 365 nights in the year. We remained in each of these places five minutes, got the merest passing glimpse of plays and operas, as the phrase goes. . . .

After having been hard at work from nine or ten in the morning until eleven at night scraping material together, I took the pen and spread this muck out in words and phrases, and made it cover as much acreage as I could. It was fearful drudgery, soulless drudgery, and almost destitute of interest. . . .

In those ancient times the counting room of the *Morning Call* was on the ground floor; the office of the Superintendent of the United States Mint was on the next floor above, with Bret Harte as private secretary of the Superintendent. The quarters of the editorial staff and the reporter were on the third floor, and the composing room on the fourth and final floor. I spent a good deal of time with Bret Harte in his office. . . . Harte was doing a good deal of writing for the *Californian* —contributing "Condensed Novels" and sketches to it and also acting as editor, I think. I was a contributor. So was Charles H. Webb; also Prentiss Mulford; also a young lawyer named Hastings, who gave promise of distinguishing himself in literature some day. Charles Warren Stoddard was a contributor. Ambrose Bierce, who is still writing acceptably for the magazine today [1906], was then employed on some paper in San Francisco — *The Golden Era*, perhaps. We had very good times together — very social and pleasant times.

It was Mr. Swain, Superintendent of the Mint, who discovered Bret Harte. . . . He was a compositor by trade and got work in *The Golden Era* office at ten dollars a week.

Harte was paid for setting type only, but he lightened his labors and entertained himself by contributing literature to the paper, uninvited. The editor and proprietor, Joe Lawrence, never saw Harte's manuscripts, because there weren't any. Harte spun his literature out of his head while at work at the case [of type], and set it up as he spun. *The Golden Era* was ostensibly and ostentatiously a literary paper, but its literature was pretty feeble and sloppy and only exhibited literary forms, without really being literature. Mr. Swain, the Superintendent of the Mint, noticed a new note in that *Golden Era* orchestra — a new and fresh and spirited note that rose above that orchestra's mumbling confusion and was recognizable as music. He asked Joe Lawrence who the performer was and Lawrence told him.

It seemed to Mr. Swain a shame that Harte should be wasting himself in such a place and on such a pittance so he took him away, made him his private secretary on a good salary, with little or nothing to do, and told him to follow his own bent and develop his talent. Harte was willing and development began.

9. The City Condemned

If the city was dramatized by novelists as a source of excitement and opportunity, it was roundly condemned by moralizers and social critics as a place of temptation and degradation. One of the strongest denunciations came from the pen of the Reverend Josiah Strong, General Secretary of the Evangelical Alliance for the United States, in a book entitled Our Country *(1886). As is clear in the excerpt given below, Strong viewed the city as a sink of corruption, a haven for undesirable foreigners, and a breeding ground for such evils as Catholicism, socialism, alcoholism, and bossism. Attacks like these, stemming from bigotry and moral blindness, clouded the real issues and delayed productive analysis of the city's problems.*

The second selection is also critical. In it Joseph Rice, who in 1892 visited schools in 36 cities on assignment for Forum *magazine, gives a discouraging report on the urban education of the time.* ∎

A. SINK OF CORRUPTION[1]

✦ *Josiah Strong*

The city has become a serious menace to our civilization . . . . It has a peculiar attraction for the immigrant. Our 50 principal cities in 1880 contained 39.3 per cent of our entire German population and

[1] Reprinted by permission of the publishers from *Our Country* by Josiah Strong, edited by Jurgen Herbst (Cambridge, Mass.: The Belknap Press of Harvard University Press, copyright 1963 by the President and Fellows of Harvard University), pp. 172–174, 176, 181–182.

45.8 per cent of the Irish. Because our cities are so largely foreign, Romanism[2] finds in them its chief strength.

For the same reason, the saloon, together with the intemperance and the liquor power it represents, is multiplied in the city. East of the Mississippi there was, in 1880, one saloon to every 438 of the population; in Boston, one to every 329; in Cleveland, one to every 192; in Chicago, one to every 179; in New York, one to every 171; in Cincinnati, one to every 124. Of course the demoralizing and pauperizing power of the saloons and their debauching influence in politics increase with their numerical strength.

Richer Rich and Poorer Poor

It is the city where wealth is massed; and here are the tangible evidences of it piled many stories high. Here the sway of Mammon[3] is widest, and his worship the most constant and eager. Here are luxuries gathered — everything that dazzles the eye or tempts the appetite; here is the most extravagant expenditure. Here, also, is the *congestion* of wealth the severest. Dives and Lazarus[4] are brought face to face; here, in sharp contrast, are the ennui of surfeit and the desperation of starvation. The rich are richer and the poor are poorer in the city than elsewhere; and, as a rule, the greater the city, the greater are the riches of the rich and the poverty of the poor. Not only does the proportion of the poor increase with the growth of the city, but their condition becomes more wretched. The poor of a city of 8000 inhabitants are well-off compared to many in New York. . . .

Socialism centers in the city, and the materials of its growth are multiplied with the growth of the city. Here is heaped the social dynamite; here roughs, gamblers, thieves, robbers, lawless and desperate men of all sorts congregate; men who are ready on any pretext to raise riots for the purpose of destruction and plunder; here gather foreigners and wage-workers who are especially susceptible to socialist arguments; here skepticism and irreligion abound; here inequality is

---

[2] **Romanism:** Roman Catholicism. Strong devotes a chapter in the book to the threat supposedly presented by the Catholic Church to the "fundamental principles of our free institutions." He also attacked the Mormon religion for its despotism.

[3] **Mammon:** personification of riches as an evil spirit.

[4] **Dives and Lazarus:** the rich man and the beggar in the story from the New Testament.

the greatest and most obvious, and the contrast between opulence and penury the most striking; here is suffering the sorest. As the greatest wickedness in the world is to be found not among the cannibals of some far-off coast but in Christian lands where the light of truth is diffused and rejected, so the utmost depth of wretchedness exists not among savages who have few wants, but in great cities, where, in the presence of plenty and of every luxury, men starve. Let a man become the owner of a home, and he is much less susceptible to socialistic propaganda. But real estate is so high in the city that it is almost impossible for a wage-worker to become a householder. In 1888 the Health Department of New York made a census which revealed the fact that there were then in the city 32,390 tenement houses, occupied by 237,972 families and 1,093,701 souls. . . .

Government by the Unfit

It is commonly acknowledged that the government of large cities in the United States is a failure. "In all the great American cities there is today as clearly defined a ruling class as in the most aristocratic countries in the world. Its members carry wards in their pockets, make up slates for nominating conventions, distribute offices as they bargain together, and — though they toil not, neither do they spin — wear the best of raiment and spend money lavishly. They are men of power, whose favor the ambitious must court, and whose vengeance he must avoid. Who are these men? The wise, the good, the learned — men who have earned the confidence of their fellow citizens by the purity of their lives, the splendor of their talents, their probity in public trusts, their deep study of the problems of government? No; they are gamblers, saloonkeepers, pugilists, or worse, who have made a trade of controlling votes and of buying and selling offices and official acts."[5] It has come to this, that holding a municipal office in a large city almost impeaches a man's character. Known integrity and competency hopelessly incapacitate a man for any office in the gift of a city rabble. In a certain western city, the administration of the mayor had convinced good citizens that he gave constant aid and comfort to gamblers, thieves, saloonkeepers, and all the worst elements of society. He became a candidate for a second term. The prominent men and press of both parties and the ministry of all denominations united in a Citizens' League to defeat him, but he was

[5] Henry George, *Progress and Poverty* (New York, 1879), p. 480.

triumphantly returned to office by the "lewd fellows of the baser sort." And again, after a desperate struggle on the part of the better elements to defeat him, he was re-elected to a third term of office. . . .

Destructive Elements Multiplied

As a rule, our largest cities are the worst governed. It is natural, therefore, to infer that, as our cities grow larger and more dangerous, the government will become more corrupt, and control will pass more completely into the hands of those who themselves need to be controlled. If we would appreciate the significance of these facts and tendencies, we must bear in mind that the disproportionate growth of the city is undoubtedly to continue, and the number of great cities to be largely increased. . . . When the public lands are all taken, immigration . . . will continue and will crowd the cities more and more. This country will undoubtedly have a population of several hundred millions, for the simple reason that it is capable of sustaining that number. And it looks as if the larger proportion of it would be urban. . . . the city of the future will be more crowded than that of today because the elevator makes it possible to build, as it were, one city above another. Thus is our civilization multiplying and focalizing the elements of anarchy and destruction. Nearly forty years ago De Tocqueville wrote: "I look upon the size of certain American cities, and especially upon the nature of their population, as a real danger which threatens the security of the democratic republics of the New World."

B. THE SCHOOLS INDICTED[6]

✦ *Joseph M. Rice*

The elements that exert an influence on the condition of the schools of every city are four in number: the public at large, the board óf education, the superintendent and his staff, and the teachers.

First, the public at large. As to the attitude of the public toward the schools, it must unfortunately be said that in the large majority

[6] Joseph M. Rice, *The Public School System of the United States* (New York: Century Publishing Company, 1893), pp. 10–11, 13–15, 38, 40, 65, 80, 98, 170, 221, 230.

of instances the people take absolutely no active interest in their schools. . . . It is indeed incomprehensible that so many loving mothers whose greatest care appears to be the welfare of their children are willing, without hesitation, to resign the fate of their little ones to the tender mercies of ward politicians, who, in many instances have no scruples in placing the children in classrooms the atmosphere of which is not fit for human beings to breathe, and in charge of teachers who treat them with a degree of severity that borders on barbarism.

Second, the boards of education. These boards are selected according to whims. . . . In some cities the board of education is formed by two or three distinct bodies, each of which is so constituted that while it has enough independent power to create a considerable amount of mischief on its own account, it is nevertheless sufficiently dependent on the others to be able to prove that the latter are at fault when anything goes amiss. . . .

Third, the superintendent and his staff. The office of the superintendent is, in my opinion, one the importance of which cannot be overestimated. . . . As a rule, however, superintendents do not remain long in any one place, and this is particularly true of the smaller cities. They frequently, for political or other reasons, fail to be reappointed, or they accept other positions by reason of higher salaries. By reason of these changes the schools of many cities are always in a transitional stage, never reaching any distinctive character. . . .

Last, the teachers. This is, after all, the greatest problem. . . . Indeed the professional weakness of the American teacher is the greatest sore spot of the American schools.

And once a teacher is appointed, her position, in many cities, is secure. The office of teacher in the average American school is perhaps the only one in the world that can be retained indefinitely in spite of the grossest negligence and incompetency.

In describing the schools of our cities, I begin with the discussion of the schools of New York City because they represent a condition that may be regarded, in many respects, as typical of the schools of all of our large cities.

In reading, the word method is followed. The pupils are taught to read the number of words prescribed for the grade and no more, and they are taught to spell the words as they learn to read them. . . .

By the use of this method the child is prevented from exercising his reasoning faculties and reading is actually converted into a pure and simple process of memorizing word-forms. In New York City the primary reading is, as a rule, so poor that the children are scarcely able to recognize new words at sight at the end of the school year. Even the third-year reading is miserable. . . .

The public schools of Buffalo, like those of Baltimore, belong, in my opinion, to the mechanical order of schools. By mechanical schools I mean, . . . those schools that aim to cram the minds of children with words without regard to the things they represent, with abstract ideas without regard to the concrete, and where, in consequence, the instruction appeals to the mechanical memory rather than to the reasoning faculties.

The schools of Cincinnati are, in my opinion, upon much the same level as those of Buffalo and Baltimore. . . .

But there are a number of things besides mechanical methods that serve to render miserable the lives of the children attending the public schools of Cincinnati. The child requires air and sunshine, but a large number of the buildings are dark and gloomy, and in many of them the laws of health are otherwise ignored, the classrooms being overcrowded and poorly ventilated. And, to cap the climax, corporal punishment is still used to a disgraceful extent in the public schools of Cincinnati. This does not include incidental punishments, such as pulling the hair or the ears of the pupils, or pinching their cheeks.

The fact that the child is a child is entirely forgotten, and the characteristic feature of St. Louis schools — absolute lack of sympathy for the child — ensues. The unkindly spirit of the teacher is strikingly apparent; the pupils, being completely subjugated to her will, are silent and motionless; the spiritual atmosphere of the classroom is damp and chilly. . . .

In the public schools of Chicago I found the instruction, in general, so unscientific that in judging them by the minimum requirement I should regard their standard as very low. In the lowest primary grade the work is particularly dry and mechanical. There is not even a recess to break the monotony. Owing to lack of accommodation in the rapidly growing districts, a number of the primaries have been converted into half-day schools, some of the pupils attending in the morning, while others attend in the afternoon. In some of the half-day schools the pupils do not even [learn arithmetic] during the first six months, all their time being devoted to reading and writing. . . .

Although the schools of the cities I have just mentioned differ to a considerable extent in regard to details, they do not vary much, in my opinion, in their general excellence. In all of them the vast majority of the teachers lack in professional spirit, and the instruction, regardless of subject, is in the main purely mechanical. . . .

It was because I deemed it my duty to direct the attention of the public primarily to those children who are most grievously wronged, and consequently to the school most urgently in need of reform, that I was led to devote so much space to the discussion of such schools as are a disgrace to an enlightened nation.

10. A Noble Domination[1]

✦ Adna F. Weber

Despite the arraignments of critics like Josiah Strong and the very real problems of urban life, some observers continued to be optimistic. To Adna Weber, social scientist, statistician, and author of the classic Growth of Cities in the Nineteenth Century *(1899), the city was the source and the hope of civilization. Even Weber's appraisal of urban education conflicts with that of Joseph Rice given in the previous selection. Weber's historical overview leads him to see the city as the "great differentiator," an agent for change, both good and bad, of the individual and of society.* ■

Urban vs. Rural Schools

. . . As regards education, it must be obvious that an agglomeration is more favorable than its dispersion can be. In fact, one would naturally turn to the cities and towns for the best schools, since they alone can afford to provide the expensive advantages incident to the grading of pupils and the division of labor educationally. It is not surprising, therefore, that the urban schools of the United States have 190 class days per annum and the rural schools only 115; and that the attendance in the city is 70 per cent of the enrollment, while in

[1] Adna F. Weber, *The Growth of Cities in the Nineteenth Century* (New York: Columbia University Press by The Macmillan Company, 1899), pp. 397–398, 439–443.

the country it is 62 per cent. Moreover, the statistics of illiteracy in the United States are favorable to the cities, notwithstanding the reception by the cities of the bulk of illiterate foreigners.

With very few exceptions (New York City, Pittsburgh, Cleveland, Detroit), the cities have a better educated population than the rest of the state in which they are situated. . . . There can be no doubt about the superiority of the city schools, both primary and secondary. Educators in fact now recognize the inferiority of rural schools as one of their most pressing problems. . . .

But the education of the schools forms only a part of a man's education. Their discipline must be supplemented by outside reading and experience; alone it too often promotes superficiality. And this is the peculiar danger of urban habits of life. The city boy is taught to read but not to think; the result is seen in the immense constituency of "yellow journalism." . . .

The Spectroscope of Society

Henry George puts the case against city growth in its worst light when he says that "just as the wen or tumor, drawing the wholesome juice of the body into its vortex, impoverishes all other parts of the frame, so does the crowding of human beings in the city impoverish human life in the country. The unnatural life of the great cities means an equally unnatural life in the country."

What, if any, are the benefits secured to the entire social body in compensation for these evil effects of concentration of population upon the life of the nonurban population? And is there no advantage to the villages themselves?

Economically, . . . the concentration of large masses of people upon small areas at once multiplies human wants and furnishes the means of their satisfaction; and the benefits are communicated to the surrounding country, which finds in the cities a market for its production and a stimulus to the diversification of the same.

Socially, the influence of the cities is similarly exerted in favor of liberal and progressive thought. The variety of occupation, interests, and opinions in the city produces an intellectual friction which leads to a broader and freer judgment and a great inclination to and appreciation of new thoughts, manners, and ideals. City life may not have produced genius, but it has brought thinkers into touch with one another and has stimulated the divine impulse to originate by sympathy or antagonism. As the seat of political power, as the nursery of the arts and sciences, as the center of industry and commerce, the city represents the highest achievements of political, intellectual, and industrial life. The rural population is not merely conservative; it is full of error and prejudice; it receives what enlightenment it possesses from the city. . . .

It is emphatically true that the growth of cities not only increases a nation's economic power and energy, but quickens the national pulse. In the present age, the influence of the cities is perhaps not so strong in the direction of the noblest thought and culture because the present age is essentially materialistic. But there is some reason for believing that materialism is gradually giving way before humanitarianism. . . .

The city is the spectroscope of society; it analyzes and sifts the population, separating and classifying the diverse elements. The entire progress of civilization is a process of differentiation, and the city is the greatest differentiator. The mediocrity of the country is transformed by the city into the highest talent or the lowest criminal. Genius is often born in the country, but it is brought to light and developed by the city. On the other hand, the opportunities of the city work just as powerfully in the opposite direction upon the countrymen of an ignoble cast; the boy thief of the village becomes the daring bank robber of the metropolis.

Taking this view of the cities as the central instruments of the process of differentiation, we shall be able to reconcile the differences of those who regard the cities as "ulcers on the body politics" (Jefferson) and those who place them at the apex of civilization. The fact that the cities make the opinions, fashions, and ideals of mankind rests upon the vastness of opportunity that they afford. But it is clear that opportunity to do good and become great involves opportunity to accomplish evil, that is, temptation. . . . A progressive or dynamic civilization implies the good and bad alike. The cities, as the foci of progress, inevitably contain both good and bad. . . .

IV. Into the Twentieth Century

In 1893 the elaborate Columbian Exposition commemorating the four-hundredth anniversary of Columbus's discovery of the New World opened in Chicago. Its gleaming buildings and its scientific and cultural exhibits symbolized the pride, excitement, and optimism of the nation on the threshold of the twentieth century. Most people saw the coming era as a time when the new technology, together with hard work and good will, would make urban life a pleasure for all.

Visionary city planners like Daniel Burnham, architect of the Exposition, hoped to provide an impressive and inspiring physical setting. Social reformers like Jane Addams would elevate the minds and souls of city-dwellers. Political leaders would bring an end, once and for all, to municipal corruption. And a determined band of zealots guaranteed that the moral tone of the whole country would be improved if the manufacture and sale of alcohol were banned by a constitutional amendment.

But a succession of events upset the plans of the doers and the dreamers. The gasoline-powered vehicle, mass-produced by Henry Ford and others, revolutionized every aspect of American life, both expanding and fragmenting the city. A severe economic depression cut deeper and lasted longer than anyone had expected it could. Millions of Negroes fled poverty and degradation in the rural South only to find more of the same in cities of North and South. And finally, a second world war, which the nation had tried to avoid, came to absorb its total energies for four years.

Viewed from the vantage point of the present, the period from 1900 to 1945 might be considered as a kind of seedtime for the urban crises which exploded through the nation in the 1960's and the 1970's.

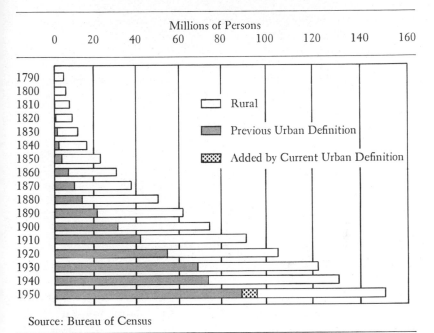

Millions of Persons

Source: Bureau of Census

From its beginning the nation has moved steadily away from a rural-agricultural way of life toward a predominantly urban, industrialized culture.

1. Great Urban Disasters

When natural disasters occur in crowded, built-up areas, the amount of death and destruction they cause is many times greater than it would be in rural areas. Early in the twentieth century catastrophes struck two American cities, one a hurricane-produced flood and the other a major earthquake. Each city's response to disaster was determined in part by its existing political structure.

In 1901 when Galveston, Texas, was inundated, the municipal government proved inadequate to deal with the situation and was soon after changed, the mayor and city council being replaced by an elected commission with full administrative and legislative powers. Reformers, always on the lookout for more efficient methods of city management, were impressed, and within a decade a hundred of the country's second-rank cities had adopted the "Galveston Plan." The calamity which brought about this innovation is described in the first selection. The flood caused a greater loss of life than any other disaster which has occurred in the United States: the death toll was 5000.

A few years later, a larger American city faced an equally terrible situation. In April, 1906, San Francisco was hit by an earthquake followed by great fires. In all 700 died, 490 city blocks were destroyed, 2593 acres were burned out, and 216,000 people evacuated. To keep order, a "Committee of Fifty" was formed; it in turn created subcommittees to deal with specific problems. The second selection is an eyewitness account of the quake and its aftermath. ■

A. THE GALVESTON FLOOD[1]

✤ Paul Lester

One of the most awful tragedies of modern times has visited Galveston. The city is in ruins, and the dead will number many thousands. I[2] am just from the city, having been commissioned by the Mayor and Citizens' Committee to get in touch with the outside world and appeal for help. Houston was the nearest point at which working telegraph instruments could be found, the wires as well as nearly all the buildings between here and the Gulf of Mexico being wrecked.

When I left Galveston, the people were organizing for prompt burial of the dead, distribution of food, and all necessary work after a period of disaster.

The wreck of Galveston was brought about by a tempest so terrible that no words can adequately describe its intensity, and by a flood which turned the city into a raging sea. The Weather Bureau records show that the wind attained a velocity of 84 miles an hour when the measuring instrument blew away, so it is impossible to tell what the maximum was.

The storm began at two o'clock Saturday morning. Previous to that a great storm had been raging in the Gulf, and the tide was very high. The wind at first came from the north, and was in direct opposition to the force from the Gulf. Where the storm in the Gulf piled the water up on the beach side of the city, the north wind piled the water from the bay onto the bay part of the city.

---

[1] Paul Lester, *The Great Galveston Disaster* (Philadelphia: Globe Bible Publishing Co., 1900), pp. 32–36, 37, 46, 65, 67 *passim*.

[2] I: Richard Spillane, editor of the *Galveston Tribune*.

About noon it became evident that the city was going to be visited with disaster. Hundreds of residences along the beach front were hurriedly abandoned, the families fleeing to dwellings in higher portions of the city. Every home was opened to the refugees, black or white. The wind was so fierce that the rain cut like a knife.

By three o'clock the waters of the Gulf and bay met, and by dark the entire city was submerged. The flooding of the electric light plant and the gas plants left the city in darkness. To go upon the streets was to court death. The wind was then at cyclonic velocity, roofs, cisterns, portions of buildings, telegraph poles, and walls were falling, and the noise of the wind and the crashing of buildings were terrifying in the extreme. The wind and waters rose steadily from dark until 1:45 o'clock Sunday morning. During all this time the people of Galveston were like rats in a trap. The highest portion of the city was four to five feet under water, while in the great majority of cases the streets were submerged to a depth of ten feet. To leave a house was to drown. To remain was to court death in the wreckage.

Such a night of agony has seldom been equaled. Without apparent reason the waters suddenly began to subside at 1:45 A.M. Within twenty minutes they had gone down two feet, and before daylight the streets were practically freed of the flood waters. . . .

Catalogue of Destruction

Very few if any buildings escaped injury. There is hardly a habitable dry house in the city. . . .

The whole of the business front for three blocks in from the Gulf was stripped of every vestige of habitation, the dwellings, the great bathing establishments, the Olympia, and every structure having been either carried out to sea or its ruins piled in a pyramid far into the town, according to the vagaries of the tempest. The first hurried glance over the city showed that the largest structures, supposed to be the most substantially built, suffered the most.

The Orphans' Home, Twenty-first Street and Avenue M, fell like a house of cards. How many dead children and refugees are in the ruins cannot be ascertained. Of the sick in St. Mary's Infirmary, together with the attendants, only eight are understood to have been saved. The Old Women's Home, on Roosenburg Avenue, collapsed, and Roosenburg School is a mass of wreckage. The Ball High School is but an empty shell, crushed and broken. Every church in the city, with possibly one or two exceptions, is in ruins.

At the forts nearly all the soldiers are reported dead, they having been in temporary quarters which gave them no protection against the tempest of flood. . . .

The bay front from end to end is in ruins. Nothing but piling and the wreck of great warehouses remain. The elevators lost all their superstructures, and their stocks are damaged by water. The life-saving station at Fort Point was carried away, the crew being swept across the bay fourteen miles to Texas City. . . .

The shore at Texas City contains enough wreckage to rebuild a city. Eight persons who were swept across the bay during the storm were picked up there alive. . . . In addition to the living and dead which the storm cast up at Texas City, caskets and coffins from one of the cemeteries at Galveston were being fished out of the water there yesterday. In the business portion of the city two large brick buildings . . . collapsed. . . .

The cotton mills, the bagging factory, the gas works, the electric light works, and nearly all the industrial establishments of the city are either wrecked or crippled. The flood left a slime about one inch deep over the whole city, and unless fast progress is made in burying corpses and carcasses of animals, there is danger of pestilence.

It will take a week to tabulate the dead and the missing and to get anything near an approximate idea of the monetary loss. It is safe to assume that one half the property of the city is wiped out and that one half of the residents have to face absolute poverty.

Looting, Profiteering, and Disorder

G. W. Ware, teacher of penmanship in a Dallas educational institution, was in Galveston during the hurricane. He reached Dallas on Tuesday, the 11th, and made the following statement:

> It was a godsend, the placing of the city under martial law. The criminal element began looting the dead, and the cold-blooded commercial element began looting the living. The criminals were stealing anything they could with safety lay hands on, and the mercenary commercial pirates began a harvest of extortion. The price of bacon was pushed up to 50 cents a pound, bread 60 cents a loaf, and owners of small schooners and other sailing craft formed a trust and charged eight dollars a passenger for transportation across the bay from the island to the mainland.

Mayor Jones and other men of conscience were shocked at these proceedings, and the Mayor decided that the only protection for the citizens would be to declare martial law, confiscate all foodstuffs and other necessities for the common good, and thus stop the lootings and holdups.

The price of bread was reduced to 10 cents a loaf, bacon was placed at 15 cents a pound, and the price of a voyage across the bay was set at $1.50 a passenger. . . .

The situation has gotten beyond the control of the authorities. The powers in control have been quarreling. Last night at seven o'clock every citizen soldier under the command of Major Fayling was called in, disarmed, and mustered out of service. Chief of Police Ketchum then took charge, and the Major was relieved of his command. During an hour and a half the city was unguarded. . . .

As the Major's work was unusually brilliant, the citizens are furious. This morning the situation from the police standpoint is improved. A hundred of the state militia . . . have arrived. They are patrolling the west end of the city. . . .

At a meeting of the Relief Committee held this morning reports were received from the various wards. The chairman called for armed men to assist in getting labor to bury the dead and clear the wreckage, and arrangements were made to supply this demand. The situation in the city today is that there are plenty of volunteers for this service, but an insufficiency of arms. There have been two or three small riots, but the officers have managed to quell them. The committee rejected the proposition of trying to pay for work, letting the laborers secure their own rations. It was decided to go ahead impressing men into service, if necessary, issuing orders for rations only to those who worked or were unable to work.

All of the ward chairmen reported the imperative need of disinfectants. A committee was appointed to sequester all the disinfectants. . . .

No liquor is permitted to be sold under any circumstances, unless ordered by the chairman of one of the committees or by a physician. . . . All persons not having business on the streets after dark must be identified before they will be allowed to pass. . . . No person is allowed to work in or about any building unless he has a written permit signed by the Chief of Police or Deputy Chief. No person is permitted to carry furniture or other property through the streets unless he has a written permit from the proper authority. No gambling is permitted, and violations of this rule are prosecuted to the fullest extent.

✤ James B. Stetson

On the morning of April 18th at 5:15 I was awakened by a very severe shock of earthquake. The shaking was so violent that it nearly threw me out of bed. It threw down a large bookcase in my [bedroom] and broke the glass front; another bookcase fell across the floor. The bric-a-brac was thrown from the mantel and tables, and strewed the floor with broken china and glass. It is said to have lasted 28 seconds, but as nearly as I can estimate the violent part was only about 12 seconds.

As soon as it was over, I got up and went to the window, and saw the street filled with a white dust, which was caused by the falling of St. Luke's stone church on the diagonal corner from my room. I waited for the dust to settle, and I then saw the damage which had been done to Claus Spreckels' house and the church. The chimneys of the Spreckels mansion were gone, the stone balustrade and carved work were wrecked. The roof and the points of the gables and ornamental stonework of the church had fallen, covering the sidewalk and lying piled up against the sides of the building to the depth of eight or ten feet. . . .

I then started on foot downtown; no cars were running on any line. The sidewalks in many places were heaved up, chimneys thrown down, and walls cracked. I went on California Street, over Nob Hill, and as I got in sight of the business part of the city, I saw as many as ten or twelve fires in the lower part of the city. When I arrived at California and Montgomery Streets, the lower part of both sides of the former seemed to be all on fire. . . . I next went up to Third Street and found the fire raging strong at the corner of Third and Mission. My son was passing in his automobile, and I got in with him. He said he was going to the Mechanics' Pavilion, where, he said, he could do some work for the temporary hospital established there. When we reached the Pavilion, they said there were 200 wounded inside. We went around to drugstores and hardware stores to get hot-water bags and oil and alcohol stoves and surgeons'

[2] James B. Stetson, *San Francisco During the Eventful Days of April, 1906. Personal Recollections* (San Francisco: The Murdock Press, 1906), pp. 3–5, 7–11, 13–14, 18–23.

appliances. We took with us Miss Sarah Fry, an ex-Salvation Army woman, who was energetic and enthusiastic. When we arrived at a drugstore under the St. Nicholas, she jumped out, and, finding the door locked, seized a chair and . . . smashed the glass doors and helped herself to . . . anything which would be useful in an emergency hospital. . . .

At eleven o'clock I found myself in the Pacific Union Club with a cup of coffee and a sandwich. I went out from the club and saw the fire raging on Market Street below Sansome, halfway between First and Second. . . . About this time I went into the Western Union Telegraph office, and while writing a telegram [I heard the announcement] that no more telegrams would be received. I then walked home, and at that time the streets leading to Lafayette Square and the Presidio[3] were filled with people dragging trunks and valises along, trying to find a place of safety. They generally landed in the Presidio.

As night came on the fire made it as light as day, and I could read without other light in any part of the house. At eight in the evening I went downtown to see the situation. . . . The fire was then burning the eastern half of the Occidental Hotel and the Postal Telegraph Company's office and other buildings adjoining. . . . I next went to Pine and Dupont Streets, and from that point could see that the Hall of Justice and all the buildings in that vicinity were on fire. Very few people were on the street. I came back to my house at 9:30. . . . I felt tired and went to bed at 11 P.M. and slept until 2:30 A.M. I got up and went downtown again to see what the situation was. . . . The St. Francis [Hotel] was on fire. I went from Pine and Mason to California and Mason. From there I could see that old St. Mary's Church and Grace Cathedral were on fire. To the north Chinatown was in a whirlpool of fire. I returned home on California Street and Van Ness Avenue. Both streets were thronged with men, women, and children — some with bundles, packages, and baby carriages; but the usual method was to drag a trunk, which made a harsh, scraping noise on the sidewalk. I overtook a man dragging a trunk with a valise on top which kept . . . falling off. As I approached him I took the valise in my hand and with the other took hold of the rope and helped him drag the heavy trunk. As we were strangers, I am sure that he at first took me for a thief who intended to steal the valise. I at once entered into conversation with him, and from his manner later on I

---

[3] **the Presidio:** fort established by the Spanish in 1776.

think he changed his mind, for when I left him a few blocks away he was hearty in his thanks. . . .

At three o'clock the soldiers drove the people north on Van Ness and west up Franklin Street, saying that they were going to dynamite the east side of Van Ness. From my window I watched the movements of the firefighters and dynamiters. They first set fire to every house on the east side of Van Ness Avenue between Washington and Bush Streets, and by 3:30 nearly every one was on fire. Their method was this: A soldier with a vessel . . . containing some inflammable stuff, would enter the house, climb to the second floor, open it, pull down the shade and curtain, and set fire to the contents of his dish. In a short time the shades and curtains would be in a blaze. . . . At about this time they began dynamiting. This was called backfiring, and as the line of fire was at Polk Street, the idea was to meet the flames and not allow them to cross Van Ness Avenue. The explosions of dynamite were felt fearfully in my house. . . .

I afterwards walked down into the business part of the city. The streets in many places were filled with debris — in some places . . . to the depth of four feet in the middle of the street and much greater depth on the sidewalk. I found it then, and ever since, very difficult to locate myself when wandering in the ruins and in the rebuilt district, as all the old landmarks are gone and the only guide often is a prominent ruin in the distance.

The water supply in our house was gone, as was also the gas and electric light. The only light we could use was candlelight, and that only until 9 P.M. The city authorities issued an order that no fires could be built in any house until the chimneys were fully rebuilt and inspected by an officer. The water we used was brought by my son in a washboiler in his automobile. He got it out near the Park. People all cooked on improvised kitchens made in the street. Our doorbell was rung several evenings, and we were ordered to "put out that light." . . .

The afternoon after the fire had exhausted itself the atmosphere was hot, the great beds of coals gave out heat and glowed brightly at night. The more I see of this desolation, the worse it looks. The front of my house was blistered and blackened by the intense heat, and over two of the windows it hung like drapery. The telegraph and telephone wires made a network on every street, and for more than two weeks I carried in my pocket a pair of wire cutters, which I had often occasion to use.

On May 3rd we were able to buy food. Up to that time we obtained what we needed from the Relief Committee, such as canned
meats, potatoes, coffee, crackers, etc. Bread we were able to buy after
a few days. . . .

Being busy in the work of restoration, I forget what a terrible calamity has befallen the city and the people, but I sometimes realize
it and it comes like a shock. I find that people lost the power of
keeping time and dates, and if I had not made notes at the time I
would be unable to recollect the events of these three days with any
degree of accuracy.

The feeding of 300,000 people suddenly made destitute is a matter
of great difficulty, but it has been done. It rained two nights — one
night quite hard — but the health of the people has been remarkably
good.

We got water in the house on the 1st of May, gas on the 5th of
June, electric light on the 7th of June, and cooked on the street until
the 8th of May.

2. Recreation for the Young[1]

✤ *Jane Addams*

*The surge of industrialization and the tremendous increase in
city populations both intensified urban problems and spurred
efforts to do something about them. Movements directed toward
social and political reform multiplied; civic leagues, boards, and
commissions took up specific issues and causes; innovative individuals outlined theories and strategies.*

*Perhaps the best-known social reformer of the period was Jane
Addams (1860–1935), who founded Chicago's first settlement
house. In Hull-House and outside it, Miss Addams constantly
worked to improve the life of children and protect them from the
evils of the city. Excerpts from her book* The Spirit of Youth
and the City Streets (1909) *reveal Jane Addams' remarkable
empathy with the young as well as a typical reformer's concern
over vice.* ■

[1] Jane Addams, *The Spirit of Youth and the City Streets* (New York: The
Macmillan Company, 1909), pp. 4–7, 75–76, 95–97, 102–103. Reprinted by
permission.

The classical city promoted play with careful solicitude, building the theater and the stadium as it built the market place and the temple. The Greeks held their games so integral a part of religion and patriotism that they came to expect from their poets the highest utterances at the very moments when the sense of pleasure released the national life. In the medieval city the knights held their tourneys, the guilds their pageants, the people their dances, and the church made festival for its most cherished saints with gay street processions. . . . Only in the modern city have men concluded that it is no longer necessary for the municipality to provide for the insatiable desire for play. In so far as they have acted upon this conclusion, they have entered upon a most difficult and dangerous experiment; and this at the very moment when the city has become distinctly industrial, and the daily labor is continually more monotonous and subdivided. We forget how new the modern city is, and how short the span of time in which we have assumed that we can eliminate public provision for recreation.

Youth's Love of Pleasure Exploited

A further difficulty lies in the fact that this industrialism has gathered together multitudes of eager young creatures from all quarters of the earth as a labor supply for all the countless factories and workshops upon which the present industrial city is based. Never before in civilization have such numbers of young girls been suddenly released from the protection of home and permitted to walk unattended upon city streets and to work under alien roofs; for the first time they are being prized more for their labor power than for their innocence, their tender beauty. . . . Never before have such numbers of young boys earned money independently of the family life, and felt themselves free to spend it as they choose in the midst of vice deliberately disguised as pleasure.

This stupid experiment of organizing work and failing to organize play has, of course, brought about a fine revenge. The love of pleasure will not be denied, and when it has been turned into all sorts of malignant and vicious appetites, then we, the middle aged, grow quite distracted and resort to all sorts of restrictive measure. . . .

Quite as one set of men has organized the young people into industrial enterprises in order to profit from their toil, so another set of men and also of women, I am sorry to say, have entered the neglected field of recreation and have organized enterprises which make profit out of this invisible love of pleasure.

In every city arise so-called "places" — "gin-places," they are called in fiction; in Chicago we . . . say merely "places" — in which alcohol is dispensed, not to allay thirst, but, ostensibly, to stimulate gaiety; it is sold really in order to empty pockets. Huge dance halls are opened to which hundreds of young people are attracted, many of whom stand wistfully outside a roped circle, for it requires five cents to procure within it for five minutes the sense of allurement and intoxication which is sold in lieu of innocent pleasure. . . . We see thousands of girls walking up and down the streets on a pleasant evening with no chance to catch a sight of pleasure even through a lighted window, save as these lurid places provide it. Apparently the modern city sees in these girls only two possibilities, both of them commercial: first, a chance to utilize by day their new and tender labor power in its factories and shops, and then another chance in the evening to extract from them their petty wages by pandering to their love of pleasure.

As these overworked girls stream along the street, the rest of us see only the self-conscious walk, the giggling speech, the preposterous clothing. And yet through the huge hat, with its wilderness of bedraggled feathers, the girl announces to the world that she is there. She demands attention to the fact of her existence, she states that she is ready to live, to take her place in the world. . . .

The young creatures themselves piteously look all about them in order to find an adequate means of expression for their most precious message. One day a serious young man came to Hull-House with his pretty young sister who, he explained, wanted to go somewhere every single evening. . . . In the difficult role of elder brother, he had done his best, stating that he had taken her "to all the missions in the neighborhood, that she had had a chance to listen to some awful good sermons and to some elegant hymns, but that she did not seem to care for the society of the best Christian people. . . ."

But quite as the modern city wastes this most valuable moment in the life of the girl and drives into all sorts of absurd and obscure expressions her love and yearning . . . so it often drives the boy into gambling and drinking in order to find his adventure. . . .

One of the most pathetic sights in the public dance halls of Chicago is the number of young men, obviously honest young fellows from the country, who stand about vainly hoping to make the acquaintance of some "nice girl." ...

One Sunday night at twelve o'clock I had occasion to go into a large public dance hall. . . . a young man approached me and quite simply asked me to introduce him to some "nice girl". . . . On my replying that a public dance hall was not the best place in which to look for a nice girl, he said: "But I don't know any other place where there is a chance to meet any kind of a girl. I'm awfully lonesome since I came to Chicago." ... He was voicing the "bitter loneliness" that many city men remember to have experienced during the first years after they had "come up to town." ...

Perhaps never before have the pleasure of the young and the mature become so definitely separated as in the modern city. The public dance halls filled with frivolous and irresponsible young people in a feverish search for pleasure are but a sorry substitute for the old dances on the village green in which all of the older people of the village participated. Chaperonage was not then a social duty but natural and inevitable, and the whole courtship period was guarded by the conventions and restraint which were taken as a matter of course and had developed through years of publicity and simple propriety. . . .

The City's Responsibility to Provide Recreation

We cannot afford to be ungenerous to the city in which we live without suffering the penalty which the lack of fair interpretation always entails. Let us know the modern city in its weakness and wickedness, and then seek to rectify and purify it until it shall be free at least from the grosser temptations which now beset the young people who are living in its tenement houses and working in its factories. The mass of these young people are possessed of good intentions and they are equipped with a certain understanding of city life. This itself could be made a most valuable social instrument toward securing innocent recreation and better social organization. They are already serving the city in so far as it is honeycombed with mutual benefit societies, with "pleasure clubs," with organizations connected with churches and factories which are filling a genuine social need. And yet the whole apparatus for supplying pleasure is wretchedly inadequate and full of danger to whosoever may approach it.

"Going to the show" for thousands of young people in every industrial city is the only possible road to the realms of mystery and romance; the theater is the only place where they can satisfy that craving for a conception of life higher than that which the actual world offers them. The theater becomes to them a "veritable house of dreams," infinitely more real than the noisy streets and the crowded factories. . . .

Well-considered public games easily carried out in a park or athletic field might both fill the mind with the imaginative material constantly supplied by the theater, and also afford the activity which the cramped muscles of the town-dweller so sorely need. . . .

Already some American cities are making a beginning toward more adequate public recreation. . . . Chicago has seventeen parks with playing fields, gymnasiums, and baths, which at present enroll thousands of young people. These same parks are provided with beautiful halls which are used for many purposes, rent free, and are given over to any group of young people who wish to conduct dancing parties subject to city supervision and chaperonage. . . .

Let us cherish these experiments as the most precious beginnings of an attempt to supply the recreational needs of our industrial cities. To fail to provide the recreation of youth is not only to deprive all of them of their natural form of expression, but is certain to subject some of them to the overwhelming temptation of illicit and soul-destroying pleasure.

3. Cleaning Up the Air[1]

✤ Civic League of St. Louis

Another serious problem resulting from industrialization was the contamination of the urban environment by coal dust and soot. In the days when soft coal was widely used, air pollution was in some respects more obnoxious than it is today. Billowing black smoke often blotted out the sun, and in some cities street lights had to be turned on in the early afternoon. The smoke nuisance, as it was known, was partially reduced by the introduction of bituminous or hard coal and by the substitution of electric for steam power. Cleaning up the air required the mobilization of public opinion. Toward that end the following report from the St. Louis Civic League was directed. ■

[1] The Civic League of St. Louis, *The Smoke Nuisance; Report of the Smoke Abatement Committee of the Civic League* (St. Louis, 1906), pp. 4, 7, 28, 31–32.

It does not require the testimony of an expert to convince the people of St. Louis that the smoke nuisance has by no means been satisfactorily abated. The dense clouds of smoke that daily hang over the city, the layers of soot that filter into office, parlor, and sleeping rooms, the throat irritation due directly to the sulfur fumes in the smoke-laden air, the injured trees and plants, the soiled linen, and the damaged merchandise are all good and sufficient evidence of the continued prevalence of this exasperating nuisance.

The assertion has been made that a considerable portion of the smoke in this city comes across the river from East St. Louis and that any effort to reduce it to a minimum must prove futile until East St. Louis sees fit to adopt and enforce rigid smoke regulations. The Committee questioned this statement at the outset of the investigation, and members visited the roofs of various high office buildings to make observations on this point. It is the judgment of the Committee that this assertion is inaccurate and that a safe estimate of the amount of smoke received from East St. Louis, even when the winds are favorable, does not exceed 10 per cent of the total amount produced on this side of the river.

While there is a considerable quantity of smoke blown across the river at times, the smoke in this city is primarily the product of St. Louis' boiler plants and furnaces and would be practically as much of a nuisance if no city existed on the other side of the Mississippi.

The task before the Committee has, however, been not to determine the amount of smoke produced in St. Louis, but rather to find an answer, if possible, to the constant inquiry why the nuisance continues to exist and what are the remedies for it.

The citizen who is interested in the general improvement of urban conditions naturally asks the question, "Is there to be no permanent solution of the smoke nuisance in our cities? Must it necessarily be a constant conflict between the city and the smoke-maker? And is the 'City Beautiful' of the future to be enveloped in a cloud of smoke or a coating of soot?" The answer of the defiant smoke-maker would no doubt be in the affirmative, but the student of heat and power production takes a more optimistic view of the situation as he looks more deeply into the rapid development in the production and utilization of heat and power for domestic, manufacturing, and transportation purposes. . . .

These rapid changes are leading to one end — the centralization of power development and distribution. They point to the time, and at no distant day, when great central plants will be located at the various mine centers, and the electric power will be transmitted and distributed to railroads, industrial plants, cities, and the various institutions where electrical energy is needed. The great railroads will operate their trains by electricity, and the passengers will be freed from the annoyance of smoke and cinders; and the railroad locomotives and the railroad yards which are now the most unsightly places in our cities will become comparatively clean and free from smoke. Furthermore, the introduction of cheaper electric power will displace the scores of smoke-belching chimneys and the befogged atmosphere of our cities will be cleared and the city clean and comfortable will become a reality and not a dream.

But this optimistic view of the future solution of the smoke problem does not relieve the present insufferable nuisance. Whatever may be the industrial and economic changes in the next ten or twenty years which will of themselves eliminate smoke, the average citizen is more deeply interested in immediate relief from the damages inflicted by the clouds of free carbon and sulfur which fill the air in this city, and the only immediate solution which will be really effective is the adoption and rigid enforcement of a broad and comprehensive ordinance similar to the one attached to this report.

4. "Where Can a Man Get a Drink in This Town?"[1]

✤ Herbert Asbury

For decades reformers of another sort had been agitating for legislation outlawing the use of liquor in the United States. In 1917 they succeeded. Congress passed the Eighteenth Amendment, which was ratified by the states in 1919 and became law in 1920. Thus began the so-called "noble experiment," forbidding the manufacture and sale of alcoholic beverages throughout the country. No more did brightly lit bars and saloons welcome the

[1] Herbert Asbury, "The Noble Experiment of Izzy and Moe," in Isabel Leighton, *The Aspirin Age, 1919–1941* (New York: copyright © 1949 by Simon & Schuster), pp. 35–39, 45–48. Reprinted by permission of Simon & Schuster, Inc.

passerby. They were replaced by the blacked-out speakeasy, into which one slipped furtively and only if properly identified.

The noble experiment was a failure: man's thirst could not be legislated out of existence. In 1933 Congress approved the Twenty-first Amendment, which called for the repeal of the Eighteenth. While prohibition lasted, enforcing this unpopular law challenged the best efforts of the authorities, and a corps of agents was sent out to gather evidence on the lawbreakers. The most famous of these "detectives" were probably Izzy and Moe, whose antics were described in Herbert Asbury in an article appearing in Isabel Leighton's The Aspirin Age, 1919–1941. ■

Probably no one ever looked less like a detective than Izzy Einstein. He was forty years old, almost bald, five feet and five inches tall, and weighed 225 pounds. Most of this poundage was around his middle, so that when he walked his noble paunch, gently wobbling, moved majestically ahead like the breast of an overfed pouter pigeon. . . .

Izzy's first assignment was to clean up a place in Brooklyn which the enforcement authorities shrewdly suspected housed a speakeasy, since drunken men had been seen staggering from the building, and the air for half a block around was redolent with the fumes of beer and whiskey. . . . Izzy knew nothing of sleuthing procedures; he simply walked up to the joint and knocked on the door. A peephole was opened, and a hoarse voice demanded to know who was there.

"Izzy Einstein," said Izzy, "I want a drink."

"Oh, yeah? Who sent you here, bud? What's your business?"

"My boss sent me," Izzy explained. "I'm a prohibition agent. I just got appointed."

The door swung open and the doorman slapped Izzy jovially on the back. "Ho! ho!" he cried. "Come right in, bud. That's the best gag I've heard yet."

Izzy stepped into a room where half a dozen men were drinking at a small makeshift bar.

"Hey, boss!" the doorman yelled. "Here's a prohibition agent wants a drink! You got a badge, too, bud?"

"Sure I have," said Izzy, and produced it.

"Well, I'll be . . . ," said the man behind the bar. "Looks just like the real thing."

He poured a slug of whiskey, and Izzy downed it. That was a mistake, for when the time came to make the pinch Izzy had no evidence. He tried to grab the bottle, but the bartender ran out the back door with it.

"I learned right there," said Izzy, "that a slug of hooch in an agent's belly might feel good, but it ain't evidence." . . .

Izzy used his original device of giving his real name, with some variation, more than twenty times during the next five years. It was successful even after he became so well known, and so greatly feared, that his picture hung behind the bar in many speakeasies, that all might see and be warned. Occasionally Izzy would prance into a gin-mill with his badge pinned to his lapel, in plain sight, and shout jovially, "How about a drink for a hard-working prohibition agent?" Seeing the round little man trying so hard to be funny, everyone in the place would rush forward to hand him something alcoholic, and Izzy would arrest them and close the joint. . . .

After Izzy had been an enforcement agent for a few weeks, he began to miss his old friend Moe Smith, with whom he had spent many pleasant evenings in the East Side coffeehouses. . . . Moe had been a cigar salesman and manager of a small fight club at Orchard and Grand Streets, New York City, and had invested his savings in a little cigar store, where he was doing well. Izzy persuaded him to put a relative in charge of the store and to apply for a job as enforcement agent. . . .

. . . As soon as he was sworn in as an agent, he and Izzy teamed up together and most of the time thereafter worked as a pair. . . .

For more than five years the whole country laughed at the antics of Izzy and Moe, with the exception of the ardent drys, who thought the boys were wonderful, and the bootleggers and speakeasy proprietors, who thought they were crazy and feared them mightily. And their fear was justified, for in their comparatively brief career Izzy and Moe confiscated five million bottles of booze, worth $15,000,000, besides thousands of gallons in kegs and barrels and hundreds of stills and breweries. They smashed an enormous quantity of saloon fixtures and equipment and made 4392 arrests, of which more than 95 per cent resulted in convictions. No other two agents even approached this record. . . .

On one of his swings around the so-called enforcement circuit, Izzy made up a sort of schedule showing the length of time it took him to get a drink in various cities. New Orleans won first prize, a

(*Continued on page* 178)

The urban policeman's lot changes with the times. Above left, an officer, pikestaff in hand, walks a cobbled beat in the New York of 1693. Below, a determined constable in the 19th century mold pursues a young thief through a city crowd. Severe condemnation awaited those guilty of the most minor offenses.

The early 20th century demanded mechanization of the force, and one result was the use of the "prowl car," such as that in operation in St. Louis in 1920 (above). Later in the century, the great increase in urban crime and social tension caused many cities to initiate programs for improving police-community relations. The Los Angeles Police Department staffed a camp for boys (below).

four-star hiss from the Anti-Saloon League. When Izzy arrived in the Crescent City, he climbed into an ancient taxicab, and as the machine got under way he asked the driver where he could get a drink.

"Right here, suh," said the driver, and pulled out a bottle. "Fo' bits."

Time — thirty-five seconds.

In Pittsburgh, disguised as a Polish millworker, Izzy bought a drink of terrible whiskey in eleven minutes. Just seventeen minutes after he got off the train in Atlanta, he walked into a confectionery shop on Peachtree Street, bought a drink, and arrested the proprietor. In Chicago he bought a drink in twenty-one minutes without leaving the railroad station, and duplicated this feat in St. Louis. In Cleveland it took twenty-nine minutes, but that was because an usher in a vaudeville theater, who had offered to take him to a speakeasy, couldn't leave his job right away. In Baltimore, Izzy got on a trolley car and asked the conductor where he could find a speakeasy. "In the next block," the conductor replied. Time, fifteen minutes. It took longer in Washington than anywhere else; Izzy roamed the city for a whole hour before he could locate a gin-mill. He finally had to ask a policeman, who provided him with the necessary directions. . . .

5. Municipal Reform: Two Approaches

A major target for reformers in the early part of the century was municipal inefficiency and corruption. Often their efforts in this direction were frustrated by outmoded charters granted by state governments in a simpler age. In many communities, moves to gain "home rule" were launched and new types of administration adopted. Some municipalities chose the nonpartisan form of government, others the city manager system. By the 1920's several hundred of the latter were in operation.

Reform governments were disappointingly short lived. Elected officials who adhered to a rigidly nonpolitical, moralistic line found that they built up little popular support. Representative of this group was Rudolph Blankenburg, a German immigrant elected mayor of Philadelphia on a reform ticket in 1911. The "Old Dutch Cleanser's" administration was notable for honest and efficient administration, especially with regard to public

*works. But it held on for just one term. One of the causes for
its failure was Blankenburg's insistence on adhering to nonpartisanship, as expressed in the speech excerpted below.*

*A quite different kind of reformer was the flamboyant Fiorello
La Guardia, mayor of New York in 1934–1935. La Guardia
managed to combine a zeal for constructive change with sophisticated political techniques. He ran the city like a personal fiefdom and exhibited a remarkable skill for transforming his own
pet peeves into targets for citizen action. The speech below illustrates the La Guardia method for persuading the public to adopt
a voluntary program of noise abatement.* ■

A. THE RATIONAL WAY[1]

✦ Rudolph Blankenburg

. . . It has ever been my conviction that one of the weakest links in
governmental progression of our country and in the sociological development of the Republic is the confused, irrational, and improvident conduct of city business, almost universally prevalent.

The government of our municipalities, large and small, should be
on an honest, efficient, business basis, nonpolitical, nonpartisan, nonsectarian; not of bosses nor by classes, but for the masses. . . .

If a newly elected chief magistrate of city, state, or nation selects
members of his cabinet from defeated rivals, he is apt to make a mistake that will haunt him throughout the term of his office. A disappointed candidate may nurse his sore until it will break out when
least expected and most hurtful. He had better be disappointed by
never being appointed.

After my election I had offers in many quarters from those willing
to sacrifice themselves upon the altar of public office. Some were
based upon political, others upon personal grounds, and strange to say,
not one was based upon the ground of the desire and ability to give
service. . . . The pressure was great until I openly declared: "I will
no more permit you to select the members of my cabinet for me

[1] Address by Mayor Rudolph Blankenburg at the Annual Dinner of the Pennsylvania Society of New York, December 11, 1915, quoted in Lucretia Blankenburg, *The Blankenburgs of Philadelphia* (Philadelphia: John C. Winston Company, 1929).

than I would permit you to select a wife for me were I unmarried."

That settled it, and the result was the appointment of official advisers whose superiors it would be difficult to find. Everyone was told, "You have entire control over your department. The responsibility is yours. Come and consult me whenever you wish; but for results I look to you. Responsibility placed upon individual shoulders will accomplish what divided authority generally fails to do."

The government of a city should be divorced from politics; if not, politics are apt to rule the municipality six days a week. As the seventh, commonly called the sabbath, is a legal holiday, there would be scant time to devote to public work. Politics would thrive, public business come to grief.

Philadelphia awoke from its lethargy four years ago, as New York did two years ago; the results of this awakening are before us. Neither city will permanently go back to the old quagmire of political corruption, though a desperate, dying gasp for restoration to power of the old gang may be temporarily successful.

To me the ballot is the most sacred and precious secular privilege. The voter who deliberately neglects to exercise the right of an American freeman, who fails to cast his ballot without proper excuse, should for repeated offense be deprived of his citizenship. He should be made the companion of the man without a country. Then he would realize what American citizenship means and learn to appreciate it.

The cornerstones of city government should be:

Absolute elimination of partisan politics.

Business administration, clean, progressive, constructive.

Fitness, not for party service, first consideration for appointment to office.

Public place free from traders in politics and the influence of the money power that claims "The dollar can't be wrong."

A hundred cents return for every dollar expended.

All contracts to the lowest responsible and not to the highest "responsive" bidder.

Strict adherence to the merit system in the Civil Service.

Adequate care for the city's dependents.

Sound education, combined with moral, physical, technical, and civic training for our children.

Plenty of playgrounds and other breathing places for the poor.

Builded upon such a rock, any incorporated municipality, which really means any cooperative corporation in which all citizens, men, women, and children, are shareholders, should prosper and benefit all alike. If a municipal corporation suffers from lack of interest on the part of many of its shareholders, it will retrograde. If it suffers from a chronic misconception of its purposes on the part of many others, it is sure to become the victim and to fall into the hands of men always eager to take advantage of the lack of public spirit among their fellows.

Honest and efficient municipal government, once established, will leave its mark, and as good municipal government is the main foundation of good state and national government, we are doubly derelict if we fail in our civic duties. . . .

Let us . . . dedicate ourselves by giving the best there is in us to the service of city, state, and nation.

And this service should commence right at home; for woe to the city whose wealth and affluence rise while its citizenship declines! Ours must not be a loose-jointed, but a firmly knit democracy, so it may serve as a bright example to the rest of mankind.

B. PERSON TO PERSON [2]

✤ *Fiorello H. La Guardia*

. . . I am speaking from my desk in City Hall in what is going to be a heart-to-heart chat. I should like to be telling you what I have to say sitting in your living room.

You probably have noticed that during the past six weeks there has been quite a bit in newspapers about noise abatement and the efforts being made to bring about the elimination of unnecessary noises. We have arranged an elaborate campaign of education, which we hope will bring about the accomplishment of our purposes, but boiled down everything we have in mind can be accomplished without any fuss and difficulty if everyone, in a spirit of cooperation, courtesy, and neighborliness, thinks twice before causing any kind of noise which might grate in the ears of the other fellow. . . .

[2] Press release of radio address delivered by Mayor Fiorello H. La Guardia, September 30, 1935.

My purpose in this talk is not to attempt to tell you all the sounds we would like to eliminate. I should like, however, to touch on several noise nuisances regarding which we get the most complaints. One is the unnecessary use of strident automobile horns.

In England the use of automobile horns has virtually been eliminated. The results have been so good that there is no demand from any quarter for their return. Automobile accidents, fatalities, and injuries have been reduced to an appreciable extent merely because the campaign against horns there has caused drivers to drive more carefully. . . .

Official statistics show that over a period of five months from April 1st to September 1st, 1935, there were 17 per cent fewer deaths and 7 per cent fewer injuries than in the same period of 1934 before the ban on horns was invoked. In that period of 1934 England had 3117 deaths and 110,400 injuries. In the same period of 1935 England had 2580 deaths and 102,902 injuries. . . .

In addition to automobile horns, the outstanding sources of complaints are noisy cabarets in residential districts, roisterous singing and talking by their occupants after leaving cabarets, street hucksters, and the use of loudspeakers by some store for advertising purposes.

We plan to curb all these noise nuisances. Police Commissioner Valentine is keeping a rigid watch on all cabarets which now have licenses to operate in residential zones. No further licenses for this type of place are being issued. Impromptu quartets on street corners and carousing groups in the early hours of the morning will find hostile audiences in patrolmen on beat. Street hucksters and newspaper vendors will have to advertise their wares more moderately and considerately. The use of amplifiers for advertising purposes in stores will be stringently controlled and loudspeakers from radio stores will be permitted only at reasonable hours and in the event of a great emergency or an extremely popular public event.

Imported customs, such as serenading under windows, will be taboo. I don't know how that will affect cats in backyards because I am afraid they won't be susceptible to our publicity. We will ask the Health Department to attend to that. Warnings will be given to people who prefer honking their horns to attract someone's attention . . . to quietly ringing a doorbell.

The response to this appeal for co-operation in the Noise Abatement Campaign has been tremendous. About 150 large organizations reaching into every walk of life are actively taking part. I want to take this opportunity to thank those who have so willingly come forward. Among them are department stores, milk companies, large chain stores, radio companies, newsreels, newspapers, civic organizations, settlement houses, various chambers of commerce, medical societies, engineering societies, educational authorities, large industrial stores, as well as countless individuals who are helping.

Noise abatement drives are under way among employees and members of all these organizations. Posters, stickers, leaflets, and other forms giving the message on noise abatement to you citizens are being prepared and distributed.

But all of these elaborate arrangements will be of no avail unless we all make up our minds to do our share in our own particular pursuit.

We are very anxious not to bring hardship to anyone in effecting noise abatement. We have no desire to add to the many restrictions upon motorists already in effect. But if need be, we will pass ordinances making it easier for the police to cope with habitual offenders. . . .

My friends, this campaign is very much in earnest and if you had read as many complaints as I have about noise you would realize how serious it is to a great many people. I am going to do now what I have never done before since becoming mayor; I am going to read to you an official proclamation on noise abatement.

The proclamation relates only to the month of October, but we do not plan to stop then nor will we restrict noise abatement to the hours mentioned. "Noiseless Nights" will be followed by "Noiseless Days." Eventually we hope to have "Noiseless Twenty-four Hours." The proclamation follows:

Whereas, New York City is a city of seven million people, most of them living in close proximity to each other, and

Whereas, in a city of seven million people teeming with the hustle and bustle of industry and life, there must of necessity be noise, and

Whereas, each one at some time or another has annoyed or more seriously harmed by discordant sounds which could have been avoided, and

Whereas, there is much noise which can with very little effort be avoided, and

Whereas, there are always among us sick and feeble persons, seriously affected by unnecessary noise, and

Whereas, the city administration has undertaken an intensive campaign of education to bring about the abatement of all unnecessary noise, because it is of the opinion that the health of our people is of paramount importance, and

Whereas, such noise abatement efforts have resulted favorably in cities abroad by bringing about a reduction in traffic accidents through more careful driving necessitated by a minimum use of automobile horns, and

Whereas, the police commissioner has instructed all men of his department to issue warnings to all persons causing unnecessary noise, and

Whereas, leading business, civic, social, and professional organizations have indicated for their memberships a desire to cooperate fully in bringing about noise abatement,

Now, therefore, I, F. H. La Guardia, Mayor of the City of New York, do hereby designate and proclaim the hours between 11:00 P.M. and 7:00 A.M. during the month of October as a period in which all citizens of the City of New York shall refrain, in a spirit of cooperation, courtesy, and neighborliness from making any noise which might interfere with the peace and quiet of other citizens as far as is humanly possible.

6. The City Planning Movement

The "Great White City" of the 1893 Chicago World's Fair provided the impetus for organized city planning in the United States. The director of works for the Fair was Daniel H. Burnham, who became the recognized leader of the movement. Burnham, a world-renowned architect, devised city plans for Washington, D.C. (1902), Cleveland (1903), San Francisco (1904), and in 1909 presented his grand design for Chicago. The Chicago Improvement Plan, over which Burnham and his associates had labored for years, was accepted in 1910 and became — with some deviation — the basis for the city's development over the next half century. It is discussed in the first excerpt that follows. Chicago and other already existing cities formed impressive plans to control future development, correct old mistakes and problems resulting from haphazard growth, and beautify their appear-

ance. *Another type of planning was concerned with the creation of towns from the ground up. Usually these were residential communities, such as Shaker Heights, Ohio, described in the second excerpt.* ∎

A. THE PLAN OF CHICAGO[1]

♣ Daniel H. Burnham and Edward H. Bennett

Burnham's plan for Chicago embodied his convictions on civic improvement and his dream of a great city, the "most attractive town in the world." His friend the architect Charles McKim said that the Chicago Plan was greater than all Burnham's monuments put together. It was a comprehensive, even grandiose, vision, but as Burnham himself said: "Make no little plans; they have no magic to stir men's blood and probably themselves will not be realized. Make big plans; aim high in hope and work, remembering that a noble, logical diagram once recorded will never die, but long after we are gone will be a living thing, asserting itself with ever-growing insistency. Remember that our sons and grandsons are going to do things that would stagger us. Let your watchword be order and your beacon beauty."[2] ∎

Needs of a Great Metropolis

Chicago, in common with other great cities, realizes that the time has come to bring order out of chaos incident to rapid growth, and especially to the influx of people of many nationalities without common traditions or habits of life. . . .

To many who have given little consideration to the subject, a plan seems to call for large expenditures and a consequent increase in taxation. The reverse is the case. It is certain that civic improvement will go on at an accelerated rate; and if those improvements shall be marshaled according to a well-ordered plan great saving must result.

---

[1] Charles Moore, *Daniel H. Burnham, Architect, Planner of Cities* (Boston: Houghton Mifflin Company; copyright 1921 by Charles Moore), p. 147.

[2] Daniel H. Burnham and Edward H. Bennett, *Plan of Chicago*, ed. by Charles Moore. Prepared under the direction of the Commercial Club of Chicago, 1909, pp. 1, 4, 32–33.

Good order and convenience are not expensive; but haphazard and ill-considered projects invariably result in extravagance and wastefulness. . . .

The plan frankly takes into consideration the fact that the American city, and Chicago pre-eminently, is a center of industry and traffic. Therefore attention is given to the betterment of commercial facilities; to methods of transportation for persons and for goods; to removing obstacles which prevent or obstruct circulation; and to the increase of convenience. It is realized, also, that good workmanship requires a large degree of comfort on the part of the workers in their homes and their surroundings, and ample opportunity for that rest and recreation without which all work becomes drudgery. Then, too, the city has a dignity to be maintained; and good order is essential to material advancement. Consequently, the plan provides for impressive groupings of public buildings, and reciprocal relations among such groups. Moreover, consideration is given to the fact that in all probability Chicago, within the lifetime of persons now living, will become a greater city than any existing at the present time; and that therefore the most comprehensive plans of today will need to be supplemented in a not remote future. Opportunity for such expansion is provided for. . . .

The growth of the city has been so rapid that it has been impossible for the economical disposition of the great influx of people, surging like a human tide to spread itself wherever opportunity for profitable labor offered place. Thoughtful people are appalled at the results of progress; at the waste in time, strength, and money which congestion in city streets begets; at the toll of lives taken by disease when sanitary precautions are neglected; and at the frequent outbreaks against law and order which result from narrow and pleasureless lives. So that while the keynote of the nineteenth century was expansion, we of the twentieth century find that our dominant idea is conservation. The people of Chicago have ceased to be impressed by rapid growth or the great size of the city. What they insist [on] asking now is, How are we living? Are we in reality prosperous? Is the city a convenient place for business? Is it a good labor market in the sense that labor is sufficiently comfortable to be efficient and content? Will the coming generation be able to stand the nervous strain of city life? When [sufficient means] have been accumulated, must we go elsewhere to enjoy the fruits of independence? If the city does not become better as it becomes bigger, shall not the defects be remedied?

These are questions that will not be brushed aside. They are the most pressing questions of our day, and everywhere men are anxiously seeking the answers . . .

An Example of Burnham's Vision[3]

At the southern end of the Lake Front will begin the Shore Drive, which, going above the Illinois Central Railway to the Lake, will extend over a stone bridge of the old Roman pattern to the first great outer concourse, and thence south seven and a half miles, to the lower end of Jackson Park. This avenue should be reached from the land by seven viaducts, each passing over the Illinois Central [Railroad] and extending to a broad concourse of the great driveway itself. These viaducts should be built of stone, and between the arches should be abutments continuing upward, until they become pedestals on the parapets, on which pedestals should be statues and vases. The piers of the viaducts might be planted with clinging vines, which would emphasize and adorn the strong masonry.

The driveway itself should be protected by a sea-wall, designed to express dignity as well as to afford security. Behind it should be a broad terrace. . . . Next this wall should be a space, planted with tall shrubs, disposed partly to conceal and partly to reveal the lake. . . . Beside the drive, on the west of it, should be another terrace, with here and there old Greek resting-places, some curved into the banks, out of which should flow fountains of water. The floor of this walk and the recesses of it should be paved with small colored pebbles in geometrical patterns. The wall itself, which is to be next west of the walk, should be built of long slivers of sparkling stone, like those encircling the Roosevelt farms that skirt along the Hudson, north of Poughkeepsie. . . .

The concourse where the viaducts end should be treated in a monumental manner. There are seven of them in all, including those at each end of the Drive. . . .

A river bank six miles long, with trees, bays, and islands, is not a great enough project to accomplish the end we have in view, namely: to make the most attractive possible waterway and parkway ever known to man. If we stop with the water, the islands, and the planting, we shall have done only a half-hearted thing, which I do not

---

[3] Charles Moore, *Daniel H. Burnham, Architect, Planner of Cities, Vol. II* (Boston: Houghton Mifflin Company, copyright 1921 by Charles Moore), pp. 106–108.

believe will bring about the change in the life of Chicago that we are after. Could I have twenty to thirty millions of dollars to spend on great monuments, terraces, landing places, and sculptured objects, along the shore between the Drive and the Lagoon, I might be able to accomplish for the scheme what I now look for the residences . . . to bring about. . . . If we make a residence portion two hundred or three hundred feet wide, between the Drive and the Lagoon, and hold the owners to certain rules when building, then they will produce an effect far finer than any one designer could lay out.

B.   SHAKER HEIGHTS: FOR THE FORTUNATE FEW[4]

✤ Fred C. Kelly

> *The Van Sweringen brothers, Oris Paxton and Mantis James, are best known for the rise and fall of their Nickel Plate Railroad empire. Few people realize that they were also the creators of one of the country's more expensive suburbs. In 1906 the brothers bought a huge tract of land east of Cleveland and proceeded to lay out a development of elliptical boulevards and broad, parklike avenues, on which stood beautiful houses set well back from the street. As the Van Sweringens had intended, Shaker Heights became a very desirable residential community.* ∎

Nine or ten years ago [1906], two brothers, unassuming chaps in their twenties, O. P. and M. J. Van Sweringen by name — strolled into an open stretch of country at the edge of Cleveland, Ohio, and saw a vision.

All that the eye could see was a thinly wooded expanse of vacant land, once occupied by a colony of Shakers,[5] and lying well out of the line of transportation development. But these young Van Sweringens beheld there the future fashionable residence section of the city.

---

[4] Fred C. Kelly, "Two Young Men Who Are Real Estate Marvels," in *American Magazine*, Vol. 83, No. 3 (March, 1917), pp. 50–51.

[5] **Shakers:** a communistic religious sect with settlements scattered throughout the eastern United States; so called from the body movements which form part of their service.

The Van Sweringens set about trying to make their vision come true. What they needed was money, and so they conferred with financiers. They were assured that the land was too far from the city and reminded that there was no streetcar line, or even a road for automobiles. When they answered that they would build these, it was pointed out that no city person would want to live out so far.

"My idea," explained one of the young men, "is to build a few high-priced homes and offer them at so much less than cost to the people of the right sort that they will be irresistible. In that way we'll get the place pioneered. Once it is started the rest will not be difficult. We'll provide big automobile vans to take the children of our settlers to the nearest school and deliver them back home again each noon and evening."

The Van Sweringen imagination won the day. In an astonishingly short period, these mere boys had laid out more than four thousand acres, or the greater part of two townships, in a high-grade residence allotment; built and endowed several streetcar lines; given to the city several hundred acres of public parks; built miles of winding boulevards; made millions of dollars' worth of homes spring from vacant lands.

Within three or four years after they had glimpsed their vision in the stretch of uninhabited land, that land had become the fashionable residence locality of their city.

Some time ago the Van Sweringens arranged for a private right of way from their allotment down into the heart of Cleveland. This would cut to one third the time required to reach their property, making it just as accessible as the nearest allotments to the downtown, and at the same time as clean and free from downtown turmoil as those farthest away. . . .

In laying out boulevards and car lines, one of the Van Sweringens prepared for the day when traffic would be so thick that there would be a demand for overhead crossings. People laughed and said he was looking ahead about a thousand years. But he had enough vision to see what the automobile would do, and already one overhead crossing in his big allotment has become a reality. The boulevards are arranged so that when it becomes essential to have an overhead crossing it can be done with the least possible expense and trouble. Van Sweringen worked out this little detail of the general scheme and attached no particular importance to it. One day he learned that the idea had been copied in Germany.

Instead of streets laid out to form blocks in the ordinary fashion, all are in curves, and they cross the car tracks in bunches — thus making the fewest possible number of car stops. These stops are one third of a mile apart, which means an obvious quickening of service as compared to starting and slowing down again every time the car runs the length of an ordinary block.

7. Bohemia: Feeling Free[1]

✤ *Allen Churchill*

Within most large cities of the world there have always been special neighborhoods which draw the people who shape the artistic and intellectual life of a country. Lower living expenses and the free-and-easy atmosphere of areas considered undesirable by the middle and upper classes attract Bohemians — those who disregard conventional rules of behavior. Soon after the turn of the century, Greenwich Village in New York City became a kind of "promised land" for America's artists, intellectuals, reformers, and eccentrics. ■

While the Mabel Dodge Evenings[2] drew the attention of the country to Greenwich Village, the locality itself was well on its way to its first and — by almost unanimous agreement — happiest period as part of what Shakespeare calls "the mythical and fabulous land without seacoast called Bohemia." For this would be the truly creative era in Greenwich Village, a time when it seemed that Villagers were about to change the mores, the artistic standards, and even the political course of the United States.

[1] Allen Churchill, *The Improper Bohemians* (New York: E. P. Dutton, Inc.; Copyright © 1959 by Allen Churchill), pp. 59–66, 68–70. Reprinted with permission of the publishers.
[2] **Mabel Dodge Evenings:** Mrs. Dodge entertained the "most emancipated minds of the time" in her Greenwich Village townhouse.

Picturesque — and Cheap

"It felt free and you could live as you pleased," Max Eastman[3] has said of this Village where everything seemed possible and almost was. Not the least of the inducements offered by the burgeoning Left Bank[4] of New York remained the cheap rents and picturesque houses. A few landlords, noting the advent of the artistically radical young, had made motions toward refurbishing their properties. But they had not — as yet — raised rents, so that for thirty dollars a month it was still possible to rent an entire floor through in an atmospheric, old-fashioned red brick Village house. . . .

What tenants did with such rooms was a highly personal matter. Some went in for quaintness, with floors plainted black and chairs, tables, dressers, and beds made from packing boxes or wood of similarly humble origin. On the other hand, the apartment of the dashing sculptor William Zorach on Tenth Street and Sixth Avenue was ablaze with murals invoking Gauguin.[5] Zorach and his beautiful bobbed-haired wife Marguerite had traveled the South Seas and created quarters like a breath of lush Tahiti opposite the noisome Jefferson Market Court. Every piece of furniture in the Zorach apartment was painted a crude color: yellow, vermilion red, bright orange, purple. A huge flat group depicting Adam and Eve, the evil serpent, and the Tree of Life, all in flaming hues, covered one wall, while on the others were painted tropical foliage and flowers, orange leopards, birds, and other creatures. The pot-bellied stove, a necessary item in any Village apartment of the day, was painted dead white.

. . . Single artists, writers, and deep thinkers were likely to rent individual rooms . . . for sums like eight to twelve dollars a month. Into houses which for nearly fifty years had been thought fit only for immigrants and servants eager young people now poured, to begin a Bohemian existence in surroundings of picturesque decrepitude. Washington Mews and MacDougal Alley, hitherto deemed suitable only for horses, rose to eminence among the desirable localities in the Village. . . .

[3] **Max Eastman:** essayist and poet; author of *The Enjoyment of Laughter.*
[4] **Left Bank:** famed artist and student quarter of Paris left of the Seine River if one looks upstream.
[5] **Gauguin** (go′gan): Paul Gauguin (1848–1903) painted Tahitian scenes in a distinctive style.

To the intense disgust of members of the already entrenched Irish and Italian population, who had all but succeeded in taking over the Village area, these primitive conditions seemed to inspire rather than deter the young hopefuls. So great was the Bohemian influx that slowly the Italians and Irish began to fall back, signaling the beginning of a wary conflict between the groups old and new. To the young Villagers the old population always seemed stupid and backward, while to the foreign-born the artists were in turn eccentric and immoral. . . .

The Lively Liberal Club

By the summer of 1913, the Liberal Club was solidly entrenched as the first important Village landmark. The quarters above Polly's Restaurant on MacDougal Street comprised two large parlors and a sunroom on the first floor . . . with high ceiling, open fireplaces, and magnificent mahogany doors. Liberal Club rooms were furnished sparsely with wooden tables and chairs, but this lack of decoration was more than counteracted by the cubist, futurist, and other colorful types of art on the walls. . . . Every night was party night at the Liberal Club. . . .

On occasion the Liberal Club could be a quiet, reflective place where, as Harry Kemp wrote, "there would always be a glowing fire in the grate and the pervasive warmth would restore me . . . and I could weave fancies of the day when I would be great and famous." But such peaceful intervals were rare. More often than not it was Harry Kemp himself who, beating his manly chest in proud, pre-Hemingway fashion, provided the noise by debating poetry with Vachel Lindsay or Alfred Kreymborg. . . . Or perhaps heavy-set Theodore Dreiser, author of the just-published A *Traveller at Forty*, would be endeavoring to counter the terrier-dog opinions of pale, intense, furiously energetic Upton Sinclair. . . .

Also conspicuous around the Liberal Club was a gangling redhead named Harold Sinclair Lewis. Even then the storytelling gifts of Sinclair "Red" Lewis were exceptional, and he found himself a much admired raconteur in the early Village. . . .

On certain nights the Liberal Club presented one-act plays written and performed by members, and the germ of the eventual Theatre Guild was born in these presentations. In quest of further culture, a wall was broken down between the Club and the Washington Square Book Shop, newly established next door by Albert and Charles Boni

... in theory [this] was ... a smart financial move on the part of the Boni brothers. In practice, though, [it] was a failure. Club members selected books to read, walked back to the club premises, and read them. Then they returned the books to the bookstore, all without paying a cent. ...

With such changes in upstairs regions, Polly's Restaurant inevitably experienced transmutations. Hippolyte Havel [cook and waiter] continued as before, sneering "Bourgeois pigs!" into the faces of trusting diners. But on the yellow calcimined walls of the front dining room there began appearing an overflow of modern art from the Liberal Club exhibits upstairs ...

The Liberal Club, was, of course, kept in almost constant turmoil by its most ardent member. This was still Henrietta Rodman ... with bobbed hair, meal-sack dress, and sandals, who had moved the club downtown. Miss Rodman espoused dress reform, women's suffrage, equal rights for women, and a hundred other feminist causes. ...

To her female [disciples] in the Liberal Club, Henrietta Rodman painted a glowing picture of the New Order for the female sex. "Out of us women will come a great generation of young, free women," she would passionately assert. "These free young women will wear skirts to the knees, or maybe knickerbockers. We girls have achieved much already by discarding corsets and wearing loose clothing, not to mention the trouble of having long, thick hair that brings headaches in the summer. Yes, they laugh at us now, but the day will come when all women will wear their hair short."

8. Auto-mobilized

After industrialization and immigration, the next great city-shaper — and problem-maker — was the automobile. Unrestricted by rails or a fixed power supply, cars soon affected every phase of urban life. Their construction and operation required steel, glass, rubber, and gasoline, among other things. As a result, new industries were formed and established ones greatly expanded. The physical structure of the city was radically altered by the coming of highways and consequent shifts in commercial and residential building patterns.

But *perhaps more important than the economic impact were the social effects. Detroit, the "motor city," was a special case, as is suggested by the somewhat overoptimistic contemporary description below. Los Angeles, the other metropolis discussed, is said to have been actually* created *by the automobile. Of more general significance was the effect on smaller, established communities throughout the country. In cities like "Middletown" (actually Muncie, Indiana), increasing ownership of the automobile produced changes in customs, manners, and morals — in other words, in the American way of life.* ◼

A. DETROIT[1]

♣ R. L. Duffus

There are no two cities in the United States better illustrative of what might be called by cynics the American disease of growth than Los Angeles and Detroit. There are no two cities that differ more in their fundamental reasons for being, in the character of their populations, and in their characteristic moods. . . .

In the instance of Detroit and Los Angeles there are two more or less accidental sources of kinship. One is that each has been able to spread itself over an almost limitless area, with few natural obstacles. The other is that the most rapid growth of each city has been coincident with the almost universal adoption of the automobile and the frantic use thereof. Detroit and Los Angeles are cities on wheels. I would go so far as to say of Detroit that even its buildings somehow give the impression of being parked rather than rooted in the ground. . . . In finding one's way about one looks not so much for street numbers as for license plates.

Motorized cities, with an unlimited supply of easily accessible land at their peripheries, go through unbelievable transformations overnight. . . .

A city growing by jerks, too rapidly for planning, presents a curious pattern. Perhaps one should say absence of pattern or jumble of patterns. Old Detroit, hugging the river, had its slums, its business dis-

[1] R. L. Duffus, "Detroit: Utopia on Wheels." Copyright © 1930 by Harper's Magazine, Inc. Reprinted from the December, 1930, issue of *Harper's Magazine* by permission of the author.

trict, its middle-class residential areas, and its preserves for the aristocracy — the latter within easy horse-and-carriage distance of downtown.
The automobile necessarily worked havoc with this arrangement.
But the automobile with a million and more new inhabitants riding
on the running board shattered it completely. It scrambled it. It
made an omelet of it. As soon as workingmen could afford to buy
motor cars the autocracy of space vanished. Beginning with the downtown section of Woodward Avenue, which may fairly be classified as
Detroit's main stem, one comes at irregular intervals upon the abandoned outposts of a retreating exclusiveness. Some quiet old residential sections were destroyed by retail trade. Others gave way with
the advance of successive waves of newcomers — newcomers on
wheels, who suddenly discovered that it was no longer necessary to
live near their jobs or even near the car lines.

Poles, Negroes, Russian Jews, Italians, Belgians, Hungarians, they
came in big and little waves, got a foothold, edged their fastidious
betters out. Sometimes they encountered resistance and flowed
around it, leaving an island to be conquered at leisure or in some cases
to be left intact. . . .

Detroit has literally no tenement houses and only a few blocks
which could be correctly described as slums. One is shown houses as
good as those of the average smalltown professional man or businessman. They belong to foremen or skilled mechanics. In good times a
man beginning as a sweeper in Mr. Ford's plant[2] may look forward to
owning a house costing five or six thousand dollars. If bad times come
he may be unable to complete his payments; but that is another story.
And this agreeable picture is the result of a happy combination of
level or gently rolling land, the gasoline-propelled vehicle, and industries which demand skilled or semiskilled labor and are able to pay a
fair price for it. . . .

Detroit has bridged the river to Canada; it is preparing to tunnel
under it; it is considering a 35-mile elevated highway over the Grand
Trunk Railway to Pontiac; it has a municipal airport as well as that
laid out by Mr. Ford, and I think it must have more interurban bus
lines than any other city in the country. I do not doubt that Detroit
can adapt itself to any possible development in transportation.

So far our picture of Detroit is one which, if universally studied

---

[2] **Mr. Ford's plant:** Henry Ford (1863–1947) made his first car in 1896 and
founded the Ford Motor Company in 1903. In 1914 his assembly line for the
production of the Model T Ford went into operation.

and believed, might double the population again in considerably less than ten years. We have here, evidently, a kind of gasoline Utopia, at least in the making.

B. LOS ANGELES[3]

✣ Henry Carr

Los Angeles is more than a city; it is a major controversy.

To scornful young sophisticates, we are a hick town populated by Iowans who hold Wednesday night prayer-meetings and shout at revivals. We are told in one breath that we are racketeers drawing the unwary flies into our webs; that we are boobs; that we are crossroads Puritans trying to sock the joy out of life by ringing curfew bells; that we are bawdy proprietors of a modern Sodom and Gomorrah[4] where the population swims naked by moonlight in wicked marble pools and have — as our one important industry — the divorce court. We are at once gold-brick buyers [dupes] and slickers.

Bored young Bohemians from New York tell us that this is the town where nothing ever happens; and the news associations put in extra wires for the reason that Los Angeles is on the front pages more frequently than any other city in the world — with the exception of Washington.

To the literati[5] we seem to be an affliction. We worry the writers of the world to a point of frenzy almost beyond human endurance.

We scarcely recover from the horror of being told that our town is a prostitute, when the next writer turns his ink-stained thumb down on us as being the Old Lady from Dubuque — daring someone to have a good time.

An irate Hearst editor who departed the town in high indignation because we were unable to get excited over a little lost child, said in a poison farewell from the back platform of the train: "This isn't a city; this is a [blasted] conspiracy. It isn't interested in anything except selling vacant lots and cures for consumption."

[3] From the book *Los Angeles, City of Dreams* by Henry Carr. Copyright © 1935 by Henry Carr. Published by D. Appleton and Co., 70 Fifth Avenue, New York.

[4] **Sodom and Gomorrah:** in the Old Testament two ancient cities destroyed for their wickedness (Genesis 18–19).

[5] **literati** (*lit'*uh-*ray'*tye): scholarly or literary people.

What these literary hatcheck boys — giggling over the discovery of cat's fur masquerading as sable — have not realized is that they are missing a great drama.

Los Angeles is an epic — one of the greatest and most significant migrations in the long saga of the Aryan race.[6]

Whether we were sun-worshippers coming here to thaw out [or] real estate subdividers seeking to coax the innocent into our clutches, is a detail without significance. The point is, Los Angeles was a milepost of destiny. It happened because it could not help itself.

It is impossible to describe the business section of Los Angeles. How can one describe a Mulligan stew?

More than anything else, it looks as though Titan in frolicsome mood had picked up a handful of modern and very handsome skyscrapers, moldy old brick shacks, freak cafés built like derby hats . . . thrown them up in the air, and let them come down where they would.

Fifth Avenue is New York. Market Street is San Francisco. Paris is the Champs [Élysées]. Berlin is looking through the Brandenburger Tor down the Linden. Shanghai is the Bund. Peking is the Forbidden City. But there isn't any place that is Los Angeles.

Approximately one thousand correspondents came here for the Olympic Games [in 1932] and they all felt a sacred duty to describe Los Angeles. They all said it was "sprawling." That adjective went sizzling over the cables in just about every language that can be put into words.

Nine out of ten visitors coming to Los Angeles for the first time will mention the drab, uninteresting-looking crowds on the streets and the variegated colors of the buildings. It does not seem quite respectable to them that we should have a limit-height skyscraper painted black and gold like a débutante in an evening gown. We have office buildings that look like Persian palaces, another that looks like an imperial tomb — Spanish, Italian ducal castles — stolid Gibraltars with windows cut in the precipice sides.

On the whole the architecture is pleasing and good; but magnificent and stately office buildings have shabby little ducklings clucking at their feet.

Spilled out over 450 square miles, Los Angeles had too much room to grow. In cities like New York, where the area is restricted and

[6] **Aryan race:** descendants of a prehistoric people who spoke Indo-European; Europeans.

there can be no spread, old buildings are torn to make way for new. The growth of metropolitan Los Angeles was like a child biting a cookie and throwing it down half-eaten to run after another cookie. Each generation has picked up and moved farther out on the level plain.

The residence district is as much a crazy-quilt patchwork as the downtown district. If you ask a native to see the residence part, he will say: "Which residence district?" There are dozens — separated by miles.

There is one district out in San Fernando Valley, 27 miles from the city hall; another on West Adams Street; another at Los Feliz; another in Hollywood — from there it streams down in broad rivers of houses to the sea.

It is impossible to understand Los Angeles unless you realize that it is not a town; it is a lot of towns. For a quarter of a century it has not been safe for the mother of any attractive village to leave it alone in the house; Los Angeles would kidnap it before she got back. The map of Los Angeles looks as though someone had dropped it and the pieces had scattered.

C. MIDDLETOWN[3]

✦ Robert and Helen Lynd

In the 1920's sociologists Robert S. and Helen M. Lynd attempted to capture the essence of an average American city. Muncie, Indiana, estimated population 38,000, was the setting of the study and Middletown *(1929) was the result. In an excerpt from this landmark work, the Lynds discuss some social effects of the automobile on small-city life.* ■

Although lectures, reading, music, and art are strongly intrenched in Middletown's traditions, it is none of these that would first attract the attention of a newcomer watching Middletown at play.

[3] From *Middletown* by Robert S. and Helen Merrell Lynd, copyright, 1929, by Harcourt Brace Jovanovich, Inc.; copyright, 1957, by Robert S. and Helen Merrell Lynd. Reprinted by permission of the publisher.

"Why on earth do you need to study what's changing this country?" said a lifelong resident and shrewd observer of the Middle West. "I can tell you what's happening in just four letters: A-U-T-O!"

In the 1890's the possession of a pony was the wildest flight of a Middletown boy's dream. In 1924 a Bible class teacher in a Middletown school concluded her teaching of the Creation: "And now, children, is there any of these animals that God created that man could have got along without"? One after another of the animals from goat to mosquito was mentioned and for some reason rejected; finally, "The horse!" said one boy triumphantly, and the rest of the class agreed. Ten or twelve years ago a new horse fountain was installed at the corner of the Courthouse square; now it remains dry during most of the blazing heat of a midwestern summer, and no one cares. The "horse culture" of Middletown has almost disappeared.

Nor was the horse culture in all the years of its undisputed sway ever as pervasive a part of the life of Middletown as is the cluster of habits that have grown up overnight around the automobile. . . .

The first real automobile appeared in Middletown in 1900. About 1906 it was estimated that "there are probably 200 in the city and county." At the close of 1923 there were 6221 passenger cars in the city, one for every 6.1 persons, or roughly two for every three families. . . . These cars average a bit over 5000 miles a year. For some of the workers and some of the business class, use of the automobile is a seasonal matter, but the increase in surfaced roads and in closed cars is rapidly making the car a year-round tool for leisure-time as well as getting-a-living activities. As, at the turn of the century, business-class people began to feel apologetic if they did not have a telephone, so ownership of an automobile has now reached the point of being an accepted essential of normal living.

Into the equilibrium of habits which constitutes for each individual some integration in living has come this new habit, upsetting old adjustments, and blasting its way through such accustomed and unquestioned dicta as "Rain or shine, I never miss a Sunday morning at church"; "A high school boy does not need much spending money"; "I don't need exercise, walking to the office keeps me fit"; "I wouldn't think of moving out of town and being so far from my friends"; "Parents ought always to know where their children are." The newcomer is most quickly and amiably incorporated into those regions of behavior in which men are engaged in doing impersonal, matter-of-fact things; much more contested is its advent where emotionally charged sanctions and taboos are concerned. No one questions the use of the auto for transporting groceries, getting to one's place of work or to the golf course, or in place of the porch for "cooling off after supper" on a hot summer evening; however much the activities concerned with getting a living may be altered by the fact that a factory can draw from workmen within a radius of 45 miles, or however much old labor union men resent the intrusion of this new alternate way of spending an evening, these things are hardly major issues. But when auto riding tends to replace the traditional call in the family parlor as a way of approach between the unmarried, "the home is endangered," and all-day Sunday motor trips are a "threat against the church"; it is in the activities concerned with the home and religion that the automobile occasions the greatest emotional conflicts.

Group-sanctioned values are disturbed by the inroads of the automobile upon the family budget. A case in point is the not uncommon practice of mortgaging a home to buy an automobile. . . .

Even food may suffer: "I'll go without food before I'll see us give up the car," said one woman emphatically, and several who were out of work were apparently making precisely this adjustment.

Many families feel that an automobile is justified as an agency holding the family group together, "I never feel as close to my family as when we are all together in the car," said one business-class mother, and one or two spoke of giving up Country Club membership or other recreations to get a car for this reason. . . .

But this centralizing tendency of the automobile may be only a passing phase; sets in the other direction are almost equally prominent. . . . "In the nineties we were all much more together," said another wife. "People brought chairs and cushions out of the house and sat on the lawn evenings. We rolled out a strip of carpet and put cushions on the porch step to take care of the unlimited overflow of neighbors that dropped by. We'd sit out so all evening. The younger couples perhaps would wander off for half an hour to get a soda but come back to join in the informal singing or listen while somebody strummed a mandolin or guitar." . . .

The boys who have cars "step on the gas," and those who haven't cars sometimes steal them: "The desire of youth to step on the gas when it has no machine of its own," said the local press, "is considered responsible for the theft of the greater part of the 154 automobiles stolen from Middletown during the past year."

The threat which the automobile presents to some anxious parents is suggested by the fact that of thirty girls brought before the juvenile court in the twelve months preceding September 1, 1924, charged with "sex crimes," for whom the place where the offense occurred was given in the records, nineteen were listed as having committed the offense in an automobile. Here again the automobile appears to some as an "enemy" of the home and society.

Sharp also, is the resentment aroused by this elbowing new device when it interferes with old-established religious habits. The minister trying to change people's behavior in desired directions through the spoken word must compete against the strong pull of the open road strengthened by endless printed "copy" inciting to travel. If we except the concentrated group pressure of wartime, never perhaps since the days of the camp-meeting have the citizens of this community been subjected to such a powerfully focused stream of habit diffusion. . . . To get the full force of this appeal, one must remember that the nearest lake or hills are one hundred miles from Middletown in either direction and that an afternoon's motoring brings only mile upon mile of level stretches like Middletown itself.

9. Bread Line[1]

✦ *Hugo Johanson*

The twenties gave way to the thirties, prosperity to depression, and the quickened pace of urban growth to the dispirited creep of the bread line. The stock market crash of October, 1929, signaled a general economic collapse; sales and profits declined; thousands of banks failed; and hundreds of thousands of people lost their jobs. The impact of the depression was greatest and its effects most visible in the cities. The following excerpt comes from the account of a man down and out in San Francisco, but his experience could have taken place in any large American city. ■

[1] Hugo Johanson, "Bread Line," *The Atlantic Monthly*, Vol. 158, No. 2 (August, 1936), pp. 164–166, 169–170, 173–174. Copyright © 1936 by The Atlantic Monthly Company, Boston, Mass. Reprinted by permission.

December, 1931

A wet and cold day in December, 1931, I was an active member of the bread line on Ritch Street in San Francisco. The line ahead of me was two thousand strong, and I knew by bitter experience that it would be at least two hours before I could dip into a bowl of waterlogged stew. I was ravenously hungry, friendless, homeless, and far removed from the possibilities of obtaining a job.

It was four o'clock in the morning, and still pitch-dark; when our advance guard appeared and took up its position six abreast outside the municipal kitchen. . . . By six o'clock, when the actual feeding started, the line had reached as far as Folsom Street, when every moment brought its quota of semistarved, shabby, despairing men. In the meantime a second, smaller line was forming, hugging the kitchen wall. This was the dreadful "Lost Battalion." To be eligible there a man had to be of extreme age . . . or else blind, badly crippled, partly paralyzed, or feeble-minded.

At last, after hours of nervous shuffling on the sidewalk, it was my turn to enter the kitchen. From the counter I grabbed a bowl of mush without milk or sugar and a tin cup of coffee likewise without any sweetening. One attendant handed out a spoon, while another tossed slices of bread in the mush, or, if he happened to be a poor marksman, on the floor. Everybody except the badly crippled men, who were furnished benches to sit upon, ate standing up, resting the dishes on narrow boards about five feet from the floor. After a short time the concrete floor became mired with an inch-deep film of spilled mush and coffee. The air was indescribably foul — clammy with vapors from the huge steam cookers, plus the thousand and one stenches of unwashed bodies, dirty clothing, and wet brogans.

I always ended breakfast cursing under my breath, determined never to return, but when it was time for the afternoon handout this twentieth-century inferno found me waiting outside, tail wagging, heart aflutter, anxious to put up with anything, be it ever so filthy and meager.

Well, out on the street again, the fresh air and a pipeful of . . . tobacco jacked up my spirit. It was eight o'clock and time to go to work. In those days I started out convinced that sometime and somewhere a job was bound to turn up. . . . I used to "work" one side of the street a day. First the even numbers and later, returning, the odd ones. Factories, warehouses, retail houses, stores, and restaurants

— wherever a man was likely to be needed, I was present. With hat in hand and lips twisted into what I hoped resembled an engaging smile, I spoke my little piece, affecting a gruff, cheery heartiness. "We ain't takin' on. When we're doin' anything at all, we're layin' off," grumbled elderly shop bosses not unkindly. "Sorry, buddy," or "Can't you read signs?" were other standard signing-off signals. . . .

. . . If one wished to spend the night under a roof, another line-up had to be faced. "Sally" (the Salvation Army) issued bed tickets at its post on Harrison Street at 5 p.m. This time it paid to be well ahead in the line. . . .

The flophouse itself was on Ninth Street, in a two-story building shortly before vacated by the San Francisco *News*. The ground floor was reasonably well heated, but the second floor, a big, barnlike hall, was a veritable icebox. If a lodger couldn't squeeze into the bottom floor, he might as well spend the night walking the streets. Therefore, as soon as the bed tickets were given out, a weird marathon race took place. The disturbance was five blocks, and the swiftest bums had the pick of the place. The inhabitants of the neighborhood took great interest in the spectacle; small boys rooted and the sporting element placed bets on long-legged individuals.

The first to arrive found broken-down, rusty, iron cots. The problem of furnishing bedclothes to so many guests was solved in a surprisingly ingenious way. A rubber mat did the combined duties of mattress, sheets, blankets, and pillow. Undressing was, of course, out of the question. The fashion plates put on all the sweaters and overcoats they had taken off during the race, the remaining poorly dressed majority produced newspapers, which they tied with strings around their chests. If I ventured to take off my shoes, I had to stay awake guarding them, or some poor devil, prowling around after the lights had gone out, his own footgear worn to shreds, would be certain to confiscate them. After a while I used them as a pillow, securing them by tying the laces around my neck.

In less than fifteen minutes the shelter was filled to capacity. Hundreds of men were turned away and forced to sleep in boxcars, doorways, empty packing cases, or else to pound the pavement. . . .

May, 1932

In Sacramento the [work] gang broke up. Some of the men went East; quite a number stopped in the Sacramento Valley to look for work. The hard-earned five dollars burning in their pockets, others went in pursuit of pleasures long denied. San Francisco was my goal, and I reached it late the next day. Covered with soot and dust, tattered, bewhiskered, and hungry, I went to the cheapest hotel I knew, a small disreputable place on the Embarcadero. . . . I had decided not to go near the Skidroad until absolutely forced to. In a pinch the five dollars could be stretched to last two weeks. The budget was not complicated: three dollars for room rent and two dollars for food. . . . I took my meals in the room twice a day. For breakfast I had kippered herring, tap water, and stale bread. At dinner I simply reversed the bill of fare and enjoyed stale bread, tap water, and kippered herring.

During the daylight hours I roamed all over the city looking for work. Hatless, clad in overalls and heavy, hobnailed boots, peaked and hungry-looking, badly in need of a haircut, I must have been a sight. People didn't waste promises or interviews when I turned up. With a few exceptions they gave me the cold shoulder or muttered, "Nothing doing."

When the kippered-herring interlude ended, I returned to the Skidroad and its charity institutions. Before I could eat and sleep as a guest of the city I had to go through a mild third degree in a recently opened registration bureau for unemployed men. The qualifications were a year's residence in San Francisco and a solemn declaration that I had no money in the bank and owned no stocks, bonds, or real estate. I received a meal ticket and a bed card good for seven days. . . . I took my meals in the municipal kitchen on Ritch Street and slept in a flophouse sponsored by the Volunteers of America, 1261 Howard Street, an organization divorced from the Salvation Army and successfully engaged in the second-hand-clothes business with the saving of souls as a sideline. Double-decked bunks were installed to accommodate the ever-increasing number of applicants. The bunks were placed so close together that if an occupant moved his arms a bit carelessly he was bound to hit his neighbors, one on each side, in the face. Naturally the place was swarming with vermin of all descriptions.

By the summer of 1932, I looked at least ten years older. My weight under normal conditions is about 170 pounds. After four months in the bread line I tipped the scales at 125. My ribs protruded like laths, and my lusterless eyes had retreated way back into dark-ringed sockets.

I didn't beg or ransack the garbage cans; nor did I rob or steal.

Instead, I walked about for hours, eyes glued to the sidewalk, looking for lost coins and cigar and cigarette butts. Money I never found; tobacco enough to fill my pipe. . . .

May, 1933

The caring for the jobless had taken a slight turn in the right direction during the winter months. Responsible, thoughtful citizens and the police department had tired of seeing hordes of indigents swarm over the city, poke into the garbage cans, and panhandle on the principal streets. To prevent this, a day shelter was established on Folsom Street. Here we could rest our weary legs, read the day-before-yesterday's newspapers . . . and play cards and chess or checkers. The shelter, a large onetime warehouse, was a decided success. New flophouses sprouted like mushrooms and thrived under somewhat similar conditions, as far as dampness and darkness were concerned. . . .

I ate and slept in the San Francisco bread line and flophouses from the first of May to the first of December, 1933. The five dollars I had earned in the last labor camp came in handy during this period. . . . My total monthly expenses amounted to seventy cents. Thirty cents went for the purchase of a daily loaf of stale bread, at a penny a loaf, the remaining forty cents kept me in tobacco — or, to be more exact, cigar clippings swept off the floor in a tobacco factory. The bread helped to eke out the bread-line fare, and the cigar clippings saved me from the gutter safari.

10. Urban In-migration

In the first half of the twentieth century, crushing poverty and the degradation of their existence in the rural South drove black Americans into the cities, especially into northern cities. They arrived in two waves, which coincided roughly with the two World Wars, periods of greater employment opportunity. Impressed by the prosperity and freedom they found in the North, yet nostalgic for the South, transplanted Negroes displayed an ambivalent attitude toward their new environment, as is evidenced in the following documents. The first selection is composed of excerpts drawn from letters written in 1917 by southern Negro emigrants to friends left behind. The second consists of testimony given in 1940 before the House Select Committee to Investigate the Inter-state Migration of Destitute Citizens. Even during the Depression, prospects seemed better in the urban North than they did in the South. ■

A. LETTERS HOME[1]

PITTSBURGH, PENNSYLVANIA
May 11, 1917

MY DEAR PASTOR AND WIFE:

It affords me great pleasure to write you. This leaves me well. . . . I am in this great city and you know it's cool here right now, the trees are just peeping out, fruit trees are now in bloom, but it's cool yet. We set by a big fire at night. I like the money O.K. but I like the South better for my pleasure. The city is too fast for me. They give you big money for what you do but they charge you big things for what you get. And the people are coming by carloads every day. . . . Listen, Hayes, I am here and I am going to stay until fall if I don't get sick. It's the largest city I ever saw, 45 miles long and equal in breadth, and a smoky city. So many mines of all kinds; some places look like torment [hell] or how they say it look and some places look like Paradise.

CLEVELAND, OHIO
August 28, 1917

HELLO, DOCTOR, MY OLD FRIEND:

. . . I am doing fine. Plenty to eat and drink and I'm making good money. In fact I am not in the best of health . . . since I've been here. . . . I have several notions of coming back, yet I am doing well. No trouble whatever except I cannot raise my children here like they should be. This is one of the worst places in principle you ever look on in your life, but it is a fine place to make money. All nations is here, and let me tell you this place is crowded with the lowest Negroes you ever met. . . . I have made as high as $7.50 per day and my wife $4.00, Sundays my son $7.50 and my two oldest girls $1.25, but

[1] Adapted from letters of Negro migrants in *Journal of Negro History,* Vol. IV, pp. 459–461, 464. Reprinted by permission.

my regular wages is $3.60 for eight hours' work. Me and my family make $103.60 every ten days. It don't cost no more to live here than it does there, except house rent. . . . I am able to farm without asking any man for anything on credit. I cannot enjoy this place. Let me tell you this is a large place.

PHILADELPHIA, PENNSYLVANIA
October 7, 1917

DEAR SIR:

. . . Well, Doctor, with the aid of God I am making very good. I make $75 per month. I am carrying enough insurance to pay me $20 per month if I am not able to be on duty. I don't have to mister every little white boy comes along. I haven't heard a white man call a colored "nigger" . . . since I been in the state of Pennsylvania. I can ride in the electric street- and steam-cars anywhere I get a seat. I don't care to mix with whites . . . but if I have to pay the same fare I . . . want the same accommodation. And if you are first in a place shopping you don't have to wait until the white folks get through trading. Yet amid all this I shall ever love the good old South, and I am praying that God may give every well wisher a chance to be a man regardless of his color.

EAST CHICAGO, INDIANA
June 10, 1917

DR. ⸺

UNION SPRINGS, ALABAMA
DEAR OLD FRIEND:

These moments I thought I would write you a few true facts of the present condition of the North. Certainly I am trying to take a close observation — now it is true the colored men are making good. Never pay less than three dollars a day or ten hours. . . . I do not see how they pay such wages the way they work laborers. They do not hurry or drive you. Remember this is the very lowest wage. Piece-work men can make from six to eight dollars per day. . . . This city I am living in [has a] population of 30,000 [and is] 20 miles from Big Chicago, Illinois. Doctor, I am somewhat impressed. My family also. They are doing nicely. . . . I often think . . . of the conversation we engaged in concerning this part of the world. I wish many times that you could see our people up here as they are entirely in a different light. . . . Let me know what is my little city [Union Springs, Alabama] doing. People are coming here every day and are finding employment. Nothing here but money and it is not hard to get. . . . Oh, I have children in school every day with the white children. I will write you more next time. How is the lodge?

B. "A WHOLE LOT BETTER HERE"[2]

Testimony of Spurgeon Hayden (Chicago), August 20, 1940.

Mr. Curtis: Mr. Hayden, give your full name to the reporter, please.

Mr. Hayden: Spurgeon Hayden.

Mr. Curtis: How old are you?

Mr. Hayden: Forty-three.

Mr. Curtis: Are you married?

Mr. Hayden: Yes.

Mr. Curtis: How old is your wife?

Mr. Hayden: About thirty-nine.

Mr. Curtis: Do you have any children?

Mr. Hayden: Seven.

Mr. Curtis: Where were you born?

Mr. Hayden: Mississippi.

Mr. Curtis: Was Mrs. Hayden born there, too?

Mr. Hayden: Yes.

Mr. Curtis: How much schooling have you had?

Mr. Hayden: I ain't had much.

Mr. Curtis: Have you had some?

Mr. Hayden: Yes, I have had some.

Mr. Curtis: Mrs. Hayden has had some schooling?

Mr. Hayden: Yes.

Mr. Curtis: You went a few years to grade school?

Mr. Hayden: Yes; public school, a country school.

Mr. Curtis: Where was that school?

Mr. Hayden: That was in Mississippi, in Carroll County.

Mr. Curtis: Did you spend all of your time in Mississippi until you came to Chicago?

---

[2] Interstate Migration: Hearings before the House of Representatives, Select Committee to Investigate the Interstate Migration of Destitute Citizens, Washington, D.C. Part III, Chicago Hearings, pp. 961–966.

Mr. Hayden: Yes, all the time.

Mr. Curtis: When did you come to Chicago?

Mr. Hayden: December 7, 1939.

Mr. Curtis: In other words, you have been here about six months.

Mr. Hayden: Yes.

Mr. Curtis: What did you do for a living in Mississippi?

Mr. Hayden: Well, I farmed, and day-worked some. I worked in the sawmill, corn press, and so forth. . . .

Mr. Curtis: When you say "farmed some," what do you mean? Were you a sharecropper?

Mr. Hayden: Yes, a sharecropper.

Mr. Curtis: You did not own any land?

Mr. Hayden: No, sir.

Mr. Curtis: How many acres did you handle when you were a share-cropper?

Mr. Hayden: Well, we would have from 12 to 14 or 15 acres in cotton, something like that. We would have 5 or 6 acres in corn, or something like that.

Mr. Curtis: Did the landlord permit you to have space for a garden?

Mr. Hayden: Yes, he gave me a garden.

Mr. Curtis: Were you and your family able to get enough food that way?

Mr. Hayden: Well, not exactly. Sometimes we would and some-times we wouldn't.

Mr. Curtis: You could not make any money to buy anything else?

Mr. Hayden: No. Money was scarce. I would make a crop, and sometimes collect from $25 to $30.

Mr. Curtis: How much would you get working around in the saw-mills, and so forth?

Mr. Hayden: Well, they paid at that time — they paid a dollar a day, or $1.25 down there. For cotton picking you would get about 50 cents a hundred. For plowing all day long, you would get 60 cents a day, from sunup to sundown. . . .

Mr. Curtis: Well now, what have you done since you have been in Chicago?

Mr. Hayden: Well, I worked a little. I — well, I paint a little. I have calcimined. I tear down paper, clean buildings, and all like that.

Mr. Curtis: Did you know someone who gave you that work?

Mr. Hayden: Yes. I didn't know them until I came up here though. I didn't know them before.

Mr. Curtis: During the year 1940, this year, have you had work most of the time?

Mr. Hayden: No. I ain't got no regular job now.

Mr. Curtis: About how many days' work do you suppose you would have each month?

Mr. Hayden: I don't know, sir. I worked last month pretty regular. I haven't done much this month.

Mr. Curtis: How about the winter months — January, February, and March? Did you have any work?

Mr. Hayden: No, sir. I didn't have no work.

Mr. Curtis: How did you live?

Mr. Hayden: Well, charity helped me some. . . .

Mr. Curtis: How much money did you have when you arrived in Chicago?

Mr. Hayden: I had when I got here, about $25 or $30.

Mr. Curtis: Did you come up in a car?

Mr. Hayden: No. I came up on the train.

Mr. Curtis: You were able to buy your tickets and had $25 or $30 when you got here?

Mr. Hayden: Yes; I was about two years or longer saving that up to get up here.

Mr. Curtis: You have not had any work this month of August?

Mr. Hayden: Yes. I had a little work, the same place, cleaning buildings.

Mr. Curtis: Have you any work now?

Mr. Hayden: I worked yesterday until 12. The man told me might have some more tomorrow.

Mr. Curtis: How much do you make?

Mr. Hayden: He gave me $1.50.

Mr. Curtis: $1.50 for the morning?

Mr. Hayden: No; for the whole day. . . .

Mr. Curtis: How did it happen you decided to leave Mississippi?

Mr. Hayden: I just got tired of that job we had. We didn't have enough to live. We couldn't send the children to school.

Mr. Curtis: Why did you pick out Chicago?

Mr. Hayden: Well, I heard a whole lot of talk about Chicago. . . .

Mr. Curtis: Well, would you rather stay here in Chicago?

Mr. Hayden: Yes. I would rather stay here. I ain't done bad here.

Mr. Curtis: You can get along better here?

Mr. Hayden: Yes. A heap better. Of course, it is a little tight now, because I ain't got no job. It is kind of tight. Times is kind of tight, anyhow. It's a whole lot better than Mississippi.

Mr. Curtis: Is it easier to raise vegetables down there?

Mr. Hayden: Yes. It is very easy to raise vegetables. You can raise plenty of vegetables up and down them breaksides, and one thing and another — cabbage and one thing and another.

Mr. Curtis: But you could not make any cash money?

Mr. Hayden: Oh, no, sir. Cash money was scarce. When they pay a man 60 cents a day from sunup to sundown, that ain't much money.

Mr. Curtis: You could not educate your children?

Mr. Hayden: No. I couldn't go to school any. My dad would keep me working. I didn't have a chance to go to school.

Mr. Curtis: We are glad to have had you here as a witness, because you have given us some information that is typical of a certain group that are involved in this problem. Thank you. That is all I have, Mr. Chairman.

11. Explosion in Detroit[1]
✤ National Urban League

Coincidental with their appearance in large numbers, forced to live in fixed locations within the cities, black urbanites found themselves objects of violence. In 1917 there were race riots in East St. Louis and Philadelphia; in 1919, it was Washington, D.C., and Chicago; and in 1943, Detroit and Harlem. The following are selections from a report by the National Urban League on the Detroit riot of 1943. ■

Two Rumors Make a Riot

On Sunday, June 20, 1943, thousands of Detroit war workers went to Belle Isle, city-owned recreation center located on an island in the Detroit River, to seek relief from the intense heat that gripped the

[1] National Urban League, *Racial Conflict — a Home Front Danger: Lessons of the Detroit Riot* (New York: National Urban League, 1943), pp. 4–7.

city. The majority of this holiday crowd were Negroes and a considerable number were servicemen, Negro and white. Throughout the day there were minor clashes between Negroes and whites, but they were promptly handled by the police. On Sunday evening, as the crowd shoved and elbowed its way homeward, fighting broke out on the bridge that connects the island with the mainland. Reports differ as to who or what started the trouble but it is generally agreed that an altercation between a white sailor and a Negro precipitated a free-for-all which spread to all sections of the bridge. By 2:00 A.M. the situation was considered under control.

Meanwhile the disturbances had reached the city proper. Two rumors, emanating from the fighting on the bridge, had been widely circulated simultaneously. "A Negro shot a white woman on the bridge" is the story that reached whites. Negroes in their turn heard that "a Negro woman and her baby had been thrown into the river by whites." Without confirmation of either rumor, whites and Negroes gathered in threatening groups in their respective neighborhoods.

Police attempted to disperse the groups of Negroes on Hastings Street, principal thoroughfare in the Negro district, and fighting broke out. White persons in the district were attacked as were business establishments owned by whites. Streetcars and automobiles were stopped and white occupants were assaulted. On Woodward Avenue, Detroit's main street, gangs of whites attacked Negroes. Streetcars were searched for Negro passengers and automobiles driven by Negroes were stopped and their occupants beaten. In many instances the automobiles were burned.

The rioting continued all day Monday, increasing in intensity as evening approached. At no time did large groups of Negroes and whites clash. A mob of whites attempted to penetrate the Negro district at one point but was turned back by the police. By midnight Monday, federal troops reached the city and the rioting ceased. To prevent further disorders, a state of emergency was declared and the city was placed under partial martial law. A curfew regulation was imposed throughout the city. Places of amusement and liquor stores were closed and all large meetings were banned.

Twenty-four hours of lawlessness, fighting, and looting took a heavy toll of life and property. Thirty-four persons were killed, 500 were injured, and 1800 rioters were arrested. Of the dead 25 were Negroes and 9 were whites. Seventeen of the Negro dead were reported killed by the police. The Department of Public Welfare reported 250 whites and 211 Negroes injured, and 1300 of the 1800 rioters under arrest were Negroes.

The Role of the Police

Disappointment and resentment over the weak and ineffective attempts to control the rioting were openly expressed throughout the city by both white and Negro citizens. Some members of the city's police department were severely criticized for what was described by many as "wanton murder of innocent people." Eyewitness accounts of the conduct of many police officers in the Negro district as well as on Woodward Avenue where the majority of Negroes were attacked by whites revealed numerous instances of absolute disregard for the plight of Negro victims of the mob. Police gunfire was held responsible for the deaths of 17 Negroes who, according to official records of the police department, were killed "while looting, resisting an officer, and rioting." No white persons were reported killed by the police.

The timidity and helplessness of the police department in the face of the rapidly spreading disorders were obvious early Monday morning. Representatives of numerous groups and organizations appealed to Mayor Jeffries to request that troops be sent in without delay. At a meeting of an Interracial Citizens' Committee at noon on Monday, the Mayor declared that "calling for troops would be a reflection on the fair name of the city." It was not until Governor Kelly, who was attending a meeting in Columbus, Ohio, was informed of the seriousness of the situation that this action was taken. A delay of twelve hours before federal troops arrived allowed the disorders to continue unabated. The Mayor and the Police Commissioner held army authorities responsible for the delay; and army officials charged these city officials with stupidity in not realizing that they could not intervene until the President of the United States had taken appropriate action. A Presidential proclamation was officially issued on Monday, June 21.

The ancient game of "passing the buck" was indulged in by several official and unofficial groups and organizations during and after the riot. But a disturbing phase of the aftermath of the riot was the [issuing of] "white papers" by the Police Commissioner and subsequently by the Mayor, in which the police performance was praised. The reaction to the treatment at the hands of the police in the Negro community was bitter and at times openly hostile. One observer said, "You don't know whether they (the police) are for you or against you, but most of the time they seem to be against you regardless of what you are doing." This statement appears to have been substantially true, although there were several reports of the courageous efforts of several policemen to protect the lives of Negroes and to prevent clashes between groups of whites and Negroes. Two police officers were among the white victims of the rioting.

A History of Racial Trouble

Race clashes have been frequent in Detroit's stormy history during the past 25 years. In 1918 when the Negro population numbered less than 40,000, there were reports of minor neighborhood conflicts most of which arose over housing. In 1926, Dr. O. H. Sweet, a Negro physician, purchased a house in a neighborhood in which Negroes had not previously lived. A white mob attempted to force him out of his home and he fired into it, killing two members and wounding several others. He was arrested and tried for manslaughter, but was acquitted of the charge.

Minor incidents involving Negroes and whites have been reported in Detroit papers almost weekly since that date. In 1942, a mob of whites prevented Negroes from moving into the Sojourner Truth[2] Housing Project, constructed for their use by the federal government. The Housing Authority with the aid of Detroit police, state police, and Michigan state troops later moved Negro families into the houses.

Immediately before and after this incident, there were several racial clashes of more or less serious nature in the Detroit area. They ranged from street fights among gangs of Negro and white youths and stoning of houses and churches recently acquired by Negroes, to outright murder. Among . . . incidents to gain public attention was the Packard strike in June, 1943, in which it is reported that 25,000 white workers staged a strike because three Negro workers were upgraded. Two weeks before the June 20th riot, street brawls broke out spontaneously between colored and white youths in Inkster, a suburb of Detroit, and a few days later, white sailors and civilians attempted to run Negroes from Eastwood Park. Belle Isle saw its first big race disturbance in August, 1942, which started from a quarrel among children on the playground. It is not difficult to understand, therefore, why Detroit residents were not surprised when the recent riots occurred.

[2] **Sojourner Truth:** A former slavewoman who could neither read nor write, yet conducted her own antislavery campaign in the 1850's.

V. The Age of the Metropolis

After World War II came to an end, the satisfying of pent-up consumer desires helped spark unprecedented economic growth and affluence. As returning veterans settled into suburban development houses and more city-dwellers moved out to claim their quarter-acres, urban growth became urban sprawl. The big city was transformed into the metropolis, a vast conglomeration of communities around a deteriorating core. In 1920 just over half of all Americans lived in cities; in 1960 the figure reached 70 per cent; by 1980 it was expected to be 90 per cent, or almost total urbanization. Most of this growth was in suburban development.

As a result, the inner city was deprived of the tax income as well as the concern of the middle class. During the 1950's, some effort was made to alleviate urban ills through programs of slum clearance, public housing, renewal, and commercial revitalization. But in most cities it was a case of too little and too late. Longstanding indifference to the problems, especially to the plight of those trapped within the black ghettos, created a situation from which violence was almost certain to result. In the 1960's the ghettos of America did explode in a nightmare of killing, burning, and looting. National commissions which studied the riots arraigned white racism and neglect as prime causes.

As the nation entered the 1970's, the word most often associated with cities continued to be "crisis." Progress was painfully slow. Perhaps the most hopeful aspect of the situation was the good will and energy with which individuals and groups such as the Urban Coalition struggled to eliminate the causes of urban disorder and suburban anxiety, through efforts in the areas of education, housing, employment, transportation, and the environment. ■

Urban Growth Since Mid-Century*

	1950	1960	1970	Per Cent Increase 1950 to 1970
The Big Three:				
New York	9,556,000	10,695,000	11,410,000	19%
Los Angeles	4,152,000	6,039,000	6,962,000	68%
Chicago	5,178,000	6,221,000	6,894,000	33%
Cities Registering Large Gains:				
Atlanta	727,000	1,017,000	1,374,000	89%
Dallas	744,000	1,084,000	1,539,000	107%
Honolulu	353,000	500,000	613,000	74%
Houston	807,000	1,244,000	1,958,000	143%
Miami	495,000	935,000	1,259,000	170%
Phoenix	331,770	664,000	963,000	190%
San Diego	557,000	1,033,000	1,311,000	135%

* Figures are for Standard Metropolitan Statistical Areas; 1970 data is preliminary.

In recent decades urban areas in warmer regions have attracted vast numbers of new residents.

1. Megalopolis: Main Street of the Nation[1]

✦ Jean Gottmann

The most striking fact about modern American society is the dominance of the city, and nowhere is the supremacy of urban life so apparent as in the oldest parts of the nation, in the region of the first settlements. The whole coastal area of what was once the northern colonies became a continuous ribbon of urban development, the vital center of regional activity, and an important influence in national life. The sociologist Jean Gottmann first saw the broader significance of this development. In his influential book, Megalopolis, *he also gave a name to the phenomenon.* ■

[1] Jean Gottmann, *Megalopolis: The Urbanized Northeastern Seaboard of the United States* (New York: The Twentieth Century Fund, copyright © 1961), pp. 3–9. Reprinted by permission.

The northeastern seaboard of the United States is today the site of a remarkable development — an almost continuous stretch of urban and suburban areas from southern New Hampshire to northern Virginia and from the Atlantic shore to the Appalachian foothills. The processes of urbanization, rooted deep in the American past, have worked steadily here, endowing the region with unique ways of life and of land use. No other section of the United States has such a large concentration of population, with such a high average density, spread over such a large area. And no other section has a comparable role within the nation or a comparable importance in the world. Here has been developed a kind of supremacy, in politics, in economics, and possibly even in cultural activities, seldom before attained by an area of this size.

This region has indeed a "personality of its own, which for some three centuries past has been changing and evolving, constantly creating new problems for its inhabitants and exerting a deep influence on the general organization of society. The modern trends in its development and its present degree of crowding provide both examples and warnings for other less urbanized areas in America and abroad and call for a profound revision of many old concepts, such as the usually accepted distinctions between city and country. . . .

An Old Name for a New Urban Structure

. . . It is difficult to single this area out from surrounding areas, for its limits cut across established historical divisions, such as New England and the Middle Atlantic states, and across political entities, since it includes some states entirely and others only partially. A special name is needed, therefore, to identify this special geographical area. . . .

. . . The name applied to it should . . . be new as a place name but old as a symbol of the long tradition of human aspirations and endeavor underlying the situations and problems now found here. Hence the choice of the term Megalopolis [*meg'*uh-*lop'*uh-lis]. . . .

Some two thousand years before the first European settlers landed . . . [in America], a group of ancient people planning a new city-state in the Peloponnesus[2] in Greece called it *Megalopolis,* for they dreamed of a great future for it and hoped it would become the

[2] **Peloponnesus** (*pel'*uh-puh-*nee'*sus): southern peninsula of Greece, where Sparta and Argos are located.

largest of the great cities. Their hopes did not materialize. Megalopolis still appears on modern maps of the Peloponnesus, but it is just a small town nestling in a small river basin. Through the centuries the word *Megalopolis* has been used in many senses . . . [and] has even found its way into Webster's dictionary, which defines it as a "very large city." Its use, however, has not become so widespread that it could not be applied in a new sense, as a geographical place name for the unique cluster of metropolitan areas of the northeastern seaboard of the United States. . . .

A Continuous Community

As one follows the main highways or railroads between Boston and Washington, D.C., one hardly loses sight of built-up areas, tightly woven residential communities or powerful concentrations of manufacturing plants. Flying this same route one discovers, on the other hand, that behind the ribbons of densely occupied land along the principal arteries of traffic, and between the clusters of suburbs around the old urban centers, there still remain large areas covered with woods and brush alternating with some carefully cultivated patches of farmland . . . many of these sections that look rural actually function largely as suburbs in the orbit of some city's downtown. Even the farms, which occupy the larger tilled patches, are seldom worked by people whose occupation and only income are properly agricultural. . . .

Thus the old distinctions between rural and urban do not apply here any more. Even a quick look at the vast area of Megalopolis reveals a revolution in land use. Most of the people living in the so-called rural areas . . . have very little to do with agriculture. . . .

In this area, then, we must abandon the idea of the city as a tightly settled and organized unit. . . . Every city in this region spread out far and wide around its original nucleus. . . . Such coalescence can be observed, for example, along the main lines of traffic that link New York City and Philadelphia. Here there are many communities that might be classified as belonging to more than one orbit. It is hard to say whether they are suburbs, or "satellites," of Philadelphia or New York, Newark, New Brunswick, or Trenton [New Jersey]. . . .

Thus an almost continuous system of deeply interwoven urban and suburban areas, with a total population of about 37 million people in 1960, has been erected along the northeastern Atlantic seaboard. It straddles state boundaries, stretches across wide estuaries and bays, and encompasses many regional differences. In fact, the landscapes of Megalopolis offer such variety that the average observer may well doubt the unity of the region. And it may seem to him that the main urban nuclei of the seaboard are little related to one another. This region indeed reminds one of Aristotle's saying that cities such as Babylon had "the compass of a nation rather than a city."

Focus and Façade of the Nation

. . . Megalopolis provides the whole of America with so many essential services, of the sort a community used to obtain in its "downtown" section, that it may well deserve the nickname of "Main Street of the nation." And for three centuries it has performed this role, though the transcontinental march of settlement has developed along east-west axes perpendicular to this section of the Atlantic seaboard.

In recent times Megalopolis has had concentrated within it more of the Main Street type of functions than ever, and it does not yet seem prepared to relinquish any of them. Witness, for example, the impact of the federal government in Washington, D.C., as it tightens up over many aspects of national life; the continued crowding of financial and managerial operations in Manhattan; New York's dominance of the national market for mass communication media, which resists all attempts at erosion; and the pre-eminent influence of the universities and cultural centers of Megalopolis on American thinking and policy-making. Megalopolis is also the country's chief façade toward the rest of the world. From it, as from the Main Street of a city, local people leave for distant travel, and to it arriving strangers come. And just as passing visitors often see little of a city except a few blocks of its Main Street, so most foreign visitors see only a part of Megalopolis on their sojourns in the United States. . . .

Cradle of a New Order?

Modern technology and social evolution provide increasing opportunity in urban pursuits on the one hand, and on the other steadily improving means of producing more agricultural goods with less manpower. The forces at work in our time, coupled with the growth in population, are, therefore, bound to channel a rising tide of people toward urban-type occupations and ways of life. As this tide reaches more and more cities, they will burst out of old bounds to expand and scatter all over the landscape, taking new forms like those already observable throughout Megalopolis. . . .

. . . So great are the consequences of the general evolution heralded by the present rise and complexity of Megalopolis that any analysis of the region's problems often gives one the feeling of looking at the dawn of a new stage in human civilization. . . . Indeed, the area may be considered the cradle of a new order in the organization of inhabited space.

2. Making a City: Levittown[1]

✤ Penn Kimball

The pace of urban development quickened dramatically after World War II. Not only did older cities fill up rapidly, but everywhere "new towns" appeared at the edge of the metropolis. No name was so closely connected with this movement as "Levitt." The Levitt family designed and built middle-income housing on an unprecedented scale. Actually, their projects were new suburbs rather than "new towns." Although they managed to produce good housing and lots of it, these "instant communities" came under criticism from many quarters. ■

The sparkling vision of new towns in America, graceful and spacious cities with attractive homes and progressive civic planning, has danced on the drafting boards of idealistic young architects for years immemorial. A few tentative experiments in greenbelt living actually advanced beyond the blueprint stage prior to World War II. Some were an aesthetic success; most were financial failures. . . .

Yet forces are being turned loose by an explosive American technology which — potentially at least — are capable of transforming yesterday's wild dream into tomorrow's commonplace. Building is being revolutionized by assembly-line construction with standardized

---

[1] From "Dream Town—Large Economy Size," by Penn Kimball (*New York Times Magazine*, December 14, 1952), pp. 12, 36, 43. © 1952 by The New York Times Company. Reprinted by permission.

materials. Geography is being upset by the movement and growth of mammoth new facilities for making aluminum, steel, power, atomic weapons.

The vital ingredient for the planners' brave new world is finally within reach. Industry, bursting at the seams, is . . . creating the demand for new plant sites and new homes for shifting thousands of factory workers; relocated industry, more than that, promises new sources of stable and taxable wealth to support the planners' schemes, an indispensable artery to pump life into the phantom carcass of a model town.

Thus it is that on the Pennsylvania bank of the Delaware River, not far from where Washington crossed to surprise the Hessians at Trenton, an astonishing pattern begins these days to unfold. A fabulous new skyline of masonry and metal soars from the river flats — a half-billion dollars in blast furnaces, stacks, coke ovens, rolling mills for United States Steel's giant new Fairless Works. . . . Conveniently close to thousands of new jobs and already starting to fill with married couples, baby carriages, respectability, and hopes . . . is the preplanned new town of the preplanned frontier. . . .

. . . Through the wide windows of Bill Levitt's farmhouse headquarters are plainly visible the first rooftops and light poles of a booming new Levittown — the first batch of 16,000 houses to go up on 1100 streets cut through acreage where but a few months ago local farmers raised only spinach. The view from this farmhouse window three years from now will have erupted into the tenth largest city in the State of Pennsylvania.[2]

Starting from scratch the Levitts will have converted eight square miles of open farm country into a densely populated community of 70,000. Paved streets, sewer lines, school sites, baseball diamonds, shopping center, parking lots, new railroad station, factory sidings, churches, trunk arteries, newspapers, garden clubs, swimming pools, doctors, dentists, and town hall — all conceived in advance, all previously planned in one of the most colossal acts ever of mortal creation. . . .

The Levittown Way of Life

[The Levitts'] self-confidence is one of the byproducts of the fact that customers have been registering faith in Levitt decisions for a

[2] Levittown has a population of 69,000, making it, in fact, the tenth largest city in Pennsylvania.

quarter of a century, and spectacularly so during the mass migration to Levittown, Long Island, after [World War II]. William, his brother Alfred, and father Abraham designed, built, and sold 17,500 homes there in five and one-half years. The four-room Levitt house, appearing on the market in the midst of a shortage, offered light, air, convenience, and value — selling for substantially less than $10,000 with closing fees, landscaping, and kitchen appliances thrown in.

Mass production methods right on the building site . . . made the Levitt price feasible. But they also defined the massive contours of a rather formidable-looking city. . . . Late commuters, lost among the identical blocks, sometimes reported a sense of panic like bewildered children suddenly turned loose in a house of mirrors. . . . When the lady of the house hung out the wash, the awesome result was 17,500 pairs of shorts flapping in 17,500 backyards. The struggle for identity in these prefabricated circumstances reduced itself occasionally to a pretty fine point — like the tone of a door chime or a novel idea for a wastebasket. People liked it anyhow, were grateful for it, got used to it, grew fond of it. . . . Levittowners, mostly young ex-G.I.'s just getting started acquired a certain esprit de corps.[3] The crime rate was phenomenally low. By some mysterious process . . . Levittowners seemed to grow progressively healthier. . . .

Levittown, Pennsylvania, will be subdivided into sixteen separate "neighborhoods," each bearing a distinctive place name like Stonybrook, Lakeside, Birch Valley . . . "Birch Valley lies in a little vale where hundreds of birch trees grow," a publicity release idyllizes. . . .

Two or three of these integrated neighborhoods center upon a single school site, with adjacent recreational and athletic facilities. Children can walk to each hub, away from the circumferential boulevards enclosing each community unit, without ever crossing a through street. No school buses will be necessary, another money-saver.

What the Critics Say

How does all this stack up against professional theory about the ideal town?

Lewis Mumford, a demanding critic of many recent housing developments conceded that the Levitt house by itself has a "superior interior design" and offers the public "a great deal of value for the price." After a recent trip to Bucks County, however, he observed

---

[3] **esprit de corps** (es-*pree*'duh kor'): group spirit which develops among persons associated together.

that, outside, the Levitts appeared to be using "new-fashioned methods to compound old-fashioned mistakes."

"Most of the open space is in the form of streets instead of gardens," Mumford said. "Endless roads and lengthy sewer lines cost money that might better be spent on reducing the number of houses per acre."

The most pressing requirement of the ideally planned town, Mumford believes, is diversity. "Levittown offers a very narrow range of house type to a narrow income range. It is a one-class community on a great scale — too congested for effective variety and too spread out for social relationships necessary among high school children, old folks, and families who can't afford outside help. Mechanically it is admirably done. Socially the design is backward." . . .

Mumford and other experts agree that the Levitts are aimed in the right direction with their plans for identifiable neighborhoods, interior school locations, shade trees, swimming pools, and built-in community services. These are ideas which have been set down for years in planning textbooks. The sight of actual earth-moving machines, actual warehouses jammed with crates of home appliances, the sawmills sawing, the trenchdiggers digging, the miles of sewer pipe, the miles of brick, the cement plant (worth $165,000), the pumping station, the 48 carloads of material arriving in the rail yards each morning — all this suggests the immensity of the investment required, the enormousness of the gamble.

"You have to have nerve," Bill Levitt said. "You have to think big."

Experts are also agreed on the difficulties of creating new communities that can be self-supporting and self-regulating, that is, neither "company towns" nor "government towns," and still boast all modern conveniences. There never was an acute need for industrial acreage in the settled suburban tract over which the Levitts first expanded in Nassau County [Long Island]. With U.S. Steel's giant plant only two miles away, however, the demand of suppliers and satellites for industrial sites in the unsettled Levittown, Pennsylvania, area is expected to be tremendous.

The New Town vs. the Existing Community

New industry is important to independent communities because factories add to the tax list needed to support municipal services. The Levitts estimate that there is already nearly $1500 worth of community facilities in the $10,500 price they are asking for their 1953 house. . . . . Although the builders turn over streets, swimming pools, water mains, sewage lines, and town hall free and clear to civic authorities, local residents are going to have to solve the problem of maintaining them.

The dilemma was graphically illustrated when it came time to turn on the street lights for Pennsylvania Levittown's first completed and occupied neighborhood. The stout farmers of Tullytown, one of the four boroughs in which Levittown's 5000 acres happen to fall, simply refused to switch on any juice for those city fellows over the hill. There never had been any street lights in Tullytown before. Besides, who was going to put up $4200 a year to pay for them? The Levitt lawyers stepped in and the lights were lit.

As far as local government is concerned, Levittown, Pennsylvania, doesn't really exist — just Tullytown, Falls Township, Middletown, and Bristol. Politically, the new arrivals have thus been gerrymandered[4] in advance. . . . Part-time road commissioners in these places used to handle most of the public issues which ever popped up prior to the arrival of Bill Levitt's bulldozers. Levitt's dream is to incorporate all of his preplanned town under one political roof, "It would cost me a million in capital assets," Levitt sighed. "But what a town we could make then, what a town!"

[4] **gerrymandered**: the political divisions already existing were maintained, thus depriving the Levittowners of the opportunity to act as a municipal unit. Today the community is designated as a "minor zoned city."

3. The New Slums[1]

✦ *Michael Harrington*

In 1962 a book caused many people to "discover" the problem of poverty in affluent America. Most analyses of the postwar period had concentrated on the explosive economic growth of a country getting wealthier by the hour. But in The Other America *Michael Harrington focused on the forgotten millions who*

*had dropped out of, or never even started, the race for riches.
His book, widely circulated among the New Frontiersmen of the
Kennedy administration, provided the rationale for the War
against Poverty of the 1960's. The excerpt that follows describes
the differences between the slums of the past and the present,
and suggests a new and better concept for public housing.* ■

In 1949 the Housing Act authorized the construction of 810,000
new units of low-cost housing over a four-year period. Twelve years
later, in 1961, the AFL-CIO proposed that the new housing law
should provide for 400,000 units in order to complete the total projected in 1949. The Kennedy administration asked for 100,000 new
units.

This has been one of the greatest single domestic scandals of postwar America. The statistics have all been nicely calculated; everyone
knows the dimension of the problem; and articles appear regularly,
predicting the next catastrophe that will come from inaction. But
nothing is done to attack the basic problem, and poor housing remains one of the most important facts about the other America. This
is where the nation builds the environment of the culture of poverty. . . .

As the AFL-CIO Civil Rights Department put it, "It seems, therefore, certain that 30 per cent of American families are living in substandard homes today." . . .

Perhaps a more dramatic statement of the problem was made by
Charles L. Farris, the president of the National Association of Housing Officials: at the end of the fifties there were more Americans
living in slums than on farms. . . .

The Environment of the Other America

A slum is not merely an area of decrepit buildings. It is a social
fact. There are neighborhoods in which housing is run down, yet the
people do not exhibit the hopelessness of the other Americans. Usually, these places have a vital community life around a national culture
or religion. In New York City, Chinatown is an obvious example.
Where the slum becomes truly pernicious is when it becomes the
environment of the culture of poverty, a spiritual and personal reality
for its inhabitants as well as an area of dilapidation. This is when the

slum becomes the breeding ground of crime, of vice, the creator of people who are lost to themselves and to society.

Thus, there are in the United States old slums where the buildings are miserable and decayed; and there are new slums in which the culture of poverty has been imported into the modern housing projects. Both are parts of the other America.

First, take the obvious slum of tenements and hovels. The most important fact about these places in the sixties is that they are the environment of pessimism and of hopelessness.

The Old "Ethnic" Slum

Indeed, there is a sense in which the "old" slums are new. There once was a slum in American society that was a melting pot, a way station, a goad to talent. It was the result of the massive European immigration in the late nineteenth and early twentieth centuries. That flood of human vitality came to an end after World War I when the nation established quota systems [of immigration], but the tradition of the ethnic groups survived for a generation. Symbolically, the tenements in which these newcomers lived had been built for them and had not trickled down after the middle class found them inadequate. The neighborhoods were dense and the housing was inadequate, yet the people were not defeated by their environment. There was community, there was aspiration. . . .

. . . As Oscar Handlin wrote in *The Newcomers*, "The ethnic community supplied its members with norms and values and with the direction of an elite leadership." Tenements did not prevail against people.

Now the incredible American adventure of the ethnic slums is coming to an end. There are those from the old experience who remain behind — in New York, the Irish and Germans of the South Bronx, the Jews of Williamsburg, the Italians of the South Village. . . .

The New Slum

Where the ethnic slum once stood, in the "old" slum neighborhood, there is a new type of slum. Its citizens are the internal migrants, the Negroes, the poor whites from the farms, the Puerto Ricans. They join the failures from the old ethnic culture and form an entirely different kind of neighborhood. For many of them the crucial problem is color, and this makes the ghetto walls higher than

they have ever been. All of them arrive at a time of housing shortage
. . . , and thus it is harder to escape even when income rises. But,
above all, these people do not participate in the culture of aspiration
that was the vitality of the ethnic slum. . . .

. . . This new type of slum groups together failures, rootless people,
those born at the wrong time, those in the wrong industry, and the
minorities. . . .

Failure of the Public Housing Program

The current American answer to the problem of the slum is the
low-cost housing project. The theory behind this approach contains
at least the beginnings of an attack upon the culture of poverty: a
public commitment to create a new environment for human beings.

But the practice has lagged far behind the intention. The concerned citizen . . . sees that tenement eyesores have been torn down,
and he is satisfied. He does not understand that the number of
units that have been built do not equal the number that have been
destroyed in clearing the project sites. In New York in 1954, for
instance, there was one unit for every 7.1 eligible new families; in
1956, one for every 10.4 eligible new families. And these figures are
roughly typical of the nation as a whole. . . .

So, first of all, there is not enough public housing to go around.
But there are some hundreds of thousands of people who have gone
into projects recently, and their experience is perhaps even more significant than that of those who were simply displaced. . . .

. . . [M]ost public housing, even at its best, fails to solve the problem of the slum and, above all, the problem of slum psychology. In
some cases the gains appear minimal, for one must balance the physical improvement (and, hopefully, the consequent improvement in
health) against the new forms of alienation and, at the extreme, of
violence. But, perhaps most crucial, the housing policy of America
has sought the integration of the poor with the poor — which is to
say, the segregation of the other Americans from society at large.

For some people the failures of public housing are cited as an argument against national involvement in this problem. This is a disastrous and wrong-headed deduction.

With all that has been said about the inadequacies of the housing
projects, it is clear that only one agency in America is capable of
eradicating both the slum and slum psychology from this land: the
federal government. Time and time again, private builders have

demonstrated that they are utterly incapable of doing anything. If the federal government deserts the field, that would be tantamount to a decision to enlarge the slums of America. A new determination and imagination are needed, not a retreat. . . .

Second, under the present setup, it is the poor who are victimized by urban renewal. In 1959 Charles Abrams told a Senate Committee that the public housing program had become "tattered, perverted and shrunk . . . little more than an adjunct of the publicly subsidized private urban renewal program. This urban renewal program, too, while it does help the cities to get rid of slums, has developed into a device for displacing the poor from their footholds to make way for higher rental dwellings which those displaced cannot afford. . . ."

The "Mixing" Concept

Public housing must be conceived as something more than improved physical shelter with heat and plumbing. It must be seen as an important organism for the creation of community life in the cities. First and foremost, public housing should avoid segregating the poor off in some corner of the metropolis. That is the "modern poor-farm mentality," as one critic described it. The projects and subsidized homes should be located as parts of neighborhoods, so that income groups, races, and cultures will mingle. . . .

Private ownership is one of the great myths of American life — for more than half the people do not, and cannot, own their homes. In 1959 Charles Abrams estimated that an annual income of over $6000 was required before an American family could seriously think of buying a home. . . . It would be magnificent if America were to make home ownership a goal of national policy. As it is today, the poor are completely excluded from this possibility, and even the great middle third of the income pyramid have considerable difficulties.

The Need for Social Guidance

Where projects are undertaken (and it must be emphasized that the reference is not to huge high-rise ghettos, but to a new kind of public housing), there must be an adequate budget for social work. You cannot take people out of an old-fashioned slum, where reality has been giving them a grim, distorted education for years, place them in a project, and expect them to exhibit all kinds of gentle, middle-class virtues. This transition is a crucial moment. If the people are left to themselves, then the chances are that they will import the culture of poverty into the public housing. If they are helped, if there is a real effort to forge neighborhood communities, this need not happen.

Many of the public-housing administrators are sincere and imaginative public servants, but they have been frustrated at every turn by the inadequacy of funds and by the fact that the nation has yet to make a real commitment to build a human environment.

The Cost and the Payoff

And the cost? The point has already been made, but it deserves repeating: we already pay an inordinately high price for poverty in the United States. Misery generates social chaos, and it takes money just to police it, just to keep it from becoming so explosive that it will disturb the tranquillity of the better off. In cold [financial] terms, there would be a long-range payoff if slums were abolished in the United States. In human terms, such an action would mean that millions of people would be returned to . . . society and enabled to make their personal contributions.

4. Urban Renewal[1]

✦ *Herbert J. Gans*

> *One of the tools of slum clearance and new housing was "urban renewal." Financed and directed largely by the federal government, it was designed to wipe out dilapidated and unsound housing and redevelop "blighted" neighborhoods. Since every city had large areas of cancerous slums in the postwar period, most applied for federal help and put together their own programs. Launched with much hope and extravagant rhetoric, the concept of urban renewal soon fell under attack. The range of this criticism is illustrated in the following passages taken from an article by sociologist Herbert J. Gans, concerning the impact of urban renewal on America's cities.* ■

[1] Herbert J. Gans, "The Failure of Urban Renewal, a Critique and Some Proposals," *Commentary*, Vol. 39, No. 4, April, 1965, pp. 29–37. Reprinted from *Commentary* by permission; copyright © 1965 by the American Jewish Committee.

Suppose that the government decided that jalopies were a menace to public safety and a blight to the beauty of our highways, and therefore took them away from their drivers. Suppose, then, that to replenish the supply of automobiles, it gave these drivers a hundred dollars each to buy a good used car and also made special grants to General Motors, Ford, and Chrysler to lower the cost — though not necessarily the price — of Cadillacs, Lincolns, and Imperials by a few hundred dollars. Absurd as this may sound, change the jalopies to slum housing, and I have described, with only slight poetic license, the first fifteen years of a federal program called urban renewal.

Since 1949, this program has provided local renewal agencies with federal funds and the power of eminent domain[2] to condemn slum neighborhoods, tear down the buildings, and resell the cleared land to private developers at a reduced price. In addition to relocating the slum-dwellers in "decent, safe, and sanitary" housing, the program was intended to stimulate large-scale private rebuilding, add new tax revenues to the dwindling coffers of the cities, revitalize their downtown areas, and halt the exodus of middle-class whites to the suburbs.

Attacks on Urban Renewal

For some time now, a few city planners and housing experts have been pointing out that urban renewal was not achieving its general aims, and social scientists have produced a number of critical studies of individual renewal projects. These critiques, however, have mostly appeared in academic books and journals; otherwise there has been remarkably little public discussion of the federal program. Slum-dwellers whose homes were to be torn down have indeed protested bitterly, but their outcries have been limited to particular projects. . . . In the last few years, the civil rights movement has backed protesting slum-dwellers, while [right-wing conservatives] have opposed the use of eminent domain to take private property from one owner in order to give it to another. . . .

Slum clearance has also come under fire from several prominent architectural and social critics, led by Jane Jacobs, who have been struggling to preserve neighborhoods like Greenwich Village, with their brownstones, lofts, and small apartment houses, against the

---

[2] **eminent domain:** the right of the government to appropriate private property for public use, compensation being given.

encroachment of the large, high-rise projects built for the luxury market and poor alike. But these efforts have been directed mainly at private clearance outside the federal program, and their intent has been to save the city for people (intellectuals and artists, for example) who, like tourists, want jumbled diversity, antique "charm," and narrow streets for visual adventure and aesthetic pleasure. . . .

But if criticism of the urban renewal program has in the past been spotty and sporadic, there are signs that the program as a whole is now beginning to be seriously and tellingly evaluated. . . . [O]ne highly negative analysis by an ultraconservative economist . . . has already appeared: Martin Anderson's *The Federal Bulldozer.* Ironically enough, Anderson's data are based largely on statistics collected by the Urban Renewal Administration. What, according to these and other data, has the program accomplished? It has cleared slums to make room for many luxury-housing and a few middle-income projects, and it has also provided inexpensive land for the expansion of colleges, hospitals, libraries, shopping areas, and other such institutions located in slum areas. As of March, 1961, 126,000 dwelling units had been demolished, and about 28,000 new ones built. The median monthly rental of all those erected during 1960 came to $158, and in 1962, to $192 — a staggering figure for any area outside of Manhattan.

The Relocation Shuffle

Needless to say, none of the slum-dwellers who were dispossessed in the process could afford to move into these new apartments. Local renewal agencies were supposed to relocate the dispossessed tenants in "standard" housing within their means before demolition began, but such vacant housing is scarce in most cities, and altogether unavailable in some. . . . Thus, a 1961 study of renewal projects in 41 cities showed that 60 per cent of the dispossessed tenants were merely relocated in other slums; and in big cities, the proportion was even higher. . . .

Moreover, those dispossessed tenants who found better housing usually had to pay more rent than they could afford. In his careful study of relocation in Boston's heavily Italian West End, Chester Hartman shows that 41 per cent of West Enders lived in good housing in this so-called slum (thus suggesting that it should not have been torn down) and that 73 per cent were relocated in good housing — thanks in part to the fact that the West Enders were white. This improvement was achieved at a heavy price, however, for median rents rose from $1 to $71 per month after the move.

According to renewal officials, 80 per cent of all persons relocated now live in good housing, and rent increases were justified because many had been paying unduly low rent before. Hartman's study was the first to compare these official statistics with housing realities. . . .

As for the substandard rents paid by slum-dwellers, this is true in only a small proportion of cases, and then mostly among whites. Real-estate economists argue that families should pay at least 20 per cent of their income for housing, but what is manageable for middle-income people is a burden to those with low incomes who pay a higher share of their earnings for food and other necessities. Yet even so, Negroes generally have to devote about 30 per cent of their income to housing, and a Chicago study cited by Hartman reports that among nonwhite families earning less than $3000 a year, median rent rose from 35 per cent of income before relocation to 46 per cent afterward.

To compound the failure of urban renewal to help the poor, many clearance areas (Boston's West End is an example) were chosen, as Anderson points out, not because they had the worst slums, but because they offered the best sites for luxury housing — housing which would have been built whether the urban renewal program existed or not. Since public funds were used to clear the slums and to make the land available to private builders at reduced costs, the low-income population was in effect subsidizing its own removal to benefit the wealthy. What was done for the slum-dwellers in return is starkly suggested by the following statistic: *only one-half of one per cent* of all federal expenditures for urban renewal between 1949 and 1964 was spent on relocation of families and individuals; and 2 per cent if payments are included.

The Psychological Costs of Relocation

Finally, because the policy has been to clear a district of all slums at once in order to assemble larger sites to attract private developers, entire neighborhoods have frequently been destroyed, uprooting people who had lived there for decades, closing down their institutions, ruining small businesses by the hundreds, and scattering families and friends all over the city. By removing the structure of social and emotional support provided by the neighborhood, and by forcing people to build their lives separately and amid strangers elsewhere, slum clearance has often come at a serious psychological as well as financial cost to its supposed beneficiaries. Marc Fried, a clinical psychologist who studied the West Enders after relocation, reported that 46 per cent of the women and 38 per cent of the men "give evidence of a fairly severe grief reaction or worse" in response to questions about leaving their tight-knit community. . . .

People like the Italians or the Puerto Ricans who live in an intensely group-centered way among three-generation "extended families" and ethnic peers have naturally suffered greatly from the clearance of the entire neighborhoods. It may well be, however, that slum clearance has inflicted yet graver emotional burdens on Negroes who lack a stable family life and have trouble finding neighbors, shopkeepers, and institutions they can trust may have been hurt even more by forcible removal to new areas. . . .

Little Economic Return to the City

These high financial, social, and emotional costs paid by the slum-dwellers have generally been written off as an unavoidable byproduct of "progress," the price of helping cities to collect more taxes, bring back the middle class, make better use of downtown land, stimulate private investment, and restore civic pride. But, as Anderson shows, urban renewal has hardly justified these claims either. For one thing, urban renewal is a slow process: the average project has taken twelve years to complete. Moreover, while the few areas suitable for luxury housing were quickly rebuilt, less desirable cleared land might lie vacant for many years because developers were — and are — unwilling to risk putting up high- and middle-income housing in areas still surrounded by slums. Frequently, they can be attracted only by promises of tax write-offs, which absorb the increased revenue that renewal is supposed to create for the city. . . . Thus, all too few of the new projects have produced tax gains and returned suburbanites, or generated the magic rebuilding boom. . . .

A Comprehensive Program of Urban Rehousing

The solution is not to repeal urban renewal, but to transform it from a program of slum clearance and rehabilitation into a program of urban rehousing. This means, first, building low- and moderate-cost housing on vacant land in cities, suburbs, and new towns beyond the suburbs, and also helping slum-dwellers to move into existing

(*Continued on page 236*)

Jacob Riis's picture of an East Side (New York City) hovel in 1890 (above) and the Depression-era shack in St. Louis (below) represent slums of an earlier day.

In recent years slum dwellings such as the one at the right have been demolished to make way for high-rise housing projects some have labeled "vertical ghettos." The units below in Hartford, Conn., a city noted for its renewal program, reflect an effort to give variety and livability to public housing.

housing outside the slums; and then, *after* a portion of the urban low-income population has left the slums, clearing and rehabilitating them through urban renewal. This approach is commonplace in many European countries, which have long since realized that private enterprise can no more house the population and eliminate slums than it can run the post office.

Of course, governments in Europe have a much easier task than ours in developing decent low-income projects. Because they take it for granted that housing is a national rather than a local responsibility, the government agencies are not hampered by the kind of real-estate and construction lobbies which can defeat or subvert American programs by charges of socialism. Moreover, their municipalities own a great deal of the vacant land and have greater control over the use of private land than do American cities. But perhaps their main advantage is the lack of popular opposition to moving the poor out of the slums and into the midst of the more affluent residents. Not only is housing desperately short for all income groups, but the European class structure, even in western socialist countries, is still rigid enough so that low- and middle-income groups can live near each other if not next to each other, and still "know their place."

In America, on the other hand, one's house and address are major signs of social status, and no one who has any say in the matter wants people of lower income or status in his neighborhood. Middle-class homeowners use zoning as a way of keeping out cheaper or less prestigious housing, while working-class communities employ less subtle forms of exclusion. Consequently, low-income groups, whatever their creed or color, have been forced to live in slums or near-slums and wait until they could acquire the means to move as a group, taking over better neighborhoods when the older occupants were ready to move on themselves.

5. The Ghettos

Most of the nation's black population now lives in cities, and the number is steadily increasing. Racism is at the heart of America's urban dilemma. The first of the three following documents is from Dark Ghetto *(1965), a report on Harlem attitudes by the eminent black social psychologist Kenneth Clark. It is a brief but compelling analysis of "the ghetto," its sharp contrasts and potential fury.*

In the mid-1960's some of this fury was released in rioting. And in 1967 President Johnson established the National Advisory Commission on Civil Disorders under the chairmanship of Governor Otto Kerner of Illinois to find out "What happened? Why did it happen? What can be done to prevent its happening again?" The second selection is drawn from the Kerner Commission's widely read but largely ignored final report and deals with the problems and options facing American cities.

Against a background of continued urban rioting and violence, the assassinations of Dr. Martin Luther King, Jr., and Senator Robert F. Kennedy in 1968 were the specific incidents which prompted President Johnson to create the National Commission on the Causes and Prevention of Violence under the chairmanship of Dr. Milton S. Eisenhower. A selection from The Politics of Protest, a special report to the Commission, indicates the problems of those left-behind ethnic groups who are the other pole of the black-white confrontation which the Kerner report feared and predicted. ■

A. THE INVISIBLE WALL[1]

✦ Kenneth B. Clark

"Ghetto" was the name for the Jewish quarter in sixteenth-century Venice. Later, it came to mean any section of a city to which Jews were confined. America has contributed to the concept of the ghetto the restriction of persons to a special area and the limiting of their freedom of choice on the basis of skin color. The dark ghetto's invisible walls have been erected by the white society, by those who have power, both to confine those who have *no* power and to perpetuate their powerlessness. The dark ghettos are social, political, educational, and — above all — economic colonies. Their inhabitants are subject peoples, victims of the greed, cruelty, insensitivity, guilt, and fear of their masters.

The objective dimensions of the American urban ghettos are over-crowded and deteriorated housing, high infant mortality, crime, and disease. The subjective dimensions are resentment, hostility, despair, apathy, self-depreciation, and its ironic companion, compensatory grandiose behavior.

The ghetto is ferment, paradox, conflict, and dilemma. Yet within its pervasive pathology exists a surprising human resilience. The ghetto is hope, it is despair, it is churches and bars. It is aspiration for change, and it is apathy. It is vibrancy, it is stagnation. It is courage, and it is defeatism. It is cooperation and concern, and it is suspicion, competitiveness, and rejection. It is the surge toward assimilation, and it is alienation and withdrawal within the protective walls of the ghetto.

. . . Yet the ghetto is not totally isolated. The mass media — radio, television, moving pictures, magazines, and the press — penetrate, indeed, invade the ghetto in continuous and inevitable communication, largely one-way, and project the values and aspirations, the manners and the style of the larger white-dominated society. Those who are required to live in congested and rat-infested homes are aware that other young people have been taught to read, that they have been prepared for college, and can compete successfully for white-collar, managerial, and executive jobs. Whatever accommodations they themselves must make to the negative realities which dominate their own lives, they know consciously or unconsciously that their fate is not the common fate of mankind. . . .

The privileged white community is at great pains to blind itself to conditions of the ghetto, but the residents of the ghetto are not themselves blind to life as it is outside of the ghetto. They observe that others enjoy a better life, and this knowledge brings a [mixture] of hostility, despair, and hope. If the ghetto could be contained totally, the chances of social revolt would be decreased, if not eliminated, but it cannot be contained and the outside world intrudes. The Negro lives in part in the world of television and motion picture[s], bombarded by myths of the American middle class, often believing as literal truth their pictures of luxury and happiness, and yet at the same time confronted by a harsh world of realities where the dreams do not come true or change into nightmares. The discrepancy between the reality and the dream burns into their consciousness. The oppressed can never be sure whether their failures reflect personal inferiority or the fact of color. This persistent and agonizing conflict dominates their lives.

B. THE NATION'S OPTIONS[2]

✦ Kerner Commission

The most basic of [the forces contributing to civil disorder] is the accelerating segregation of low-income, disadvantaged Negroes within the ghettos of the largest American cities. . . . Prospects for domestic peace and for the quality of American life are linked directly to the future of these cities. Two critical questions must be confronted: Where do present trends now lead? What choices are open to us?

The Key Trends

Negro Population Growth. The size of the Negro population in central cities is closely related to total national Negro population growth. In the past sixteen years, about 98 per cent of this growth has occurred within metropolitan areas, and 86 per cent in the central cities of those areas.

A conservative projection of national Negro population growth indicates continued rapid increases. For the period 1966 to 1985, it will rise a total of 30.7 million, gaining an average of 484,000 a year, or 7.6 per cent more than the increase in each year from 1960 to 1966.

. . . Further Negro population growth in central cities depends upon two key factors: in-migration from outside metropolitan areas, and patterns of Negro settlement within metropolitan areas . . . .

As of 1966, the Negro population in all central cities totaled 12.1 million. By 1985, we have estimated that it will rise 68 per cent to 20.3 million. We believe that natural growth will account for 5.2 million of this increase and in-migration for 3.0 million. . . . Growth projected on the basis of natural increase and in-migration would raise the proportion of Negroes to whites in central cities by 1985 from

---

[2] Chapter 16, "The Future of the Cities," *Report of the National Advisory Commission on Civil Disorders* (Washington, D.C.: U.S. Government Printing Office, March 1, 1968), pp. 215–226.

the present 20.7 per cent to between an estimated 31 and 34.7 per cent.

. . . These, however, are national figures. Much faster increase will occur in the largest central cities, where Negro growth has been concentrated in the past two decades. Washington, D.C., Gary [Indiana], and Newark are already over half Negro. A continuation of recent trends would cause the following 10 major cities to become over 50 per cent Negro by the indicated dates.

New Orleans	1971	St. Louis	1978
Richmond	1971	Detroit	1979
Baltimore	1972	Philadelphia	1981
Jacksonville	1972	Oakland	1983
Cleveland	1975	Chicago	1984

. . . Experience indicates that Negro school enrollment in these and other cities will exceed 50 per cent long before the total population reaches that mark. In fact, Negro students already comprise more than a majority in the public elementary schools of 12 of the 13 cities mentioned above. . . . If present trends continue, many cities in addition to those listed above will have Negro school majorities by 1985, probably including Dallas, Pittsburgh, Buffalo, Cincinnati, Harrisburg, Louisville, Indianapolis, Kansas City, Mo., Hartford, and New Haven. . . .

We estimate that the nation's white population will grow 16.6 million, or 9.6 per cent, from 1966 to 1975, and the Negro population 3.8 million, or 17.7 per cent, in the same period. The Negro age group from 15 to 24 years of age, however, will grow much faster than either the Negro population as a whole, or the white population in the same age group. . . . The rapid increase in the young Negro population has important implications for the country. This group has the highest unemployment rate in the nation, commits a relatively high proportion of all crimes, and plays the most significant role in civil disorders. By the same token, it is a great reservoir of underused human resources which are vital to the nation.

The Location of New Jobs. Most new employment opportunities do not occur in central cities, near all-Negro neighborhoods. They are being created in suburbs and outlying areas. . . . Providing employment for the swelling Negro ghetto population will require society to link these potential workers more closely with job locations. This can be done in three ways: by developing incentives to industry to create new employment centers near Negro residential areas; by opening suburban residential areas to Negroes and encouraging them to move closer to industrial centers; or by creating better transportation between ghetto neighborhoods and new job locations. . . .

Choices for the Future

The complexity of American society offers many choices for the future of relations between the central cities and suburbs and patterns of white and Negro settlement in metropolitan areas. For practical purposes, however, we see two fundamental questions:

Should future Negro population growth be concentrated in the central cities, as in the past 20 years, thereby forcing Negro and white populations to become even more residentially segregated?

Should society provide greatly increased special assistance to Negroes and other relatively disadvantaged population groups?

For purposes of analysis, the Commission has defined three basic choices for the future embodying specific answers to these questions:

The Present Policies Choice. Under this course the nation would maintain approximately the share of resources now being allocated to programs of assistance for the poor, unemployed, and disadvantaged. These programs are likely to grow, given continued economic growth and rising federal revenues, but they will not grow fast enough to stop, let alone reverse, the already deteriorating quality of life in central city ghettos. This choice carries the highest ultimate price, as we will point out.

The Enrichment Choice. Under this course the nation would seek to offset the effects of continued Negro segregation and deprivation in large-city ghettos. The enrichment choice would aim at creating dramatic improvements in the quality of life in disadvantaged central-city neighborhoods — both white and Negro. It would require marked increases in federal spending for education, housing, employment, job training, and social services. . . .

The Integration Choice. This choice would be aimed at reversing the movement of the country toward two societies, separate and unequal. The integration choice — like the enrichment choice — would call for large-scale improvement in the quality of ghetto life. But it would also involve both creating strong incentives for Negro movement out of central-city ghettos and enlarging freedom of choice concerning housing, employment, and schools. . . .

The Present Policies Choice

Powerful forces of social and political inertia are moving the country steadily along the course of existing policies toward a divided country. . . . Of the three future courses we have defined, the present policies choice — the choice we are now making — is the course with the most ominous consequences for our society.

. . . We believe that the present policies choice would lead to a larger number of violent incidents of the kind that have stimulated recent major disorders.

First, it does nothing to raise the hopes, absorb the energies, or constructively challenge the talents of the rapidly growing number of young Negro men in central cities. The proportion of unemployed or underemployed among them will remain very high. These young men have contributed disproportionately to crime and violence in cities in the past, and there is danger, obviously, that they will continue to do so.

Second, under these conditions, a rising proportion of Negroes in disadvantaged city areas might come to look upon the deprivation and segregation they suffer as proper justification for violent protest or for extending support to now isolated extremists who advocate civil disruption by guerrilla tactics. . . .

In fact, the likelihood of incidents mushrooming into major disorders would be only slightly higher in the near future under the present policies choice than under the other two possible choices. For no new policies or programs could possibly alter basic ghetto conditions immediately. . . . In the long run, however, the present policies choice risks a seriously greater probability of major disorders, worse, possibly, than those already experienced.

If the Negro population as a whole developed even stronger feelings of being wrongly "penned in" and discriminated against, many of its members might come to support not only riots, but the rebellion now being preached by only a handful. Large-scale violence, followed by white retaliation, could follow. This spiral could quite conceivably lead to a kind of urban *apartheid*[3] with semimartial law in many major cities, enforced residence of Negroes in segregated areas, and a drastic reduction in personal freedom for all Americans, particularly Negroes.

[3] apartheid (ah-*part'*hite): racial segregation of the kind practiced in South Africa.

The same distinction is applicable to the cost of the present policies choice. In the short run, its costs — at least its direct cash outlays — would be far less than for the other choices. . . . But it would be a tragic mistake to view the present policies choice as cheap. Damage figures measure only a small part of the costs of civil disorder. They cannot measure the costs in terms of the lives lost, injuries suffered, minds and attitudes closed and frozen in prejudice, or the hidden costs of the profound disruption of entire cities. . . .

Polarization. Another and more serious consequence is the fact that this course would lead to the permanent establishment of two societies: one predominantly white and located in the suburbs, in smaller cities, and in outlying areas, and one largely Negro located in central cities. We are well on the way to just such a divided nation. This division is veiled by the fact that Negroes do not now dominate many central cities. But they soon will, as we have shown, and the new Negro mayors will be facing even more difficult conditions than now exist.

As Negroes succeed whites in our largest cities, the proportion of low-income residents in those cities will probably increase. . . . Moreover, many of the ills of large central cities spring from their age, their location, and their obsolete physical structures. . . .

These facts underlie the fourfold dilemma of the American city:

Fewer tax dollars come in, as large numbers of middle-income taxpayers move out of central cities and property values and business decline.

More tax dollars are required to provide essential public services and facilities, and to meet the needs of expanding lower income groups.

Each tax dollar buys less, because of increasing costs.

Citizen dissatisfaction with municipal services grows as needs, expectations, and standards of living increase throughout the community.

These are the conditions that would greet the Negro-dominated municipal governments that will gradually come to power in many of our major cities. The Negro electorates in those cities probably would demand basic changes in present policies. Like the present white electorates there, they would have to look for assistance to two basic sources: the private sector and the federal government.

. . . The withdrawal of private capital is already far advanced in most all-Negro areas of our large cities. Even if private investment continued, it alone would not suffice. Big cities containing high proportions of low-income Negroes and block after block of deteriorating older property need very substantial assistance from the federal government to meet the demands of their electorates for improved services and living conditions.

It is probable that Congress will be more heavily influenced by representatives of the suburban and outlying city electorate. These areas will comprise 40 per cent of our total population by 1985, compared with 31 per cent in 1960; and central cities will decline from 32 per cent to 27 per cent.[4]

Since even the suburbs will be feeling the squeeze of higher local government costs, Congress might resist providing the extensive assistance which central cities will desperately need.

Thus the present policies choice, if pursued for any length of time, might force simultaneous political and economic polarization in many of our largest metropolitan areas. Such polarization would involve large central cities — mainly Negro, with many poor and nearly bankrupt — on the one hand and most suburbs, mainly white, generally affluent, but heavily taxed — on the other hand. . . .

The acquisition of power by Negro-dominated governments in central cities is surely a legitimate and desirable exercise of political power by a minority group. . . . But such Negro political development would also involve virtually complete racial segregation and virtually complete spatial separation. By 1985, the separate Negro society in our central cities would contain almost 21 million citizens. That is almost 68 per cent larger than the present Negro population of every Negro nation in Africa except Nigeria. . . .

There are at least two possible developments under the present policies choice which might avert such polarization. The first is a faster increase of incomes among Negroes than has occurred in the recent past. This might prevent the central cities from becoming even deeper "poverty traps" than they now are. . . . The second possible development is migration of a growing Negro middle class out of the central city. . . . There is, however, no evidence that a continuation of present policies would be accompanied by any such movement. . . . Indeed, from 1960 to 1966, there was actually a net total in-migration of Negroes from the urban fringes of metropolitan areas into central cities.

---

[4] Based on Census Bureau series D projections.

The Enrichment Choice

The present policies choice plainly would involve continuation of efforts like Model Cities,[5] manpower programs, and the War on Poverty. These are in fact enrichment programs designed to improve the quality of life in the ghetto. Because of their limited scope and funds, however, they constitute only very modest steps toward enrichment — and would continue to do so even if these programs were somewhat enlarged or supplemented. . . .

Effective enrichment policies probably would have three immediate effects on civil disorders.

First, announcement of specific large-scale programs and the demonstration of a strong intent to carry them out might persuade ghetto residents that genuine remedies for their problems were forthcoming, thereby allaying tensions.

Second, such announcements would strongly stimulate the aspirations and hopes of members of these communities — possibly well beyond the capabilities of society to deliver and to do so promptly. This might increase frustration and discontent, to some extent canceling the first effect.

Third, if there could be immediate action on meaningful job training and the creation of productive jobs for large numbers of unemployed young people, they would become much less likely to engage in civil disorders. . . .

The enrichment choice is in line with some of the currents of Negro protest thought that fall under the label of "Black Power." We do not refer to versions of Black Power ideology which promote violence, generate racial hatred, or advocate total separation of the races. Rather, we mean the view which asserts that the American Negro population can assume its proper role in society and overcome its feelings of powerlessness and lack of self-respect only by exerting power over decisions which directly affect its own members. . . .

The enrichment choice by no means seeks to perpetuate racial segregation. In the end, however, its premise is that disadvantaged Negroes can achieve equality of opportunity with whites while continuing in conditions of nearly complete separation. . . .

Whether or not enrichment in ghetto areas will really work is not

---

[5] **Model Cities:** a program of federal aid to cities. Each city must prepare a comprehensive plan of health, education, and housing in order to be considered for a grant.

yet known, but the enrichment choice is based on the yet-unproven premise that it will. Certainly, enrichment programs could significantly improve existing ghetto schools, if they impelled major innovations. But "separate but equal" ghetto education cannot meet the long-run fundamental educational needs of the central-city Negro population. . . .

In the field of housing, it is obvious that "separate but equal" does not mean really equal. The enrichment choice could greatly improve the quantity, variety, and environment of decent housing available to the ghetto population. It could not provide Negroes with the same freedom and range of choice as whites with equal incomes. . . .

In the end, whatever its benefits, the enrichment choice might well invite a prospect similar to that of the present policies choice: separate white and black societies . . .

The Integration Choice

The third and last course open to the nation combines enrichment with programs designed to encourage integration of substantial numbers of Negroes into the society outside the ghetto. Enrichment must be an important adjunct to any integration course. No matter how ambitious or energetic such a program may be, relatively few Negroes now living in central-city ghettos would be quickly integrated. . . .

The goal must be achieving freedom for every citizen to live and work according to his capacities and desires, not his color.

We believe there are four important reasons why American society must give this course the most serious consideration. First, future jobs are being created primarily in the suburbs, while the chronically unemployed population is increasingly concentrated in the ghetto. This separation will make it more and more difficult for Negroes to achieve anything like full employment in decent jobs. But if, over time, these residents began to find housing outside central cities, they would be exposed to more knowledge of job opportunities, would have much shorter trips to reach jobs, and would have a better chance of securing employment on a self-sustaining basis.

Second, in the judgment of this Commission, racial and social-class integration is the most effective way of improving the education of ghetto children.

Third, developing an adequate housing supply for low-income and middle-income families and true freedom of choice in housing for Negroes of all income levels will require substantial out-movement.

We do not believe that such an out-movement will occur spontaneously as a result of increasing prosperity among Negroes in central cities. A national fair-housing law is essential to begin such movement. . . .

Fourth, and by far most important, integration is the only course which explicitly seeks to achieve a single nation rather than accepting the present movement toward a dual society. This choice would enable us at least to begin reversing the profoundly divisive trend already so evident in our metropolitan areas — before it becomes irreversible.

Conclusions

The future of our cities is neither something which will just happen nor something which will be imposed upon us by an inevitable destiny. That future will be shaped to an important degree by choices we make now.

We have attempted to set forth the major choices because we believe it is vital for Americans to understand the consequences of our present drift:

Three critical conclusions emerge from this analysis:

1. The nation is rapidly moving toward two increasingly separate Americas. Within two decades, this division could be so deep that it would be almost impossible to unite:

a white society principally located in suburbs, in smaller central cities, and [on the edges] of large central cities; and

a Negro society largely concentrated within large central cities

The Negro society will be permanently relegated to its current status, possibly even if we expend great amounts of money and effort in trying to "gild" the ghetto.

2. In the long run, continuation and expansion of such a permanent division threatens us with two perils.

The first is the danger of sustained violence in our cities. The timing, scale, nature, and repercussions of such violence cannot be foreseen. But if it occurred, it would further destroy our ability to achieve the basic American promises of liberty, justice, and equality.

The second is the danger of a conclusive repudiation of the traditional American ideals of individual dignity, freedom, and equality of opportunity. We will not be able to espouse the ideals meaningfully to the rest of the world, to ourselves, to our children. They may still recite the Pledge of Allegiance and say "one nation . . . indivisible." But they will be learning cynicism, not patriotism.

3. We cannot escape responsibility for choosing the future of our metropolitan areas and the human relations which develop within them. It is a responsibility so critical that even an unconscious choice to continue present policies has the gravest implications.

That we have delayed in choosing or, by delaying may be making the wrong choice, does not sentence us either to separatism or despair. But we must choose. We will choose. Indeed, we are now choosing.

C. URBAN WHITE MILITANCY [6]

✤ *Jerome Skolnick*

They have learned from the black people that the squeaky wheel gets the grease, so they're going to squeak, too.

—Tony Imperiale

The leading edge of the growing northern militancy lies in the largely working-class, generally ethnic neighborhoods of the cities. Given a national context in which the representatives of all three major political parties felt compelled to issue remarkably similar demands for "law and order," it is not surprising that a similar, but more strident, demand is made by those who are most directly threatened by the disorder attendant on contemporary social change. In short, the new militancy of the urban working class must be seen in proper perspective. The militancy of those in the white ghettos differs principally in being more urgent.

This urgency is anchored in a set of real and pressing problems. As Robert Wood of HUD [the Department of Housing and Urban Affairs] has put it:

> Let us consider the working American — the average white ethnic male:
> He is the ordinary employee in factory and in office. Twenty million strong, he forms the bulk of the nation's working force. He makes five to ten thousand a year, has a wife and two children; owns a house in town — between the ghetto and the suburbs, or perhaps in a low-cost subdivision on the urban fringe; and he owes plenty in installment debts on his car and appliances.

[6] Jerome Skolnick, *The Politics of Protest*, A Report Submitted to the Task Force on Violent Aspects of Protest and Confrontation, National Commission on the Causes and Prevention of Violence. (New York: Simon & Schuster, Inc., 1969), pp. 170–175.

. . . Despite the gains hammered out by his union, his job security is far from complete. Layoffs, reductions, automation, and plant relocation remain the invisible witches at every christening. He finds his tax burden is heavy; his neighborhood services poor; his national image tarnished; and his political clout d.minishing . . . one comes to understand his tension in the face of the aspiring black minority. . . . He sees the movement of black families as a threat to his home values. He reads about rising crime rates in city streets and feels this is a direct challenge to his family. He thinks the busing of his children to unfamiliar and perhaps inferior schools will blight their chances for a sound education. He sees only one destination for the minority movement — his job.

As has been the case historically, American social and political institutions have not found ways of accommodating both the legitimate grievances of aspiring minorities and the grievances of those who feel the threat of displacement. Nor have those institutions succeeded in substantially lessening the danger of physical violence or criminal victimization which accompany life on the fringes of the slums. The result has been a pervasive insecurity for the white urban dweller, which, while frequently exaggerated, nevertheless has a basis in the rather grim realities of contemporary urban life. Under present conditions, property values may indeed be threatened when blacks move in numbers into white areas; whites living near black ghettos do have to cope directly with the problem of "crime in the streets." . . . It is in the context of these conditions that urban white militancy is nourished. . . .

The Potential for White Violence

One indication of the depth of the new militancy is the body of evidence showing that a sizable segment of the urban population is willing to use violence to defend itself against black disorder. Not only do many northern whites organize in support of harsh police measures against rioters, many urban whites express a willingness to use private violence. A Harris poll taken in September, 1967, indicated that 55 per cent of a sample of white gun owners said they would use their guns to shoot other people in case of a riot. . . . A study of white reaction to the Los Angeles [Watts] riot of 1965 indicates that the willingness to use guns and personal fear of the riot are related. Twenty-three per cent of a sample of whites said that they had felt a great deal of fear for themselves and their families during the riot, and 29 per cent said that they had considered using firearms to protect themselves or their families. . . .

In general, these findings support the conception of the white working and lower-middle class on the ghetto fringe as the most violence-prone wing of the growing white militancy, but the fact that higher-income whites living close to blacks express a high degree of willingness to use violence emphasizes the point that it is the situation — rather than the character or culture of the working class — which is critical . . . .

Further light on the potential for white violence is shed by a study prepared for the Kerner Commission which attempted to pinpoint the "potential white rioter." A sample of whites was asked whether, in case of a Negro riot in their city, they should "do some rioting against them" or leave the matter for the authorities to handle. Eight per cent of male whites advocated counterrioting. Suburban whites were slightly less inclined to advocate a counterriot than were city whites. Less educated whites tended to support counterrioting, and there was a striking degree of advocacy of counterriot by teenage males, 21 per cent of whom agreed that they should riot against Negroes. This percentage was slightly higher than the percentage of Negro teenagers who said they would join a riot if one occurred in their city.

. . . Studies of recent riots indicate that a significant number of "riot-related" arrests of whites have taken place. Occasionally, as in the Detroit riot of 1967, whites have been arrested on charges of looting, apparently in cooperation with blacks. More frequently, however, white males have been arrested beyond or near the [edges] of riot areas for "looting outside the riot areas, riding through the area armed, refusing to recognize a police perimeter, shooting at Negroes." Such incidents were particularly apparent in the New Haven, Plainfield, Dayton, and Cincinnati riots of 1967. The white counterriot, of course, has historical precedent: most of the northern race riots before 1935 involved pitched battles between whites and blacks, with working-class white youth particularly in evidence. . . .

Although youth have been prominent in relatively disorganized instances of militant white violence, the major efforts at organized militancy have been made by the adults who comprise the leadership of the various neighborhood defense organizations which have appeared in the North and West. Some of these, like the "Breakthrough" organization in Detroit, urge members to "study, arm, store provisions, and organize"; a similar group called "Fight Back" in Warren, Michigan, argues that "The only way to stop them is at the city limits." Others focus less on storage and training, concentrating on community patrols to discourage black intrusion. The most significant of these urban vigilante groups is the North Ward Citizens Committee of Newark, whose leader, Anthony Imperiale,[7] has recently been elected to the Newark City Council.

Newark's Angry Whites

Newark's North Ward is a primarily Italian-American neighborhood with a large and growing black population, adjacent to the predominantly black Central Ward, which was the scene of the Newark riot of 1967. . . .

. . . The North Ward Italians feel themselves beleaguered by a horde of criminal blacks, instigated by radicals. The North Ward Citizens Committee operates patrols of the neighborhood, and members train in karate. Their militant quest for law and order is rooted in a set of severe insecurities attendant on life in Newark, where all the problems of the urban white North exist in extreme form. Newark is over half black; it leads all cities of its size in crime rates. It was the scene of one of the most disastrous episodes of black disorder and violent official response in the sixties. The sense of fear pervading the white ghetto is reflected in Imperiale's words: "When is it gonna stop? Everybody says, 'don't bother 'em now. Leave 'em alone, and they'll calm down.' Well, it took riots that burned down half of a town before we learned."

Accompanying the fear of black violence is a strong sense of relative injustice. The citizens of the North Ward, conscious that their own neighborhood is deteriorating, strongly resent the concentration of state and federal monies being poured into the black community.

> Are there no poor whites? But the Negroes get all the antipoverty money. When pools are being built in the Central Ward, don't they think the white kids have got frustration? The whites are the majority. You know how many of them come to me, night after night, because they can't get a job? They've been told, we have to hire Negroes first.

The sense of special and unjust treatment for whites with grievances is compounded by what Imperiale regards as unfair discrimination against his organization:

[7] Imperiale was an unsuccessful candidate for mayor of Newark in the primary of May, 1970. In the runoff election a Negro, Kenneth A. Gibson, defeated the incumbent mayor, Hugh Addonizio, on trial at the time for extortion and conspiracy, of which he was convicted.

The Mayor says he is going to try to get funds to start civilian patrols in the Central Ward. He claims this should be done for the so-called ghetto area. I went to Washington to get federal funds to set up a civilian patrol program in the North Ward and the other areas of the city, black as well as white, and I was pushed from pillar to post. It is all right for the Central Ward but not for the North Ward where I am called a paramilitary organization.

In August, Imperiale's headquarters was bombed, and Imperiale has been highly critical of the lack of response by the law and city officials. "What makes me mad is that if the bombing had happened in the Central Ward, there would have been all kinds of FBI agents and authorities. When we get bombed, neither the Mayor, the Governor, nor anyone else said it was a bad thing to have happened. No statement whatsoever was made in the papers."

This sense of injustice and of exclusion from political concern could lead to a heightened political alienation. The citizens of Newark's North Ward are largely correct in feeling that the [government] has ignored them. At present, the Imperiale organization remains involved in traditional political action through the electoral process. Imperiale has insisted on this: "The Anti-Vigilante bill will do nothing because I am not a Vigilante. I am one-hundred-per-cent for a [law against paramilitary organizations] that would outlaw people dressed in uniforms getting together and practicing sabotage and overthrow of the government. I love the government and am trying to save it." Should legitimate politics bear few significant results in terms of the grievances of the white ghetto, the North Ward Citizens Committee and similar groups may feel driven beyond politics. If this were to happen, the protest of the working-class urban white could take a new and ominous form.

6. Lee of New Haven[1]

♣ *Bernard Asbell*

On of the toughest jobs in the nation today is that of mayor of a city, large or small. The multiplicity of demands, the scarcity

[1] Adapted from Bernard Asbell, "Dick Lee Discovers How Much Is Not Enough," *New York Times Magazine*, September 3, 1967, pp. 6–7, 31, 40–42. © 1967, by The New York Times Company.

of funds, the muddled demarcations of responsibility all contribute to a mayor's frustrations. Richard Lee served as chief executive of New Haven, Connecticut, from 1954 to 1970. The following article reveals the dimensions of his job, the breadth of his accomplishments, and the depth of his disappointments. ■

He couldn't know it at the time, of course, but it was only an early summer false alarm. Mayor Richard C. Lee had just received an ominous phone call from a police official, telling him that a couple of bottles of gasoline had been found in an alley. Mayor Lee was still an innocent among mayors; his city had not yet blown.

The Mayor glared out of his office window, across the expanse of the New Haven Green, at the ancient dormitories of Yale [University]. Then he strode about the room, packing his first into his palm.

"I'm supposed to give everyone confidence, including the police. But sometimes I have to exude a confidence I don't feel. Dammit, you can't tell a soul. You got to sit here lonely as hell and wonder who it is out there. They tell me I control everything. . . . But I can't sit down with that kid, whoever he is, and find out what he wants. One match, and my city — after thirteen years of work — will be down with all the rest of them."

That's the way it's been for the anguished men holding office across America in the agonizing summer of 1967, and the way it may remain for some summers to come. Yet even after Newark went down — and Detroit and Spanish Harlem [New York] and Hartford and Syracuse and all the rest — many believed . . . that it would not happen in New Haven. That small city appeared the pinnacle of enlightened, constructive effort to reach the heart of urban discontent. Then, on the sweltering Saturday night of August 19, New Haven, blew, too. . . . In three convulsive nights New Haven became a symbol of how much is not enough. Nobody knows how much *is* enough — or how much of what. Are the greatest needs tangible, to be bought with tax dollars — or intangible, the reshaping of community attitudes? . . . If nobody yet knows, almost everybody agrees . . . that New Haven's has been the most advanced, sophisticated thrust toward an answer that will eventually succeed. Thus it is important before the hot summer grows entirely cool, to take a detailed look at what New Haven and Richard C. Lee tried to do.

Fund City's Renewal Experience

New Haven, 70 miles northeast of the seething metropolis that at lighter moments is called Fun City [New York], has so disproportionately and for so long bagged federal dollars in the case of remaking itself that it has become known among bureaucrats as Fund City. The $120,000,000 for urban renewal by which New Haven has lightened the federal treasury is only surpassed by subsidies to the giant cities of New York, Philadelphia, Boston, and Chicago. . . .

New Haven has more to show for renewal than shiny new buildings. In tearing down old slum walls, New Haven found it did not relieve the real problems of the poor; it merely revealed them. So, five years ago, [the city] applied to the Ford Foundation for $2,500,000 to try what no city had ever attempted: a many-pronged project in human renewal, bringing new opportunities for education, work, and self-dependence to the poor. Its experience, perhaps more than that of any other community, provided the design for the Economic Opportunity Act of 1964, which is the main thrust of the War on Poverty. . . .

[Lee has often been criticized for] not having completed the job. He has not wiped out poverty or all poor housing although New Haven is a far better place than it was. Almost 9000 old dwelling units have been rehabilitated. Physical renewal, both in rehabilitation and new construction, has swept across an astonishing 30 per cent of the city's land area, touching 50 per cent of its population. One third of the city's aging school buildings have been replaced by bright new ones.

In the beginning, the job seemed easy. At that time, Congress had authorized $500,000,000 for urban renewal, but cities had requested an embarrassingly small sum of only $74,000,000. Local officials were afraid of the political booby traps involved in condemning slums and relocating the poor; many citizens were even more offended at the thought of taking land with public funds and turning it over to private developers for the seeking of profit. Lee was untroubled by these moral obstacles.

Financed by federal funds, Lee aimed a bulldozer through the decrepit Oak Street district and connected the Connecticut Turnpike with downtown.

For a while, it was a beautiful road leading nowhere. Lee soon learned why most mayors avoided taking leadership in rebuilding their downtown districts. Where do you put the dehoused families? Who will put up millions for gleaming new buildings before there are prosperous tenants to guarantee long-term leases? Where will you get the tenants before you have the promoters, the plans, the rental terms?

After years of excruciating suspense . . . , steel girders began to rise into a new telephone-company building, then a cluster of luxury apartments. The city's leading merchant, Malley's, erected a modern department store adjoining a multilevel parking area designed by Paul Rudolph.[2] When R. H. Macy & Company decided to become a neighbor of Malley's — and of Rudolph's garage — the turning had come. Before long, a gleaming office building and a hotel, the Park Plaza, towered over the new commercial center.

To house the poor families of Oak Street, Lee did the obvious. . . . [He] poured federal funds into an expansion, started by his predecessor, of a low-cost housing project called Elm Haven, away from the center of the city. Dispossessed families poured into the new, red-brick structures. Back came the echoes through the schools, the Police Department, the Welfare Bureau: little in the misery-ridden lives of these families had really changed. Lee and his redevelopment lieutenants came to a resolve that at the time was revolutionary: there would be no more large, low-cost housing projects. They are nothing but transplanted ghettos where the poor are lost among the other poor, the alienated among the alienated, unmotivated school children consigned to schools full of their own.

"Scatterization" and Other Lee Devices

Clearly, one alternative was to scatter small clusters of low-cost apartments among the dwellings of the middle class. The theory was fine, but the politics was murder.

The fast-growing Negro population was approaching 15 per cent of the total. Their few leaders, supported by liberal voices, particularly among the Yale faculty, were demanding that Lee do something to break open the ghetto walls. To the rest of the city, however, nothing could be less attractive. More than a third of the city's population were Italians who traditionally cling to old neighborhoods and were hardly likely to welcome intrusion by lower-class Negroes. Next in number to Italians came the Irish who, joined by middle-class Jews

[2] **Paul Rudolph:** distinguished architect, former head of the Department of Architecture at Yale.

of Westville and dwindling communities of Yankee Protestants, might go along with housing projects for the poor — "but not near our block. . . ."

With the skill of a virtuoso, Lee soft-pedaled "scatterization." He attacked the spread of slums in a way that appeared to be less drastic. He reduced the attack by separating it into less recognizable parts. A major part of the poor are old. Nobody minds little old ladies and gentlemen . . . on social security living nearby. On a half-dozen sites around town sprang up sprightly developments of senior-citizen housing. . . .

Another major group was the working poor, as distinguished from the "welfare poor." For them, Lee's staff invoked an obscure clause — Section 2219d)3 — of the Federal Housing Law. Under this clause, any nonprofit group (a church, a union, or whatever) advancing "seed money" of a few thousand dollars can get a large, federally guaranteed loan for building a development of homes. Once built, the apartments are sold as cooperatives to their tenants. A family with the most meager of savings may purchase an apartment for about $300 down and maintain it for about $115 a month.

Still, what to do about the welfare poor? Lee devised an experiment of using federal housing funds to pay a landlord the difference between the rental of a large apartment and the rental allowance permitted by state welfare regulations. This experiment covered only 27 families. It worked so well, however, that the Johnson administration established the device nationally. . . .

Another Lee device, called "turnkey housing," is just getting under way. A private building contractor may buy a tract of land, build a low-cost housing project, and sell it outright to the City Housing Authority, which becomes the landlord. Thus, by accepting the turnover of keys, the city is relatively protected from accusations of having "chosen" to scatterize a low-cost housing site "over here near us." The choice was made by a private capitalist, and who can criticize that?

Clever as these devices may be, they were small-scale. They could hardly begin to keep up with the spreading need. As the major effort, the Lee government has relied on rehabilitating neglected old homes. . . .

Lee recalls, "We provided planners, home improvement people, landscapers, architects, even some students from the Yale School of Architecture, to sit down with homeowners and advise them how to make their property more attractive, more livable — and more valuable. That had its critics, too. Some people called it tokenism. Well, we've been engaged in tokenism for a long time. Neighborhood after neighborhood, street after street. You put enough tokens together and it comes out the right way. . . ."

The Mayor's Day

Almost any day in the life of 51-year-old Richard C. Lee is a microcosm of the triumphs and agonies, the roughhousing and delicacy, the complexities and minutiae that blend into the skills of modern mayoring. . . .

Since any politician's first duty is keeping himself in office, Lee begins his day with first things — an hour at home tending to small affairs of one man here, one vote there, before proceeding to City Hall for mayoring on a grand scale. At a desk in a sunlit study off the living room, he reached for the morning paper and, with hardly a glance at the front page, turned to the obituaries.

"Here's that fellow who died of some disease in Vietnam, but I don't think they shipped him back yet," he mused aloud. "Oh, here's the lady who used to do my mother's hair. We've got to go to that one." His chauffeur made a note. Lee seldom attends fewer than two wakes a day. Over his thirteen years in office, there is hardly a voter whose hand he has not shaken in the solemnity of a funeral home. . . .

Completing his search of the obits, the Mayor reached for his telephone to bark at the city park director because a difficulty in buying a piece of land for a playground had turned up in a letter from the dissatisfied seller. "Listen," the Mayor growled, "your job is to keep those things off my desk. If you don't come to a decision with these people, they wind up in my office. And, remember, I've got to see them. *I* don't have tenure, *you* do." . . .

Arriving at his office at 10 o'clock after his circuitous ride from home, the Mayor was joined by a half-dozen aides from City Hall, from the Redevelopment Agency, from Community Progress, Inc., the antipoverty agency. The biggest business on his mind was the $100,000 he was about to receive from the Office of Economic Opportunity for summer recreation and jobs for teenagers.

"We need programs, *programs*," he exhorted. "I want programs that are original and revolutionary. I want them yesterday."

"We're meeting on this next Thursday," one aide said, but was quickly cut off.

"I'm tired of meetings. These kids in the street may not wait for your doggone meeting." . . .

A bearded Orthodox rabbi, principal of a Jewish day school, was shown in. The Mayor, suddenly a serene public official without a care in the world, joked about the Arabs and the Israelis. They talked about the rabbi's *shul*, the Mayor promising it wouldn't be demolished by a renewal project for a year and a half. The rabbi smiled in appreciation. Lee leaned forward significantly. He had not called the rabbi in for light chitchat.

"Rabbi, I've got to use that school playground of yours this summer. The new people coming into that neighborhood — their kids need it."

"All I ask is that I get it back in September."

The Mayor punched a button on his intercom unit. Through its speaker, a man's voice greeted him, that of Lawrence Spitz, director of Community Progress, whose office was two blocks away. "Larry," the Mayor said, "the rabbi is here to offer his playground. Isn't that fine?" He added, "He's here now."

Spitz picked up the cue and declaimed, "We can certainly use it, and we're sincerely gratified. . . ."

Then the day was turned in an unexpected direction by the telephone call from his police official. After the opening words, the Mayor sank thoughtfully, grimly into his chair. [His] questions were hard and specific. "Do they look like [Molotov] cocktails?" "Do they have a wick?" "Any prints?" "Any suspects?" To all the questions, the answers were uncertain. The Mayor commanded:

"Keep me informed. Say nothing to anybody. That means nobody."

Then he repeated to himself, "Dammit, you can't tell a soul."

* * *

The time was now about 1 P.M., and the threat of firebombs was heavy in the air. After an endless stretch of silent tension in the Mayor's office, another call informed Lee that the bottles, although wickless, were believed to be intended as firebombs.

Ironically, the Mayor's next visitors were a group of police officials from across the country who happened to be visiting New Haven for a conference on using computers in crime detection. They were making a courtesy call.

One of them asked, "How are things going in New Haven, sir?"
Lee shrugged. "Mondays and Tuesdays are O.K. Sometimes Wednesdays are another story."

The Long Hot Summer in New Haven

Not a man to trust to luck, Lee arranged never to spend a night out of the city all through the hot weeks [of summer, 1967]. He declined all engagements, political or social, on Friday and Saturday nights. These he spent at home in a vigil by the phone in his study. On Saturday night, August 19, the call he dreaded came. Stores in the Hill district were in flames. As word flashed around the city, the Dixwell district erupted, then the neighborhoods of Newhallville and Fair Haven. Then three horrendous nights followed.

As Lee took over a command post in City Hall, another man, apparently as surprised by the outbreak as the mayor, was taking a kind of leadership in the streets. Fred Harris seemed to be everywhere at once, pleading with roving gangs of thrill-seeking juveniles to cool it.

But that effort was premature. The people in the streets were still in need of more dramatic satisfaction of racial hostility. As one smiling 30-year-old Negro woman, gazing around at the debris, said to a reporter:

"Lee was so sure nothing would happen to his pretty city. As far as I'm concerned, this is a good thing."

As the debris was swept away, Lee wearily toured his city. Oddly, the scene was hardly as dramatic as headline readers may have been led to believe. What mainly met the eye was that a few store windows along a few commercial avenues were boarded up — some to cover broken glass, others as a precaution against breakage. Looting had not been heavy.

Reporters swarmed through the now quiet ghetto probing for analytical wisdom that few seemed ready to offer. They asked "Why?" and people shook their heads. Reporters searched for deep social causation even while it was clear that the violence was a teenage tantrum, not a programmed protest. A Hill housewife remarked, "I don't know who started it, but whoever did must have rocks in their heads."

The more socially significant the comments were, the less they explained. "Low-cost housing is the critical issue," said Willie Counsel, Hill Parents' Association vice president. Yet one of the first avenues to erupt was Dixwell, along the site of the massive Elm Haven low-cost housing project. "The job training and placement program is only tokenism," said Henry Parker, a Negro school teacher. "A kid is in training for about a year and still can't find a job." Yet Kenneth Redmond, an assistant principal, remarked that he had seen some of his former students looting the Peoples' Market — and they were kids with good jobs. The contradictions seemed to allow room for only one explanation: That it's hell to be black, poor, and ghettoed in rich white America, and that even in New Haven, teenagers had to do something with their suppressed rage.

7. Going Metro: Nashville[1]

✤ Forbes Magazine

The fragmented political framework within which they have to operate has frustrated those trying to deal with area-wide problems such as crime and pollution. One attempt at a solution has been the consolidation of core city and suburbs into one governmental unit, in much the same way that the states are linked under the federal system. Dade County (Miami), Florida, adopted such a plan in 1957 and has been modifying it ever since. In Tennessee in 1962, Nashville-area voters accepted an audacious arrangement which joined five counties under one jurisdiction. Metropolitan government is nothing new, but two factors account for renewed interest in it: first, the suburbs have come to realize that they cannot be "iron-curtained" off from the core city; and second, some whites fear that blacks will "take over" the cities unless a wider constituency is created by some form of federation. The following article reveals the reasons why Nashville finally chose to "go Metro" and describes early results.

Somewhere, somehow, the people who live in the suburbs will have to learn, maybe in a fatal way, that their whole existence depends more on the central city than on that nice house they live in. I hope they learn it quick enough so that nice houses won't have to be destroyed.

[1] From *Forbes Magazine*, Vol. 101, No. 10 (May 15, 1968), pp. 51–52. Reprinted by permission.

Mayor C. Beverly Briley of Metropolitan Nashville can afford to utter this dark warning because five years ago his city did something about its problems. It merged with the outlying suburbs to form a 535-square-mile "Metro" government with nearly half a million people. It did so because Nashville, like many another U.S. city, was beginning to rot downtown. This deeply concerned the city's banks, alert to Nashville's role as a regional financial, wholesale, and retail center drawing its customers from middle Tennessee, southern Kentucky, and northeastern Mississippi.

Businessmen for Metro

Actually, for the banks, Nashville's decay would have meant their own. Explains T. Scott Fillebrown, Jr., executive vice president of the First American National Bank: "Tennessee banks are limited to the county in which their headquarters are located. We can set up branches in this county, but we can't move into any other county in the state. If a company moves from Nashville to an adjoining county, we can't follow it. This means that our downtown headquarters in Nashville depends heavily on the health of the downtown area. That's why we were so keenly interested in Metro."

Fillebrown, who has become chairman of Nashville's Housing Authority, which is responsible for all public housing and renewal projects, says: "Eight years ago Nashville had serious problems. Land values and rentals were dropping downtown. There were few new buildings. Fortunately we caught Nashville's downtown rot in time. Property values are back up. You can see new buildings going up all over the place. Nashville recently completed its "Capitol Hill" project including a new domed auditorium. Now Fillebrown's agency is in Phase I of a $100-million downtown renewal that will start by rebuilding fourteen city blocks. . . .

The path to Metro was not a smooth one. Metro lost the first countywide charter vote in 1958. Opposed to it was a strange mix of opposition: center-city Democratic jobholders who feared the "county crowd"; Negro militants who figured it would dilute their voting power downtown; suburban businessmen who feared higher taxes; and hard-core conservatives who see any governmental centralization as part of a Moscow plot. Metro finally passed (by a comfortable majority) in 1962 largely because of the all-out support of the banks, downtown stores, and insurance companies as personified by men like Fillebrown. . . .

Suburban Taxpayers "Get Involved"

One of Metro's main advantages, says Farris A. Deep, executive director of Nashville's Metropolitan Planning Commission, is that "suburbanites had to pay taxes for downtown problems. When they had to pay, they suddenly became interested in solving those problems." Adds Professor Daniel R. Grant, political science professor at Vanderbilt and one of Metro's designers: "So often we have a government structure that permits those out in lily-white suburbs to say, 'We out in Azalea Heights can solve our (nonexistent) welfare problems, why don't you people downtown in Gutter City solve your welfare problems?' In Nashville we have brought together the human resources of both groups, compelling them to come face to face to look at the problems of the core city." . . .

The new Metro system has enabled the city's administration to be streamlined much the way the merger of two railroads can cut out overlapping jobs and duplication of service. "A city is a municipal corporation," [a City Council member] says, "and this city sells $100 million a year in services. The merger of the county and the suburbs with downtown Nashville has made it possible to give more services for a better price."

One of the major changes effected was in taxes. Prior to merger, suburbanites paid only county property taxes at a rate (in 1960) of $2.78 per $100 of assessed value — with assessments at about 40 per cent of market value. The relatively poorer downtown dwellers had to pay both county and Nashville City taxes, for a 1960 total of $5.33 per $100.

Metro Nashville now has two tax districts. The general district covers everybody: its tax money goes into area-wide services such as the unified school system, the airport, and roads. To help pay for these, suburban taxes were raised 72 cents to $3.50 per $100. . . . By establishing one school system, Nashville has cut out its double standard for schools. The system now assigns its top teachers, white or Negro, to the toughest downtown slum schools where the major effort is needed. For the first time in its history, there are a number of Negro teachers out in suburbia.

One interesting move to come out of the Metro merger was the chance to extend the city's sewer system. Prior to Metro, suburban developers just plopped new houses down wherever land would pass a septic-tank percolation test. There were no sewers. Now the downtown sewer system is being pushed throughout the suburbs, and land is being developed according to an area-wide plan.

The extension of the sewer system gave the Metro government a chance to experiment with collecting "use charge" taxes for sewer and water use from the array of government offices, religious organizations, and especially universities that account for the fact that 35 per cent of local land is tax free. . . .

Prosperity and Morale

The new blend of unified government and suburban money and brains flowing back into Nashville leads William C. Weaver, executive vice president of National Life, to say, "This city has caught fire. The scent of magnolia blossoms has been replaced by a more subtle, satisfying smell — that of money." And there is no doubt that his company, as well as most of Nashville's other major financial companies, now accounting for some four billion dollars in assets, stand to gain from today's sharply rising land values.

But there is more to it than money, more even than the arrival of new factories and the proliferation of the city's air, highway, and water transportation. Nashville was not really hit by rioting during last month's upheaval following Martin Luther King, Jr.'s, death. But Nashville businessmen reacted in a way that no one would have thought possible five years ago. A group of them invited civil rights leader Whitney Young, Jr., executive director of the National Urban League, to come to Nashville to help set up a local chapter. Even before Dr. King's death, Nashville businessmen formed a limited-profit company to build 3500 new homes in an experimental interracial development, Trinity Hill. . . .

The most interesting feature of Trinity Hill is the fact that city planners are entwining $10,000 homes in and around much more expensive homes and apartments in an interracial and intereconomic mix. Says Chief Planner Farris Deep: "There's no point building public housing on a mass scale for these people. You just transfer them from a wooden ghetto into a concrete ghetto. By mixing them in with higher-income people they have a better chance at a local walking-distance job and a better environment in which to start climbing the ladder. . . ."

Businessmen and city officials are convinced that Metro government has turned Nashville around. But will it work in other cities? Says Vanderbilt professor Grant, "For cities Nashville's size it *can* work. Their suburbs are not so powerful. Jacksonville, Florida, is starting Metro government this year. Charleston is voting on it. Atlanta, Indianapolis, Topeka, Tampa, Tacoma, Charlotte, and Seattle are studying it closely and might go Metro."

8. The New Atlanta¹

✦ William S. Ellis

The revival of downtown business districts was perhaps the most visible sign of the renewed vitality of American cities. Everywhere spectacular new skylines rose from the old centers. Shortly after World War II Pittsburgh undertook a major rehabilitation program which resulted in the celebrated "Golden Triangle." Replacing a mixture of outdated commercial facilities, rundown housing, and older public buildings (as well as some attractive and historically interesting structures), the new development placed shimmering towers of steel, aluminum, and glass at the point where the Allegheny and Monongahela Rivers join to form the Ohio. Another example of downtown rehabilitation was Atlanta where public and private funds infused new life in a declining central business district. ■

I had come to know Atlanta some fifteen years ago, when it was still a relaxed southern city on the brink of its destiny. Now I found the city caught up on a wave of development and growth, strengthening its role as a transportation hub, medical and educational center, financial capital of a large section of the country, and ballet-to-baseball sophisticate in culture and major-league sports. . . .

Today's Atlanta boils with activity. High above a downtown corner where I used to listen to the shrill admonishments of a tattooed evangelist, workmen pour concrete around a rib cage of a building under construction. Express buses to the new $18,000,000 stadium

---

¹ William S. Ellis, "Atlanta, Pacesetter City of the South," *National Geographic*, Vol. 135, No. 2 (February 1969), pp. 248–252, 271–272. Reprinted by permission.

line the curb of another block, siphoning clumps of sports fans from the sidewalk. In the hotels, hordes of convention-goers do battle with the doors of packed elevators.

Marveling at the many changes led me to wonder about the survival of the town's personality. . . .

"Atlanta's character has always been one of growth and progress, so there's no danger of that being lost," I was assured by Mayor Ivan Allen, Jr.[2] "Of course there's some nostalgia for the way things were, but we can't live in the past."

Responsibility for Atlanta's position as flagship city of the Southeast rests largely with Mayor Allen and former Mayor William B. Hartsfield. Most Atlantans credit Bill Hartsfield who held the office for 24 years, with guiding their city from the verge of bankruptcy to an enviable financial stability.

Just before succeeding Mayor Hartsfield in 1962, Ivan Allen, as president of the Chamber of Commerce, engineered the spectacular success of "Forward Atlanta," "a program aimed at selling Atlanta to the nation as a good place to do business. . . . More than 400 of the nation's 500 biggest industrial corporations now maintain operations in Atlanta. . . .

Downtown Atlanta is undergoing an imaginative facelifting that carries the promise of a new concept in urban living. Showcase of this effort to keep downtown bustling and vital is Peachtree Center, a cluster of buildings destined to become a city within a city.

Peachtree Center mirrors the vision of John C. Portman, Jr., a gifted young Atlanta architect driven by impatience. His first building in the complex was the 22-story Atlanta Merchandise Mart opened in 1961; a recent expansion made it the second largest such facility in the nation, after the Merchandise Mart in Chicago. He followed that with three office towers, a hotel, and a bus terminal. Soon to come: a 70-story skyscraper.

Talking in his office on the 21st floor of the Peachtree Center Building, Portman was full of infectious enthusiasm for the promise of cities. "As architects, we have been building . . . single buildings. We have to do more if we are to solve the problems of our complex society. What we are doing at Peachtree Center is developing coordinated urban units. There will be 45 acres where you can walk without ever getting on the same level as an automobile. . . . We're

---

[2] After eight years in office, Mayor Allen decided not to seek re-election. He was succeeded by Sam H. Massell, Jr.

planning gardens and galleries and restaurants, museums, and theaters, places to live and work — everything. This is the grand scale; this is what cities are all about."

When Peachtree Center is completed, a person will be able to live, work, shop, play, and worship without leaving the $175,000,000 complex — and do it all on foot without walking more than seven and a half minutes at a time from any one unit to another.

"The average person will walk for seven and a half minutes rather than bother to take a car or a bus," Portman explained. "So that's the limiting time factor in locating the units. You see, what we're trying to do is to turn this thing back to a man on foot in a village, but a village in the center of the whole throbbing heart of a great city."

From Portman's office window I looked across Peachtree Street to the Regency Hyatt House, the young architect's most creative work. Viewed from the outside, the hotel holds little hint of what's in store for the persons about to enter the building for the first time. The entranceways are dark and confining. But then: space expands overwhelmingly in the lobby, soaring to the heavens in a 22-story sunlit atrium. Glass-bubble elevators, festooned with rows of lights, streak up and down the columns of the great court. Water flows musically within the tubes of an unusual 70-foot mountain. A massive . . . parasol-like cover over an elevated cocktail lounge in the lobby hangs suspended from the ceiling by a single cable. Topping it off, a lounge slowly revolves on the roof. At night its Plexiglas dome glows a soft blue, adding a decorative scoop of marzipan to the city's skyline. . . .

As home for so many colleges and universities, Atlanta is a city steeped in the fine arts. The Metropolitan Opera first sent a company to Atlanta in 1910, and its appearance each year highlights not only the city's musical calendar but the bustling social season as well. In October, 1968, the city dedicated the Atlanta Memorial Arts Center, a $13,000,000 colonnaded building erected in memory of 122 Atlanta art patrons killed in 1962 when their chartered plane crashed in Paris. The French Government honored the memory of the victims by giving a six-foot-seven-inch bronze casting of Rodin's "L'Ombre" (The Shade) to the center.

Under the big roof of the center on Peachtree Street there is something for everyone interested in the arts: the High Museum of Art (including a collection of Old Masters); Atlanta School of Art; the Atlanta Symphony Orchestra under Robert Shaw's direction; and the

Atlanta Municipal Theater, Inc., which includes ballet, opera, repertory theater, and children's theater. The center houses a symphony hall with 1848 seats, an 868-seat theater for ballet, plays, and opera, and the intimate Studio theater with only 200 seats.

Instrumental in making the center a reality was Richard H. Rich [chairman of the board of Rich's department store], a name synonymous with Atlanta's growth in recent years. Under his leadership, the Atlanta Arts Alliance, the center's founding body, spearheaded drives to finance the facility.

"We [Atlanta's business leaders] got together one day, and someone said the city needs more cultural activities," Rich recalled. "So we raised $6,500,000."

9. Is There an Urban Crisis?[1]
✤ *Edward C. Banfield*

While despair characterized much writing about the problems of the contemporary city, not all experts were willing to give up. Edward Banfield of Harvard University offered a new perspective on the crisis in his book The Unheavenly City *(1970). This statement was important not only because it came from one of the most important academic specialists in urban affairs, but also because it was widely believed that his general approach was shared by key officials in the Nixon administration and probably by the President himself. The excerpts given reveal the provocative ideas of Mr. Banfield, who was chosen to head President Nixon's Task Force on Model Cities.* ∎

That we face an urban crisis of utmost seriousness has in recent years come to be part of the conventional wisdom. We are told on all sides that cities are uninhabitable, that they must be torn down and rebuilt or new ones must be built from the ground up, that something drastic must be done — and soon — or else.

[1] From *The Unheavenly City* by Edward C. Banfield, by permission of Little, Brown and Co. Copyright © 1968, 1970 by Edward C. Banfield.

On the face of it, this "crisis" view has a certain plausibility. One need not walk more than a few blocks in any city to see much that is wrong and in crying need of improvement. It is [paradoxical] that in a society as technologically advanced and as affluent as ours there should be many square miles of slums and even more miles of dreary blight and chaotic sprawl. And when one considers that as many as 60 million more people may live in metropolitan areas in 1980 than lived there in 1960, it seems clear that unless something drastic is done things are bound to get worse.

There is however, another side to the matter. The plain fact is that the overwhelming majority of city-dwellers live more comfortably and conveniently than ever before. They have more and better housing, more and better schools, more and better transportation, and so on. By any conceivable measure of material welfare the present generation of urban Americans is, on the whole, better off than any other large group of people has ever been anywhere. What is more, there is every reason to expect that the general level of comfort and convenience will continue to rise even faster through the foreseeable future.

The question arises, therefore, not of whether we are faced with an urban crisis, but rather, *in what sense* we are faced with one. Whose interests and what interests are involved? How deeply? What should be done? Given the political and other realities of the situation, what *can* be done?

Some Problems Are Really Conditions

A great many so-called urban problems are really conditions that we either cannot change or do not want to incur the disadvantages of changing. The presence of a great many people in one place is a cause of inconvenience, to say the least. But the advantages of having so many people in one place far outweigh the inconveniences. . . . To "eliminate congestion" in the city must mean eliminating the city's reason for being. Congestion in the city is a "problem" only in the sense that congestion in Times Square on New Year's Eve is one; in fact, of course, people come to the city, just as they do to Times Square, precisely because it is congested. If it were not congested, it would not be worth going to.

Most of the "problems" that are generally supposed to constitute "the urban crisis" could not conceivably lead to disaster. . . . Consider, for example, an item that often appears near the top of the list of complaints about the city — the journey to work. It takes the average worker in a metropolitan area about half an hour to get to work, and only about 15 per cent of workers spend more than three-quarters of an hour getting there. It would, of course, be very nice if the journey to work were much shorter. No one can suppose, however, that the essential welfare of many people would be much affected even if it were 15 minutes longer. Certainly its being longer or shorter would not make the difference between a good society and a bad one.

The same can be said about efforts to "beautify" the cities. That for the most part the cities are dreary and depressing, if not offensively ugly, may be granted; the desirability of improving their appearance . . . cannot be questioned. It is very doubtful, however, that people are dehumanized (to use a favorite word of those who complain about the cities) by the ugliness of the city or that they would be in any sense humanized by its being made beautiful. . . .

Air pollution comes closer than any of these problems to threatening essential welfare, as opposed to comfort, convenience, amenity, and business advantage. Some people die early because of it, and many more suffer various degrees of bad health; there is also some possibility (no one knows how much) that a meteorological coincidence (an "air inversion") over a large city might suddenly kill thousands or even tens of thousands. Important as it is, however, the air pollution problem is rather minor as compared to other threats to health and welfare not generally regarded as "crises." According to the U.S. Public Health Service, the most polluted air is nowhere near as dangerous as cigarette smoke.

Solutions Are Available

Many of the "problems" that are supposed to constitute the "crisis" could be quickly and easily solved, or much alleviated, by the application of well-known measures that lie right at hand. For example, the rush-hour traffic problem in the central cities . . . could be much reduced and in some cases eliminated entirely just by staggering working hours in the largest offices and factories. . . .

The "price" of solving, or alleviating, some much-talked-about urban problems is largely political. The proposal to reduce transit jams in Manhattan by staggering work hours was quickly and quietly killed by the city administration because the business community preferred the usual nine-to-five pattern.

If the rush-hour traffic problem is basically political, so is the revenue problem. A great part of the wealth of our country is in the cities. When a mayor says that his city is on the verge of bankruptcy, he really means that when the time comes to run for re-election he wants to be able to claim credit for straightening out a mess that was left him by his predecessor. What a mayor means when he says that his city must have state or federal aid to finance some improvements is (1) the taxpayers of the city (or some important group of them) would rather go without the improvement than pay for it themselves; or (2) although they would pay for it themselves if they had to, they would much prefer to have some other taxpayers pay for it. Rarely if ever does a mayor who makes such a statement mean (1) that for the city to pay for the improvement would necessarily force some taxpayers into poverty; or (2) that the city could not raise the money even if it were willing to force some of its taxpayers into poverty. . . .

That we have not yet been willing to pay the price of solving, or alleviating, such "problems" even when the price is very small suggests that they are not really as serious as they have been made out to be. Indeed, one might say that, by definition, a serious problem is one that people are willing to pay a considerable price to have solved.

An Inner-city, Older-suburb Crisis

The serious problems are to be found in all large cities and in most small ones. But they affect only parts of these cities (and only a minority of the city populations). In the central cities and the larger, older suburbs, the affected parts are usually adjacent to the central business district, and spreading out from it. If these inner districts, which probably comprise somewhere between 10 to 20 per cent of the total area classified as urban by the census, were suddenly to disappear, along with the people who live in them, there would be no serious urban problems worth talking about. If what really matters is the essential welfare of individuals and the good health of society as opposed to comfort, convenience, amenity, and business advantage, then what we have is not an "urban problem" but an "inner-central-city and larger-older-suburb" problem. . . .

It is widely supposed that the serious problems of the cities are unprecedented both in kind and in magnitude. Between 1950 and 1960 there occurred the greatest population increase in the nation's history. At the same time, a considerable part of the white middle class moved to the newer suburbs, and its place in the central cities was taken by the Negroes (and in New York by the Puerto Ricans as well). These and other events — especially the civil rights revolution — are widely supposed to have changed completely the character of "the urban problem."

But the facts do not compel one to take the view that the serious problems of the cities are unprecedented either in kind or in magnitude. That population growth in absolute numbers was greater in the decade 1950 to 1960 than ever before need not hold much significance from the present standpoint; American cities have frequently grown at fantastic rates. . . . In any case, the population growth of the 1950's was not in the largest cities; most of them actually lost population in that decade. So far as numbers go, the migration of rural and small-town Negroes and Puerto Ricans to the large northern cities in the 1950's was about equal to immigration from Italy in its peak decade. . . . When one takes into account the vastly greater size and wealth of the cities now as compared to half a century or more ago, it is obvious that by the only relevant measure — namely, the number of immigrants relative to the capacity of the cities to provide for them and to absorb them — the movement in the 1950's from the South and from Puerto Rico was not large but small.

Rising Expectations: Benefits and Dangers

In many important respects, conditions in the large cities have been getting better. There is less poverty in the cities now than there has ever been. Housing, including that of the poor, is improving rapidly: one study predicts that substandard housing will have been eliminated by 1980. . . . At the turn of the century only one child in fifteen went beyond elementary school; now most children finish high school. The treatment of racial and other minority groups is conspicuously better than it was. When, in 1965, a carefully drawn sample of Negroes were asked whether, in general, things were getting better or worse for Negroes in this country, approximately eight of ten respondents said "better."

If the situation is improving, why, it may be asked, is there so much talk of an urban crisis? The answer is that the improvements in performance, great as they have been, have not kept pace with rising expectations. In other words, although things have been getting better absolutely, they have been getting worse *relative to what we think they should be*. And this is because, as a people, we seem to act on the advice of the old jingle:

Good, better, best
Never let it rest
Until your good is better
And your better best.

Consider the poverty problem, for example. Irving Kristol has pointed out that for nearly a century all studies, in all countries, have concluded that a third, a fourth, or a fifth of the nation in question is below the poverty line. "Obviously," he remarks, "if one defines the poverty line as that which places one-fifth of the nation below it, one fifth of the nation will always be below the poverty line." The point is that even if everyone is better off, there will be as much poverty as ever, provided that the line is redefined upward. . . .

To a large extent, then, our urban problems are like the mechanical rabbit at the racetrack, which is set to keep just ahead of the dogs no matter how fast they may run. Our performance is better and better, but because we set our standards and expectations to keep ahead of the performance, the problems are never any nearer to solution. . . .

Some may say that since almost everything about the city can stand improvement (to put it mildly), this mechanical-rabbit effect is a good thing in that it spurs us on to make constant progress. No doubt this is true, to some extent. On the other hand, there is danger that we may mistake failure to progress as fast as we would like for failure to progress at all, and, in panic, rush into ill-considered measures that will only make matters worse. After all, an "urban crisis" that results largely from rising standards and expectations is the sort of crisis that, unless something drastic is done, is bound to lead to disaster. To treat it as if it were might be a very serious mistake.

This danger is greatest in matters where our standards are unreasonably high. The effect of too-high standards cannot be to spur us on to reach the prescribed level of performance sooner than we otherwise would, for that level is by definition impossible of attainment. At the same time, these standards may cause us to adopt measures that are wasteful and injurious and, in the long run, to conclude from the inevitable failure of these measures that there is something fundamentally wrong with our society. Consider the school dropout problem, for example. The dropout rate can never be cut to zero: there will always be some boys and girls who simply do not have what it takes to finish high school. If we continue to make a great hue and cry about the dropout problem after we have reached the point where all those who can reasonably be expected to finish high school are doing so, we shall accomplish nothing constructive. Instead, we shall, at considerable cost to ourselves, injure the boys and girls who cannot finish (the propaganda against being a dropout both hurts the morale of such a youngster and reduces his or her job opportunities) while creating in ourselves and in others the impression that our society is morally incapable of meeting its obligations.

In a certain sense, then, the urban crisis may be real. By treating a spurious crisis as if it were real, we may unwittingly make it so.

■ *The Student's Paperback Library*

The sources from which the foregoing selections were drawn furnish guidelines for further reading in the history of urban America. In addition, the following works, available in inexpensive paperback editions, provide opportunity for productive study.

A History of Urban America by Charles N. Glaab and A. Theodore Brown is a useful survey of American history from an urban perspective. Also helpful as a general work is Charles N. Glaab's The American City: A Documentary History. The recent interest of scholars is reflected in the Urban Life in American Series published by Oxford University Press, ten volumes of which have already appeared.

Materials for the colonial and Revolutionary periods include Carl Bridenbaugh's Cities in the Wilderness, Cities in Revolt, and, with his wife Jessica, the more popular Rebels and Gentlemen: Philadelphia in the Age of Franklin.

For the urban dimension of the westward movement, see Richard C. Wade, The Urban Frontier: The Rise of Western Cities, 1790–1830. An informative work about the same period is Charles Rosenberg, The Cholera Years, a study of urban epidemics in the nineteenth century. Richard C. Wade's Slavery in the Cities: The South, 1820–1860 surveys an important phase of urban life in the antebellum South.

Immigration played a major role in urban development. Works treating this aspect of city life include Oscar Handlin, Boston's Immigrants, 1790–1865 and Nathan Glazer and Daniel P. Moynihan, Beyond the Melting Pot.

Books on the development of the suburbs and the establishment of "new towns" include Sam Warner's Streetcar Suburbs: The Process of Growth in Boston, 1870–1900 and Clarence S. Stein's Toward New Towns for America, which describes planned communities of the 1930's and 1940's. The suburban way of life is analyzed in The Organization Man by William H. Whyte and more favorably described in The Levittowners by Herbert J. Gans.

Several works treat the black experience in cities. For documentation from the earliest period on, see The Negro in New York: An Informal Social History, 1626–1940, edited by Roi Ottley and William J. Weatherby. A picture of life in a more recent time is found in Black Metropolis: A Study of Negro Life in a Northern City by Horace Cayton and St. Clair Drake. Kenneth Clark's Dark Ghetto is noted for its depth of insight, and Robert E. Conot's Rivers of Blood, Years of Darkness is a vivid account of the Watts riot of 1965.

The crisis of the modern metropolis has produced a flood of books which examine, diagnose, and prescribe cures for urban America. Some of these are Jane Jacobs, The Death and Life of Great American Cities; Jeanne R. Lowe, Cities in a Race with Time; Charles Abrams, The City Is the Frontier; The Exploding Metropolis by the editors of Fortune magazine; and James Q. Wilson, ed., *The Renewal: The Record and the Controversy.*

Government publications of special relevance are the *Report of the National Commission on Urban Problems* (1968); *The Model Cities Program* by Marshall Kaplan (1969), describing the planning process in Atlanta, Seattle, and Dayton; *A Decent Home* by the President's Committee on Urban Housing (1969); and the *Report of the National Commission on the Causes and Prevention of Violence* (1969).

A final and highly rewarding source is the novel. See Upton Sinclair, *The Jungle,* Edwin O'Connor, *The Last Hurrah,* and James T. Farrell, *Studs Lonigan.*

■ *Questions for Study and Discussion*

I. The Colonial City

1. What were important considerations in the location of a colonial city? Are these equally important today?

2. What evidence is there of concern for the poor?

3. What were the signs of increasing prosperity in the colonial cities? What were the sources of this prosperity?

4. In what ways would life in Philadelphia and Boston appear to have been similar? Different? How do you account for the similarities and the differences?

5. Why were fires a great threat to colonial cities? Pestilence? What conclusion can be drawn from the advertisement in the *Boston News Letter*?

6. What evidence is there that "agitators" created problems in colonial cities? How were disorders to be quelled in Philadelphia?

7. What inferences can you draw from the regulations governing the market in Philadelphia?

8. What were the causes that provoked the "Merchants' Rebellion"? Was there any solution? Explain.

9. How did the closing of Boston Harbor following the Tea Party affect the wealthy? The middle class? The poor? Do you agree with the analysis and judgment of John Andrews?

II. The Great Era of City Building

1. In what respects did L'Enfant's plan for Washington differ from Penn's plan for Philadelphia? Which do you prefer? Why?

2. Could the prospectus for Havannah have inspired the spoof on Log-Hall? Why?

3. Why did Lowell become an important factory town? Note the four-class society that developed there. Would the same classes have been found in Waynesville (selection 2)? Why?

4. Why do you think Chicago prospered? Why, on the other hand, did Havannah never materialize?

5. What values are reflected in Cuming's description of Pittsburgh? What did he approve? Not approve?

6. Why was it necessary for New York to tap Croton's water? Would unsanitary conditions (such as those described in the account of Boston's health problems, selection 11) have been a factor? Do these account for the illness and epidemics common in the early 1800's?

7. Contrast urban firefighting in the early 1800's and today; contrast urban crime and crime prevention.

8. Were the libraries of the early 1800's "public" in our sense of the term? How were they supported? What conclusions about their purpose and functioning can you draw from Greene's account?

9. Why did New York not fear competition with Boston even if a canal from Boston to Albany were completed? What advantages did New York have over New Orleans as a port?

10. What city would have profited most from a canal between Delaware and Chesapeake bays? Why? Would that city have been able to surpass New York as a port? Why?

11. Why was St. Louis hurt by railroad bridges across the Mississippi? What was the effect of such bridges on the river's commerce? Could St. Louis hope to compete with Chicago as a railroad center? Why?

12. What is meant by "hiring out slaves"? By letting slaves "hire their time"? Why were these arrangements mutually beneficial to slave and owner? What light do these accounts shed on black-white relations just before the Civil War?

III. The New City

1. What were the advantages and limitations of the forms of urban transportation discussed (horse car, cable car, electric trolley, and elevated train)? Why did improved transportation raise the value of adjacent property? Would this always be true?

2. In what ways were Charlesbridge and Morgan Park similar? Different? Which account do you consider more reliable? Why?

3. Why were the tenements described by Riis horribly overcrowded? Why were health regulations not enforced? How did people in the Hebrew quarter earn a living? What was the special threat of disease in this section?

4. What evidence suggests that opportunities for industrial workers improved substantially in Cleveland during the 1880's?

5. According to Plunkitt, what is the secret of getting ahead in politics? How does he define "honest graft"? What is your reaction? Compare Plunkitt's views with those of Steffens. What do you conclude?

6. Why was steel-frame construction superior to solid-masonry construction? What specific need actually led Sullivan to design taller buildings?

7. What elements in urban life attracted Ragged Dick and Caroline Meeber? Does today's city exercise the same magnetic pull on young people?

8. What different facets of urban life do publications such as *The Morning Call* and *The Golden Era* reveal?

9. What major criticisms of cities are made by Glazier (selection 4B), Strong, and Rice? What are Weber's (selection 10) reactions to some of these charges? What do you conclude?

IV. Into the Twentieth Century

1. Consider the problems that confronted the people of Galveston and San Francisco following their disasters, and how the two cities coped with them. What could have been done differently and better?

2. Would Jane Addams' criticisms of commercialized recreation be equally valid today? Have local, state, and national governments done more about recreation during the last half century? Why?

3. Have the measures for reducing air pollution suggested in the Report of the Civic League of St. Louis been put into practice generally?

4. What conclusions concerning the effectiveness of prohibition can be drawn from the story of Izzy and Moe?

5. What were the goals of Mayors Blankenburg and La Guardia? How did they propose to achieve them? What are your views on political reform?

6. What goals does Burnham suggest for a city which wishes to become great? What unique ideas were contained in the plans for Chicago and Shaker Heights?

7. Why were creative people attracted to Greenwich Village? Was this a good environment for them?

8. What factors other than the automobile helped to shape the urban growth of Detroit? Los Angeles? What divergent views about the automobile's effect on ways of living are reflected in the selection by the Lynds? Are any of these opinions valid today?

9. What seems most shocking to you about the Great Depression?

10. What advantages and disadvantages for blacks living in the North and in the South are revealed in the letters home and the testimony before the Congressional committee?

11. How could the Detroit race riot have been handled more efficiently?

V. The Age of the Metropolis

1. Why does Gottmann say that Megalopolis may represent a "new stage in human civilization"?

2. What are the advantages of living in a community like Levittown? The disadvantages?

3. What does Harrington mean by the "culture of poverty"? What new approaches might be made to the development of satisfactory public housing?

4. What have been the goals of urban renewal? What mistakes have been made? With what results for whom?

5. What causes does Clark give for the "hostility, hope, despair" of ghetto-dwellers? What appraisal does the Kerner Commission make of each of its three "choices": Present Policies, Enrichment, Integration?

Why is white militancy increasing in working-class, ethnic neighborhoods of cities?

6. What are your reactions and conclusions concerning the job of a mayor?

7. What advantages have accrued from Nashville's form of government? Might such a plan help solve problems discussed in previous selections? Which ones?

8. What combination of forces achieved the results displayed in Atlanta?

9. What is your reaction to the views of Banfield on the "urban crisis"? In what ways do they differ from those expressed by Michael Harrington (selection 3), Herbert J. Gans (selection 4), the Kerner Commission (selection 5B), and Mayor Lee (selection 6)?

■ Acknowledgments

Thanks are extended to the following persons and organizations for making pictures available for reproduction.

82 — top, The Bettmann Archive; middle, Vivienne; bottom, Culver Pictures, Inc.

83 — top, The Bettmann Archive; bottom, Culver Pictures, Inc.

118 — top, Burton Historical Collection, Detroit Public Library; bottom, Carnegie Library of Pittsburgh

119 — top, Collection of George Krambles; bottom, Historical Pictures Service, Chicago

176 — top and bottom, Historical Pictures Service, Chicago

177 — top, Culver Pictures, Inc.; bottom, official photograph, Los Angeles Police Department

234 — top, Photoworld; bottom, Historical Pictures Service, Chicago

235 — top, United States Housing Authority photo by Sekaer; bottom, Robert Perron

■ *Index*

Excerpts from specific authors or sources are indicated by boldface numbers. The letter *f* indicates a footnote reference.

284   *Index*